About the Author

Nicola Jane Hobbs is an integrative counsellor and lifestyle consultant specialising in mental health and peak performance. She has a master's degree in sport and exercise psychology with a research interest in the role of sport and spirituality in post-traumatic growth. She has been teaching yoga, meditation and mindfulness for over a decade and specialises in integrating ancient wisdom practices with evidenced-based psychophysiological techniques. She runs a counselling and consultancy practice, working with individuals, sports teams and businesses.

Nicola lives in Brighton, UK. In her free time, she enjoys wild swimming, practising handstands and growing her own vegetables. You can find out more and get in touch at www.nicolajanehobbs.com or find her on social media: @nicolajanehobbs.

NICOLA JANE HOBBS

Daily Awakening

A 365-DAY JOURNEY TO HEALING, FREEDOM AND BELONGING

PIATKUS

PIATKUS

First published in Great Britain in 2021 by Piatkus

This book presents, among other things, the research and
ideas of its author. It is not intended to be a substitute for a
consultation with a professional healthcare practitioner.

ISBN: 978-0-349-42943-4

Typeset in Swift by M Rules
Printed and bound in Great Britain by
Clays Ltd, Elcograf S.p.A.

Papers used by Piatkus are from well-managed forests
and other responsible sources.

Piatkus
An imprint of
Little, Brown Book Group
Carmelite House
50 Victoria Embankment
London EC4Y 0DZ

An Hachette UK Company
www.hachette.co.uk

www.littlebrown.co.uk

for those who are hurting
and those who are healing

for those who held me
in my darkest days

and for Justin,
for being the banks to my river

Contents

Part Two: Planting the Seeds

Part Three: Pulling the Weeds

Part Four: Embracing the Bees

Part Five: Fertilising the Earth

Part Six: Letting Things Bloom

Conclusion: The Garden of Awakening

Introduction

My (continued) awakening

It was half past eight at night when I walked through the front door to my empty flat. I'd left for work at five-thirty that morning, and had only had time to grab a banana for lunch. Deadlines were weighing heavy on my mind, and my inner critic was bullying me into doing another few hours of work before I was allowed to rest. I was exhausted. Burned out. Broken-hearted. I pushed through, running the vacuum cleaner around the flat and emptying the bins before working my way through my emails, secretly hoping that by keeping busy, I could outrun my pain.

In the months before, my life had collapsed around me. My dad had just died after a long and harrowing journey with cancer. I had found out the man I once imagined I would spend the rest of my life with was having an affair with his old neighbour. And, left to pay the mortgage on my own, I was barely making ends meet while struggling to sell the flat.

I felt my eyes getting heavy and went to the bathroom to splash my face with cold water. Catching sight of my reflection in the mirror – pale, drained and hollow – I came face to face with my pain. That's when it hit me: the grief. The anger. The fear. The despair. The shame. The rage. I could not hold myself together for one moment longer.

I'm not sure how long I wept for, curled up on the bathroom floor, feeling the full force of my emotions. But, tear-stained and sorrow-filled, that's when I heard it. A tiny, tender voice inside, soft and silky and slightly wild. It reminded me to breathe deeply and feel fully and hold everything in this world gently, including myself. To stop running and numbing and self-destructing. To let myself feel and grieve and rest.

After decades of finding reasons not to, I began the long journey of healing, of getting to know myself, of coming home to myself. I committed to the process. I slept. I rested. I meditated. I journaled. I asked for help. I gave myself space to be with my pain, to listen to it, to learn from it. I began unpeeling layer after layer of childhood and cultural conditioning, untangling the knots of suffering in my soul, creating a place within my heart that felt like home.

Before work each morning, I would sit on the sofa with a steaming mug of lemon-and-ginger tea and read a verse of the *Tao Te Ching,* contemplating one verse a day, journaling about it and allowing myself to feel the emotions that were awakened within me. When I finished the *Tao Te Ching,* I did the same with translations of the *Bhagavad Gita* and the *Prajñāpāramitā Sutra,* and with the words of mystics like Rumi, Hafiz and Kabir; poets like Maya Angelou, Mary Oliver and Wendell Berry; and spiritual teachers like Thich Nhat Hanh, Clarissa Pinkola Estés and Sri Nisargadatta Maharaj. Somehow, they all found a way to say the things my heart longed to hear. Inspired by my reading, I began asking myself the deeper, braver questions. *Why am I still at war with myself? How am I contributing to my own suffering? What gifts do I carry for the world?*

In asking these questions, I found truth. And in that truth, I found healing. Now, I look back on those precious sunlit mornings when I was swimming through the icy waters of grief as essential stepping stones to the joy, peace and freedom I live with now. There is still pain and fear and sadness – because they are part of being human – but there is also a quiet strength, a deep trust that my heart can hold it all. By creating a space each day for slowing down and reflecting on who I wanted to be, and what kind of life I wanted to create, I discovered a whole new way of being: one where the self-criticism and self-hate I had known all my life began to wither, and self-acceptance and self-compassion began to bloom.

Before those mornings, I had spent most of my life in a state of anxiety, overwhelm and exhaustion. Looking back, the last time I had been truly happy was when I was about nine. Between my childhood and my early twenties, I lived with the sense that there was something wrong with me: some sin I had to atone for; something I had to achieve to prove I was worthy. In my early teens I was diagnosed with anxiety and depression, shortly followed by anorexia nervosa and obsessive–compulsive disorder. I spent the next five years in and out of psychiatric institutions – locked up, force-fed and told my brain was broken. It wasn't until much later that I realised the psychiatrists were wrong. I wasn't insane or crazy. I was a human in incredible pain, doing what she needed to do to survive.

The next few years were lonely and shame-filled as I gathered together the scattered shards of my life after so long in institutions. Instead of starving myself, I found more socially acceptable, more socially rewarded ways to numb my pain: overworking and overachieving. I chased academic, athletic and financial success.

I was always striving, always productive, always pretending everything was fine. But, despite achieving what I'd been led to believe would make me happy, I still felt hollow. I lived with a gnawing ache that told me something was missing.

It has taken me a long time to realise why I felt this way, and to connect – and stay connected – to the deepest and truest part of me, even when it would have been easier and less painful to live on the surface. To stop questioning. To stop contemplating. To fall back into unhealthy habits rooted in the work-hard-achieve-more-never-rest conditioning that is part and parcel of modern life.

Part of why my healing has taken so long, and why it still continues today, is because there are no shortcuts. No magic pills. No quick fixes. It takes time to cultivate self-awareness and self-compassion. It takes time to remember who we are, where we belong and what is sacred. I am still grieving. I am still healing. I am still learning to dance with the parts of myself I once worked so hard to hide.

I wanted to share my story because I believe we need to create space that allows for the fullness of being human, where we can speak openly about our pain and our shame, our traumas and our tragedies, the ways in which we are hurting, how we are healing and what we are discovering in our unfolding.

My experiences eventually led me to the work I do today – integrating science, spirituality, psychology and physiology. My professional journey reflects my personal one, and along the way I've studied and trained in various therapeutic techniques, including counselling, yoga, meditation, breathwork, nutrition, Ayurveda and sport psychology. Everything I offer in this book is rooted in lived experience, both from my own ongoing process of healing and awakening, and from the insights I've gained from working with hundreds of people over the past decade.

I know how much courage it takes to look deeply at yourself and the world around you, to face your fears and fragilities, to let yourself be touched by the pain and beauty of life. And every day, I feel honoured to be with those who are grieving, to hold space for those who are healing, to witness people awaken in their own wild and glorious ways.

I hope this book offers a healing space for you.

This book is for you

If you are a human being living with the pressures of modern life, this book is for you. Figures from the Mental Health Foundation suggest that almost seventy-five per cent of us admit to feeling stressed, overwhelmed or unable to cope at times. We spend our days on an anxious quest to get everything done. Exhaustion has become a way of life. And no matter how successful we appear to be outwardly, many of us live with a sense of inner failure. We have become so busy that we have little time to reflect on, let alone act on, our deepest values. We forge ahead without questioning whether we are truly happy.

Many of the people I work with come to me feeling trapped and numb. They live with an inner restlessness, a homesickness, an anxious ache that bubbles beneath the surface. Deep down they know – we *all* know – that life can be more joyful, more beautiful, more meaningful. And yet we find ourselves imprisoned by habits, fears, jobs, relationships and routines.

As they begin to question what they have been conditioned

to believe, to honour the stress they have been through, to understand the source of their pain, I see the people I work with begin to change. They begin taking care of themselves, trusting themselves, getting to know themselves in a deeper, truer, more compassionate way.

Ultimately, my work is to hold space – to be fully present in a deeply compassionate and non-judgemental way, to witness, and to ask questions that gently open the door to a richer, more meaningful life. And this is why I wrote this book. As an invitation for you to embark on your own journey of healing and awakening. Not by giving you lots of information or unsolicited advice, but by asking questions to guide you back to your own wisdom, your own truth.

Sprinkled throughout *Daily Awakening*, you'll also find psychological theories and ideas from the wisdom traditions, as well as a bibliography of scientific studies. Theories can offer us a framework to help make sense of how bewildering it can feel to be a human sometimes – but if they don't resonate with you, feel free to leave them behind.

There is nothing you will find here that I haven't struggled with personally. This book is an offering of the sacred, soul-stretching questions I have asked myself, alongside scientific studies and spiritual wisdom, synthesised into a 365-day journey. My hope is that by the time you finish reading it, you will have learned how to stop the war inside, how to savour the joyful moments in life and make room for the inevitable pain, how to live more fully, love more deeply and embrace the wild and precious adventure of being alive.

How to use this book

What comes up again and again in my work is the need for fewer answers and more questions, less information and more inspiration, less forcing and more listening. So, here you'll find 365 sacred questions, one for each day of the year, to help you gently investigate who you are, why you do what you do and what you are truly capable of. Each section contains questions centred around a common theme, including stress, rest, success, failure, perfectionism, people-pleasing, love, grief, money and God. Although these themes might seem unrelated at first, they are like threads woven into the fabric of our lives. When we begin untangling one thread, we often find it tethered to all the others.

Caught up in the breathless pace of modern life, we tend to crave quick fixes and easy solutions. But awakening is a gradual process. We cannot unravel decades of conditioning in a single day. This means that, as you embark on this journey, it's important to make a commitment to yourself to engage in reflection on a regular basis, to set aside a moment where you can pause and reflect on that day's question, noting down any insights that arise. Anything from five minutes to half an hour a day is ideal. Finding this time usually means consciously choosing *not* to do certain things (for example, browsing on social media, watching television or reading the news).

Prioritising our reflective practice despite our busy lives is rarely easy. At first, it can be easy to write off our practice as unnecessary. We might see it as selfish, a luxury we only allow ourselves once everything on our to-do list is checked off. Or we might dismiss these tiny moments of reflection as futile relative to the suffering in our lives. But, like a jug fills up drop by drop, day by day, we awaken another drop of awareness, another drop of compassion, another drop of joy, until we are overflowing. Once we have overcome the initial hurdles and made space for healing and awakening, we usually discover an evolving trust in the power of our practice, a gentle momentum that keeps it a priority in our lives.

To inspire you to begin, here are a few ways reflective practice can be healing.

- We all experience stress, pain and sorrow. And so, we all need a sacred space, an island of relief where we are free from the demands of everyday life for long enough to look more deeply at ourselves and the world.
- Healing work requires a strong container: a vessel that can hold the wild energies and emotions that may arise as we awaken. Through systematic daily practice, our journals become our anchor. Closing our journals at the end of each practice is a symbolic action of containment.
- Giving ourselves time to explore and express our deepest thoughts and emotions is an important act of validation. It shows that it's okay to feel the way we do.
- As we reflect and journal, we cultivate awareness. This awareness ripples through our daily lives, helping us to notice when we are triggered and whether we are acting in ways driven by fear and habit or rooted in our deepest values.
- Reflective writing offers us a way to translate our experiences into language. To assimilate. To understand, to integrate and to create a coherent narrative that helps us make sense of and find meaning in our lives.

- Suppressing our emotions uses psychological energy and is often experienced as a chronic, low-level stressor. As we reflect on our experiences in a safe, contained way and let our feelings flow through us as they arise, our brains are freed from the taxing job of inhibiting emotions and memories.
- As we consciously reflect and act on what we learn, excessive worrying and depressive rumination tend to reduce, because, once processed, we have no reason to rehearse or relive the experience in our minds.
- Our daily practice builds what psychotherapist Francis Weller calls 'soul muscle'. By returning again and again to our sacred space – to our journals or yoga mats or meditation cushions – we are showing that we can keep the promises we make to ourselves. That we can trust ourselves. That our voices matter. That our work is needed. That we belong.

Living the questions

The questions we ask shape the world we see. And yet we often find ourselves living on autopilot, stuck in ruts and routines, judging and criticising ourselves rather than relating to our lives with compassion and curiosity. By asking ourselves meaningful questions, we begin to wake up to the forces that have shaped us. We start to unlearn the beliefs and prejudices that were never our own. Instead of reacting automatically, we respond consciously. Instead of being driven by our conditioning, beliefs and fears, we start to drive.

Each of the questions in this book is a tool for what psychology calls introspection, religion refers to as contemplation, phi-losophy terms self-enquiry and ancient yogis called *svādhyāya* (translated as 'self-study'). These are the questions that no one ever asks us. Questions we've been avoiding our whole lives. Heart-opening questions. Questions that, like keys to the secret doors of our inner worlds, unlock the most precious and beauti-ful parts of us. Below are some tips to help you get the most out of your journaling practice.

- Play around until you find a way of journaling that works for you. Many people find it helpful to use a dedi-cated notebook for their self-reflective practice. But you might prefer to use your computer or phone.
- Don't worry about your spelling or punctuation or writing neatly. Sometimes you might want to write in full sentences; at other times, mind maps, doodles and drawings might feel more natural.
- You might like to create a sacred space for your journal-ing. Try to find a cosy chair or bean bag, or a yoga mat or meditation cushion. Choose somewhere that feels safe.
- At the beginning, you might find yourself journaling in the same way you live your life. Struggling. Striving. Trying to do it perfectly. This is part of the process. Notice how your relationship with journaling itself changes over time.
- Questioning ourselves is very different to judging our-selves. As we journal, we want to remind ourselves, as best we can, to release judgement and remain open to whatever is unfolding.
- Mindful reflection is very different from repetitive,

negative rumination. Rumination tends to be unconscious, intrusive and stress-magnifying, sucking us out of the present moment and into past regrets and future worries. On the other hand, reflection is a conscious process that always happens in the present. We recollect the past in the present. We contemplate the future in the present.

- Awakening comes from the questions we ask, not the answers we find. Maybe we find answers. Maybe we don't. Maybe we don't seek answers at all. Maybe, like the poet Rilke writes, we simply learn to love the questions and 'live along some distant day into the answer'.

- Healing comes in layers – especially if we are untangling deeply embedded beliefs and conditioning. This means that there are a few questions throughout the book that tap into similar ideas, in order to allow for deeper insights to emerge over time. Equally, you may find that questions on vastly different themes lead you back to the same wisdom, the same truth, reminding you of who you are and what really matters.

- Much of our healing happens beneath the surface. The thoughts, feelings and memories that arise as you ask each question might not make sense right away, but by anchoring yourself in the present moment and engaging with each question at the level of emotion and energy rather than just intellect, meanings will reveal themselves over time (you can find tools for grounding, centring and anchoring on pages 27–29).

Awakened action

This book is participatory. You cannot grow your own vegetables simply by reading a gardening manual: you have to be willing to roll up your sleeves, get down in the dirt and start digging. As well as developing insight, a big part of awakening is learning the psychological skills needed to untangle ourselves from difficult thoughts, emotions and conditioned beliefs, and to take awakened action, guided by our deepest values, to create rich, meaningful lives where we can flourish.

The final question in each section focuses on transforming our awareness into awakened action so we can keep our insights alive by grounding them in our daily lives. As we explore our beliefs and behaviours, we often realise that we only act in ways that are harmful – to ourselves, each other and the planet – out of habit, pain and ignorance. As we become conscious of why we do what we do, as we connect with our deepest values, as we cultivate the capacity to gently observe our thoughts and stay grounded when painful emotions arise, we discover the many 'choice points' that open up in our daily lives: thousands of little opportunities to wake up, to shift out of autopilot, and to take conscious, mindful action that will help us to be the people we want to be, live the lives we want to lead and create the kind of world we want to belong in.

You are the expert

Ultimately, this journey is yours, no one else's. This book offers tools to ground you and guide you, but you are the expert of your own experience. If life gets in the way and you miss a day or a week or a month of journaling, that's okay. If you want to explore more than one question a day, that's okay. If journaling doesn't work for you, that's okay too. Instead, you might like to explore each question with someone you can trust, someone who can hold space for you without judgement. This might be a partner, a parent, a sibling, a friend, or even a colleague; ideally it should be someone you speak to daily and who you feel safe being vulnerable with.

Crucially, learning to trust yourself means learning to listen when your soul says no; when you need to skip a question or a chapter, or take a break from your practice because it is too much for your heart to hold right now. Pausing your practice and honouring the rhythms of your soul rather than blindly following a schedule in a book is a doorway to, not a detour from, your healing and awakening.

I have done my best to create a book that is evidence-based, spiritually conscious and trauma-sensitive, but books can never replace medical advice or therapeutic support. If you feel you need to consult a medical practitioner or therapist before continuing, or at any point throughout the book, please do so. This book is not designed to stand in for treatment of any kind.

What is awakening?

Just as we cannot force ourselves to fall asleep, we cannot force ourselves to awaken. Rather, healing and awakening happen as we begin treating ourselves with compassion, as we shine light on the shadowy parts we have been trying to hide, as we embrace our fragilities and flaws and welcome the whole, wild whirlwind of life.

Our experiences of awakening will be unique to each of us, and our understanding will change as we change. Having said that, being aware of some of the misconceptions around awakening – for example, the way it has been sold to us as a glorified self-improvement project and romanticised as a way to bypass our humanness and transcend our pain – can help us to stay true to our practice when our experiences of healing and awakening don't match the ideas we have in our heads.

Awakening is messy (not linear)

There is this idea that we should always be moving forwards and making progress – but that's just not how life works. It's not how healing works. It's not how awakening works. Awakening is not linear. It has its own rhythms. Its own timings. We will go through periods of breaking, of opening, of growth, of stillness, and of spiralling downwards into the depths of ourselves and outwards into new ways of being.

Awakening happens now (not in the future)

Awakening is not a state of enlightenment that we will reach at the end of our journeys. Rather, it is here from the very beginning. Awakening is a constant process that can only ever happen exactly where we are. By coming into the present moment. By being with whatever pain, joy, boredom, love and unworthiness is here. By opening to the wild mystery of life.

Awakening allows us to fall in love with the ordinary (and stop chasing the extraordinary)

Many of us are waiting for some dramatic moment of realisation, for something momentous and profound and earth-shaking. And so, we might find ourselves chasing extraordinary experiences, all the while missing what is really happening. The irony is, when we pay attention to the simple wonders of daily life, of breathing and birdsong and the ocean breeze, we discover that our ordinary world is extraordinary. When we release the assumptions that our awakening will be loud and obvious and otherworldly, we can begin falling in love with the ordinary, with the sunrises and star-littered skies and the simple joys of being alive.

Awakening happens in everyday life (not only in ashrams and on mountaintops)

Awakening isn't reserved for mountaintops or yoga retreats or cups of ayahuasca. Awakening happens in moments that look a lot like ordinary life. In the breath-by-breath choices we make. In catching ourselves when we fall into habitual patterns and choosing to step out of them. In setting boundaries and honouring our limits. In meeting each moment of conflict or chaos or confusion with an awakened response rather than an automatic one. In learning how to take care of ourselves, each other and the natural world.

Awakening allows us to embrace the full catastrophe of life (not bypass the difficult bits)

We often hope healing and awakening will allow us to rise above our pain, but we will all face times of uncertainty, loss and heartache. Awakening is not about avoiding difficult emotions, rather it is about cultivating the capacity to rest in the unknown, to hold our pain without breaking, to embrace the whole sacred messiness of life.

Awakening is about becoming fully human (not superhuman)

We are not trying to become superhuman. We are allowing ourselves to be *fully* human. We are not striving to be perfect, with no ego, pain or fear; we are letting ourselves be the flawed, imperfect, unfinished humans that we are. We are humans that mess up and make mistakes. Humans that feel angry and ashamed and afraid. Humans that can be selfish and judgemental and unkind *and* loving and gentle and brave. The whole journey of awakening is one of accepting *all* of who we are, of becoming *more* of who we are.

Unlearning our way back to love

Awakening is largely a process of unlearning rather than learning. Of undoing rather than doing. Of untangling. Untaming. Uncaging. So many of the decisions we make are influenced by the thoughts, habits and belief systems we have absorbed from our families, friends, education, media and the society we live in. Without taking time for conscious self-reflection, we tend to remain blind to the limiting beliefs that distort the way we see ourselves and the world.

As we begin reflecting on our beliefs, exploring the forces that drive our behaviour and paying attention to the ways in which we habitually cope with our pain, we make our conditioning conscious. And once our conditioning becomes conscious, we can do something with it. We can question it, grieve for it, grow from it. We can step out of the stories we have been telling ourselves about our unworthiness. We can begin to rewire our brains, reshape our nervous systems and rediscover who we are and what we are capable of. We can move out of survival mode and begin to thrive.

The inner world and the outer world

I spent many years trapped in an ever-deepening spiral of self-blame and shame. And it was only when I started zooming out, when I began recognising the impact of adverse childhood experiences, acknowledging the chronic stress I was going through and waking up to systems of oppression and injustice, that I realised my distress – *all* distress – is not the result of individual weakness. Rather, distress begins from the outside in. Many forms of Western psychology and modern spirituality place the onus on us, as individuals, to heal. But, if we are to heal the emotional wounds of our inner worlds, we must first acknowledge the external forces that created them.

As much as possible, I have rooted this book in a bio-psycho-eco-social-spiritual model – a holistic, multidimensional framework that helps us to understand the influence and interaction of various areas of our lives, including:

- **biology** – genetic predispositions, hormones, neuro-chemistry, allostatic load, ancestral trauma
- **psychology** – belief systems, coping skills, emotional awareness, stress appraisal, personality, health behaviours
- **society** – cultural values, oppression, prejudice, religion, education, community, poverty, peer pressure, social support systems
- **ecology** – air quality, water pollution, soil health, access to nature, climate change, urbanisation, loss of species, land degradation
- **spirituality** – sense of meaning and purpose, rituals and practices, self-evolution and self-actualisation, relationship with a higher power

As we awaken, we discover the inner world and the outer world are not separate. This reveals to us a fierce paradox: much of our inner distress is caused by external forces that we do not control, *and*, through awareness, compassion and awakened action, we have the power to not only heal the emotional wounds of our inner world, but to transform the outer world.

Body, mind and soul

Language is powerful. It can open our minds to new ways of seeing, or close them down out of fear. I have used a few terms throughout the book that I wanted to clarify to help reduce confusion. The first is 'bodymind', which I use to refer to the whole psychophysiological system, including the immune, muscular, digestive, cardiovascular, neuroendocrine and nervous systems, as well as the ways in which our thoughts and emotions influence these systems. Another word is 'soul', which I've used to refer to the deepest, truest part of ourselves: our inner power, our deepest values, our vitality, our life force, our aliveness. Finally, whenever I have used the word 'God', I have used it to refer to your own personal definition of God, which does not have to be related to any religion or belief system. Rather, God can be a divine power, a personification of love and compassion, or a sense of deep connection with the rest of humanity.

Attitudes for awakening

Although we cannot force healing and awakening, we can create the conditions for awakening to happen by consciously cultivating certain attitudes. In Buddhism, these mindsets are known as the seven factors of awakening. Like preparing the soil for sowing, each of these attitudes will create fertile ground where the seeds of healing and awakening can blossom. We will be nurturing these mental qualities throughout the book, but it can be helpful to become familiar with them from the very beginning.

- **mindfulness** – paying attention to the present moment with acceptance, curiosity and kindness
- **investigation** – non-judgementally exploring our experiences more deeply so we can see things more clearly
- **energy** – motivating ourselves and devoting ourselves to whatever we are doing

- **joy** – opening ourselves to the inner joy that is always within us; living light-heartedly amidst the heaviness of life and allowing ourselves to experience the deep, spiritual joys of the everyday (which feel different to more synthetic pleasures)
- **tranquillity** – dropping into a deep inner peace beneath the surface drama of our lives
- **concentration** – fully focusing without being distracted by thoughts, doubts, worries or desires
- **equanimity** – remaining calm and balanced, even when life doesn't go the way we would like it to

Blocks to awakening

The five *kleshas*

One of the (many) paradoxes of awakening is that it is deeply personal *and* profoundly universal. Both ancient yogis and Buddhists identified five inner obstacles that can get in the way of our healing and awakening. These are called the *kleshas*. These mental patterns distort how we think, feel and relate to ourselves and the world. When we're living on autopilot, it's easy to slip into these mental patterns, and we can become reactive, impulsive, obsessive and compulsive, acting in ways that constrict our lives and hold us back from being who we want to be. Being aware of these psychological barriers can help us to notice them when they arise so we can awaken from them instead of getting lost in them.

- **ignorance** – When we ignore our emotions and intuitions, block out elements of ourselves because we think they are unacceptable, and overlook parts of our experiences because we are so focused on how we think life should be, we suffer.
- **egoism** – When we over-identify with our ego (our habits, traits and beliefs – our false self), we suffer.
- **attachment** – When we want, crave, desire or cling to external things in the hope they will make us happy, we suffer.
- **aversion** – When we try to avoid or get rid of certain experiences and emotions, we suffer.
- **fear of change** – When we resist change and uncertainty in a world that is inherently impermanent and unknown, we suffer.

Unmet needs

Much of our inner distress is caused by unmet needs and unfaced truths, by overriding our body's limits and fighting with reality. Part of healing and awakening is accepting that we are human. We have needs. We have limits. We need sleep. We need rest. We need play. There are only twenty-four hours in a day and seven days in a week, and we cannot do it all. Even though all of us have these core human needs – essential requirements for our survival and wellbeing – we often think of having needs as a sign of weakness. We judge our need for rest as laziness, our need for food as greediness, our need to deeply intertwine our lives with another as co-dependency.

Our internalised individualism, combined with the pace and pressure of modern life, means that we are often deprived of the things we innately need. And yet, by accepting that we have needs, and by identifying our limits, we can begin to build the inner and outer resources necessary to help us meet them. There are many theories exploring the general conditions in which we flourish, each of which includes meeting the following core needs:

- **safety needs** – nourishing food, clean water, sleep, rest, warmth, shelter, financial and material resources
- **psychological needs** – agency, pleasure, play, hope, emotional regulation, meaning and purpose, a sense of achievement and contribution, self-expansion and psychological maturation
- **belonging needs** – love, connection, intimate relation-ships, feeling valued, a sense of justice and fairness in our community, feeling safe and accepted in our earliest relationships

We'll be exploring these needs and how to meet them throughout the book, but you might find it helpful to reflect on which core needs are and aren't being met in your life. Are you getting enough sleep? Do you feel valued at work and at home? When was the last time you let yourself play?

Unfaced truths

A big part of healing is learning to be with what is true: to see things as they are rather than how we want them to be or how we think they should be. Accepting the universal truths of life rather than fighting them is a necessary part of awakening. As we explore these truths, often called 'the givens of life' in existential psychol-ogy, they can become gateways to a more meaningful life. These universal truths make most sense as we discover them within ourselves, but often include the following existential insights:

- Nothing is permanent – everything changes and ages and dies.
- People will not always understand us – nor will they always be loving and kind.
- Life does not always go to plan – things we do not want to happen will happen, and things we do want to happen will not happen.
- We cannot protect ourselves from experiencing pain and loss – but we have a far greater capacity to cope with and grow from these experiences than we believe.
- Being human is hard – and realising many of our sorrows and anxieties are shared can open our hearts, awaken universal compassion and inspire us to take action to better care for each other and the world.
- The more freedom we find, the more responsibility we have to take for our lives – and the more responsibility we have to help others find freedom in their lives.

The sacred messiness of life

The deeper I travel on this journey, the more I find myself embracing the vast and mysterious paradoxes of being alive. This involves accepting that two seemingly opposing things can be true at the same time, and that there is room for everything to exist. And with this comes a kind of spaciousness. A freedom for things to be messy and wild and unknown without needing to figure it all out.

To be able to hold the paradoxes of life – to move beyond right/wrong, good/evil, either/or thinking – is a path to and a gift of awakening. As we welcome the opposites in our lives, as we make space for both/and, we allow our hearts to be stretched wider, so that we can live in harmony with the mysteries and messiness of life. As we heal and awaken, it can be helpful to remind ourselves of some of these paradoxes.

- We are good enough exactly as we are, *and* there is inner work that needs to be done.
- Healing takes conscious effort, *and* there is nothing to do and nowhere to go.
- Awakening is a solitary journey, *and* we cannot walk it alone.
- We can accept things as they are right now, *and* work towards creating personal and social change (in fact, we *need* to accept rather than deny the truth of our world – both inner and outer – in order to enact change).
- Our awakening is a personal experience *and* a political act.
- Everything we need to heal is within us, *and* some of the deeper wounds we uncover cannot be healed alone (this might mean seeing a therapist or allowing someone who loves us deeply to hold space for our pain).
- Reflective practice is a way of taking care of ourselves *and* a way of creating social change (social movements emerge when we refuse to live in a way that is not true to who we are).
- Our hearts can hold grief *and* gratitude, love *and* fear, deep suffering *and* intense joy.

- None of this is our fault, *and* it is our responsibility to develop the inner resources and psychological skills we need to heal.
- Our awakening is deeply personal *and* profoundly collective.
- We can appreciate the knowledge that science has given us *and* honour the forms of knowledge that cannot be measured objectively (e.g. intuitions, feelings, insights, myths, stories, traditions).
- Our lives are cosmically significant, *and* we are just specks in a vast and unknown universe.
- Life is hard and full of suffering, *and* life is beautiful and sacred and glorious.

The storm clouds of the heart

When we begin this inner work, we often experience a kind of thawing. As we move from a place of numbness to a place of aliveness, the emotions frozen within us begin flowing. We might experience spontaneous crying, giggling, yawning, sighing and trembling as this energy begins to release. This can be both freeing and frightening.

Without knowing that awakening can be a tear-filled process involving periods of uncertainty, sadness and grief, we might wonder whether we're doing something wrong, whether we should read a different book or try a different approach, one that is quicker or easier or more comfortable. After all, if awakening can be *this* painful, why bother? We do it because we have to. Because we must. Because we cannot resist the call to journey within, to dive beneath the surface of our lives, for one moment longer.

To begin with, it may feel like our suffering is increasing, especially if we have mistaken feeling numb for feeling better. As we awaken, we tend to see our fragilities and flaws more clearly, to grieve more fiercely, to feel the suffering of the world more deeply. And although none of us want a downward path to healing – moving through grief, through imperfections, through the parts of ourselves we would rather hide – we soon find that the more we try to avoid, the more we find ourselves struggling with life. Because the pain we avoid doesn't just disappear. It shows up in our blind reactions and anxious thoughts, our addictive patterns and constant busyness, our inability to love ourselves and be present in the world.

Gradually, as we let ourselves feel our lives fully, the storm clouds of the heart begin to clear and the process of awakening shifts, moving from the hard work of grieving, releasing and fearing the unknown to a more gentle, spacious unfolding. An opening. A softening. An ever-deepening trust in the wonder and mystery of life.

This doesn't mean that we will never experience pain. Rather, we discover that we have the capacity to be with it. To feel it. To hold it with compassion. Slowly, we realise how feeling the depths of our wounds reunites us with the depth of our love – for ourselves, each other and this wild and mysterious world.

Awakening safety

Awakening opens us to the grief, anger and betrayal that were too much for us earlier in our lives, and also to the peace, love and truth that have been hiding beneath them. As someone who has experienced the heaviness of trauma and depth of despair – both personally and professionally – I do not speak of safety lightly. One of the most essential skills for healing and awakening is the capacity to create a safe space within ourselves, an inner refuge that allows us to experience intense emotions in a fully grounded and compassionate way. We need to learn how to remain rooted in the safety of the present moment, to stay anchored in our adult selves if pain arises, to honour how much our hearts can hold and to shift our awareness back to the outer world if focusing on our inner worlds becomes too intense.

Below are three simple techniques that will help create a 'neuroception' of safety (a term coined by Dr Stephen Porges to describe the way neural circuits sense whether people, places and situations are safe or dangerous), signalling to your nervous system that there are no threats, that you are not in danger, and that right now, you are safe to feel, to grieve, to heal. You might like to experiment with each technique and see what feels best so you can be confident in your capacity to create safety before, during and after your reflective practice.

Grounding

By noticing that we are supported by the ground beneath us, we send a signal to our nervous systems that we are safe and held.

1. Begin in a comfortable seated position, ideally with your back resting against a chair or wall. You can close your eyes or leave them open.

2. Notice the general feeling of being supported by whatever you are sitting on and resting against, the embodied sense of being held.

3. With non-judgemental curiosity, move your awareness to the parts of your body that are in contact with your surroundings – your back, your bottom, the backs of your legs, your feet, your hands. Spend a few moments noticing the sensations at each point of contact in as much detail as possible – is there tension, tenderness, tingling, pressure, heaviness, warmth? – bringing your awareness back to each point of contact whenever your mind wanders.

Centring

Ancient yogic scripture speaks of a centre of spiritual consciousness, an inner dwelling place, known as the lotus of the heart. By centring ourselves in our hearts and anchoring our awareness deep inside, we can counteract our physiological stress reaction, which tends to divert our energy and awareness to our limbs (this is an evolutionary response that is helpful when we need to run away from tigers, but not when we want to explore our inner worlds).

1. Begin in a comfortable seated position. You can close your eyes or leave them open.

2. Place one hand on your chest, over your heart centre, noticing the physical sensations between your palm and your chest.

3. Slowly begin anchoring your awareness deeper inside by visualising a lotus flower unfolding in the centre of your chest. If the image of a lotus flower

doesn't come naturally, play around with other images, such as a different type of flower, a flame or simply the space itself. Dwell in this place for as long as you need.

Anchoring

When we feel overwhelmed by intense emotions or lost in anxious thoughts, we can use our senses as anchors, tethering us to the safety of the present moment.

1. Look around you and name five things you can see.
2. Become aware of four things you can feel. Reach out and touch different things if you want to.
3. Listen deeply for three things you can hear.
4. Notice two things you can smell. Sniff your clothes or skin if you're struggling to notice any subtle fragrances in the air.
5. Take one deep belly breath. Inhaling through your nose for a count of three and exhaling for a count of six.

A gentle reminder

This work can be emotionally intense, and there may be times when you need to reach out for professional support so that you can heal in the safety of a therapeutic relationship.

Awakening intention

Before you begin, you might like to explore the following questions. First, grounding yourself and centring yourself in your heart using the tools on pages 27–29, then reading and journaling about the questions below.

- **What called me to begin reading this book?**
  Our callings often present themselves unexpectedly, in ways that are rarely rational or logical. Sometimes, they can be felt as an inner pull, a synchronicity, a spark of inspiration. Other times, our callings arise in the midst of confusion, chaos and crisis.

- **Where would I like to be in 365 days' time?**
  The goals we set and intentions we make now are like seeds we plant deep within us. Each day that you return to your practice, to your journal, to yourself, you water those seeds and nurture them, allowing them to blossom in their own time. It might be helpful to ask yourself: over the next year, what kind of life do I want to create? What strengths do I want to cultivate? What kind of relationships do I want to build with myself – my thoughts, my emotions, my body – the people I love and the wider world?

- **Knowing I have planted these seeds, how would it feel to release my goals so that I can give myself fully to the practice and whatever unfolds?**

  We can plant the seeds, but we cannot force them to grow. As paradoxical as it seems, we move closer to healing when we stop striving to achieve it. As we embrace each question with gentleness and curiosity, and stay present with whatever arises, moving towards our goals takes place by itself.

- **What boundaries do I need to set to make healing and awakening a priority in my life?**

  Awakening requires a certain amount of intentionality, effort and commitment, and our lives are busy, so it is necessary to set boundaries in order to protect our practice. Making time for daily reflection and journaling is not selfish; nor is setting boundaries with ourselves about bulldozing through resistance. Rather, our boundaries give us a container that can hold us in times of pain and doubt. They offer us a gentle reminder that giving ourselves time and space for healing is important, that our inner work matters, and that our awakening is sacred.

Gentle reminders

Awakening is not becoming someone we are not. It is remembering who we *are*. Remembering our wholeness when we feel broken. Remembering to be present when we feel afraid. Remembering to hold ourselves with compassion when we are in pain. At the end of each chapter, you will find some gentle reminders to help you remember, because this journey is one of continuous forgetting and remembering, slipping into autopilot and stepping into consciousness, falling asleep and awakening to the fierce beauty of our lives once more.

Some gentle reminders as we begin:

- We are always doing our best in every moment.
- We can't always see the light at the end of the tunnel, but we can learn to see in the dark.
- The things that no longer serve us also once saved us.
- There is no hierarchy of suffering. All pain is worthy of our love and attention.
- There is no rush. Healing has its own cycles, its own rhythms.
- There is no wrong path; there are no wrong turns.
- There is nothing to fix, because we have always been whole, and there is nowhere to go, because we are already home.

Awakening compassion

This journey of healing and awakening requires compassion at every step. Compassion for our humanness. Compassion for our anger, our rage and our shame. Compassion for the goals we did not reach and mistakes we have made. Where self-esteem says, 'I am good/bad, right/wrong, ugly/beautiful,' self-compassion says, 'I am human – imperfect, unfinished and still worthy.'

Consciously cultivating self-compassion involves three elements defined by Dr Kristin Neff, a compassion researcher at the University of Texas: being mindful when we are struggling; treating ourselves with kindness instead of judgement; and remembering our common humanity (recognising that life is hard for everyone sometimes). Emerging research shows just how powerful compassion can be in reducing anxiety, depression, shame, perfectionism and body-image distress, as well as increasing happiness, self-confidence and optimism, improving immune function and time-management, and creating more caring, supportive relationships.

When was the last time I treated someone else with compassion?

Often, we struggle to offer ourselves the same compassion we give to others. We treat ourselves with harshness where we would treat others with gentleness; we judge and criticise ourselves where we would offer others tenderness and love. Bring to mind the last time you treated someone with compassion. Maybe you were able to hold them in their pain, to witness their grief, to remind them of their beauty when all they could see was their flaws. How would it feel to treat yourself with the same gentleness?

What is something I have been struggling with lately?

Identifying and acknowledging the difficulties we are experiencing instead of dismissing them can be incredibly healing. Reflect on something you have been finding difficult lately. It can be a specific situation you are struggling with, or more of an ongoing worry. What would you say to someone you loved who was experiencing this kind of confusion or pain?

What stops me from being compassionate towards myself?

We may have read about all the benefits of self-compassion and yet struggle to practise it. Sometimes this is because we fear that, without our harsh self-criticism, we'd lose control; that if we stopped berating and bullying ourselves, we wouldn't have the motivation to achieve our goals. But, without self-compassion, our striving usually ends in exhaustion, overwhelm and burnout.

Reflect on what has been stopping you from being more compassionate towards yourself in the past. Common barriers include perfectionism, people-pleasing, difficulties setting loving boundaries, cognitive fusion (getting entangled with our thoughts) and excessive experiential avoidance (trying to avoid unwanted thoughts and feelings, even when this avoidance is likely to increase our suffering in the long run).

What expectations do I have of myself that I can stop pressuring myself to meet?

Self-compassion is an emotion, an intention and a skill. It is something we can learn. As we practise it, it slowly replaces our patterns of self-judgement and self-criticism until self-compassion becomes our natural way of being. One way we can practise self-compassion is by taking the pressure off ourselves to live up to unrealistically high standards. Reflect on any areas of your life where you are putting an unnecessary amount of pressure on yourself and explore how you can release it. This might look like going through your to-do list and removing anything that is not urgent or important, or maybe it means delegating household chores, or asking for help at work instead of feeling you need to do it alone.

Where do I get caught in a comparison trap?

Social comparison is deeply human, but too much of it can make us feel that what we look like, how we live and who we are is never enough. Social media has made it easier than ever to compare our bodies, homes and lives to other people's, which can have a negative effect on our wellbeing. And while comparison might temporarily boost our self-esteem if we evaluate ourselves as prettier, richer or more successful than others, self-compassion is not dependent on anything external. Instead, we offer compassion to ourselves unconditionally – because we are human, and all humans deserve compassion.

Reflect on areas where you regularly engage in comparison. How can you practise compassion instead? For example, if you notice yourself comparing your relationship to picture-perfect ones you see on social media, the most compassionate thing to do might be to unfollow those accounts and remind yourself that, while your relationship might not look like theirs, it is still beautiful.

What things does my inner critic often say to me?

Our inner critic is the force within us that constantly criticises, compares, shames, blames and judges our worth. It makes it difficult to journey within ourselves and do the inner work needed to heal, because each time we meet a challenging emotion or a part of ourselves we have been taught to believe is unlovable, it will attack us. By becoming aware of the voice of our inner critic, we can recognise it for what is – patterns of self-limiting thoughts internalised from early life experiences and wider social expectations – and continue our healing journey with less shame and more compassion.

Make a list of the common ways your inner critic attacks you. Becoming conscious of these self-destructive thoughts can be hard so be gentle with yourself as you do this. How could you respond to each criticism with compassion to help create some space from your thoughts? For example, if you look in the mirror and your inner critic is immediately judgemental, you might like to reply with something like: 'Looking at myself in the mirror is really painful today, so I need to be extra gentle with myself.'

How can self-compassion help me make room for uncomfortable emotions (both my own and others')?

As children, we need someone to be with us in our pain, to listen to us and hold us and show us that feeling pain is a natural part of life. If we don't get this safe space, this loving ground, if we are shamed for expressing certain emotions, such as rage or fear or sadness, we find ways to repress them. This might manifest as shallow breathing, muscular tension, comfort eating, negative self-talk, emotional numbing, addictions and difficulties relaxing. Although we can't change our childhood, as adults we can create a compassionate space where all emotions are welcome, where we can gently and lovingly be present with our pain.

Reflect on how you usually cope with uncomfortable emotions. How could practising self-compassion help you experience them in a more loving and tender way?

What is one feeling I have been struggling to feel?

Often, our fear of feelings is much worse than the feelings themselves. Sometimes, our fear is so great that instead of *feeling* our feelings, we might find ourselves thinking about them, talking about them, and even trying to solve them. But feelings want to be *felt*, not fixed. Self-compassion offers us a way to move from being in our heads and fixing to being in our hearts and feeling. By practising the three elements of self-compassion – self-kindness instead of self-judgement, mindfulness instead of avoidance and awareness of our common humanity instead of isolation – we can begin to feel our feelings instead of being afraid of them.

Reflect on an emotion you've been struggling to allow yourself to feel recently. This might be an unpleasant emotion, such as anger, grief or disappointment, or you might have been finding it difficult to experience joy, peace and excitement because they have been overshadowed by guilt or shame. What strategies have you been using to try and avoid this feeling, or to fix it? How can you offer yourself self-compassion when this feeling arises?

Who are the people in my life who treat me with compassion?

There is only so much healing we can do on our own. Much of our healing and awakening happens in the safety of a relationship. This isn't co-dependency. This is co-regulation. We need people in our lives that accept us unconditionally, that hold space for our pain without trying to fix it, that offer us love even when we don't feel we are worthy of it. Through these relationships, we internalise the capacity to self-soothe, to treat ourselves with compassion, and to create a safe space within ourselves where we can rest.

Reflect on the people in your life that accept you unconditionally. Are there relationships in which you feel truly seen and safe? Who do you know that embodies self-compassion and can therefore awaken it within your heart, too?

What is one awakened action I can take to cultivate self-compassion?

We cultivate self-compassion by practising it, by experiencing it directly, by embodying it. Reflect on one way in which you can practise self-compassion by weaving it into your everyday life. This might look like placing your hand on your heart when you feel a difficult emotion arise, or speaking to yourself like you would someone you love whenever you are struggling, or noticing when your inner critic gets loud and asking, 'What is the kindest thing I can do for myself right now?'.

Awakening awareness

Awareness is indivisible from aliveness. And yet, many of us find ourselves moving through life on autopilot. Only half awake. Only half alive. Awareness offers us a different way of knowing the world, a way of noticing, of paying attention, of directly experiencing the fullness of each moment so that we can see it clearly and live it fully. Awareness returns us to this breath, this body, this moment. It reminds us that, here, now, is the only place where we will find healing, where we will find beauty, where we will find love.

How present am I in my life?

The journey and destination of awakening are the same: being fully alive in the present moment. Being with things as they are. As we learn to fully inhabit each moment instead of running away from it, even if this moment is filled with discomfort, tension or pain, we begin to see things more clearly instead of through the muddied lens of our opinions, beliefs and conditioning. And from this place of clarity, we can respond mindfully rather than react automatically. And yet, research shows we spend around fifty per cent of our day living on autopilot, with our wandering minds sabotaging our mood, focus and sleep.

Reflect on how present you are in your life. How much time do you spend ruminating about the past or worrying about the future? How aware are you of what you are thinking, what you are feeling, how you are breathing?

What gets in the way of me living in a state of present-moment awareness?

The demands of modern life can mean that it is hard to be present. There is a subtle but pervasive pressure to always be somewhere other than where we are right now, as if we should be constantly moving forwards and making progress. But when we are always striving to achieve something else or be someone else, we aren't fully present in our bodies, our relationships or our lives. Awakening happens as we strip away the things that block our awareness and learn to rest in the unfolding, flowing present.

Reflect on what stops you from being fully present. What psychological barriers and mental habits get in the way of you living mindfully? These could include planning, ruminating, fantasising, striving, judging, criticising, analysing, rushing and multitasking.

How often am I living on autopilot?

Living on autopilot means we miss what is most beautiful and meaningful in our lives. We might also find ourselves acting in ways that are not in alignment with our deepest values. But, because awareness and compulsion cannot coexist, as we learn to ground ourselves in the present moment and pay attention to our thoughts, emotions and physical sensations, we can access our agency. Our awareness creates a choice point, a pause between impulse and action where we can choose to give our energy to what truly matters.

Reflect on how often you live on autopilot. When do you find yourself acting mechanically or compulsively?

What mental chatter do I experience on a daily basis?

Awareness helps us to see the difference between what is happening and the stories we tell ourselves about what is happening. Often, these mental stories are habitual soundtracks that play on repeat in our minds. We might find our minds wandering to predictable places or being critical about the same thing over and over again. This kind of rumination traps us in a spiral of negative thinking. Buddhist writings sometimes use the term 'monkey mind', meaning the feeling that our minds are full of chattering, screeching monkeys. Instead of recognising our mental chatter as intrusive thoughts, however, we often come to see them as truths. And yet, if we can be aware that they are actually automatic – and often meaningless – thoughts that arise when our minds are restless, and practise bringing ourselves back to the present moment whenever our minds start to wander, we will be able to see things more clearly.

Reflect on the mental chatter you often experience. Where does your mind go when it wanders? What are the themes of your inner dialogue? What kind of soundtracks play on repeat?

What parts of my body exist outside my conscious awareness?

We have normalised living stressed, sleep-deprived, over-scheduled lives that force us to override our bodies' basic needs. It has become normal to diet instead of recognising our hunger, to take painkillers so we can push through injury, to work eighteen-hour days fuelled on caffeine, and to exploit our bodies in ways that force us to disassociate from them. In the short term, this disembodiment can be a protective strategy. But, over time, this level of disconnection and suppression can lead to illness and isolation.

With practice, we can reconnect with our bodies. We can become aware of when we need to eat, when we need to cry and when we need to rest. We can get to know where we hold tension and how our breath changes when we are stressed. We can learn to sense the centre of our bodies, anchoring our awareness deep inside, grounding ourselves in the safety of the present.

Reflect on how much of your body exists outside your conscious awareness. How often do you leave your body, exiting into thinking or worrying? Are there parts of your body that you feel disconnected from, that feel uninhabited, empty or numb?

What do I pay attention to in daily life? What am I leaving out?

When we are fixated on fragments of our lives – our goals, our fears, our pain – we tend to become blind to the vastness of our existence. As we start to become more present in our lives, we often realise how much of our experiences we have been ignoring. We may have spent so long living in survival mode, hypervigilant to potential danger, that we fail to notice cues of safety and moments of beauty. Or we may be so emotionally invested in things needing to be a certain way for us to be happy that we fail to see opportunities for connection, meaning and wholeness.

Reflect on what you pay attention to in daily life and what you leave out. What occupies most of your awareness? What areas are you ignoring or neglecting?

How am I avoiding uncomfortable truths?

Much of our suffering comes from being too afraid to look at ourselves and our lives gently and honestly. We often resist the truths at the edge of our awareness, because a part of us knows that facing them may mean that we need to let go of comforting illusions and identities, release beliefs and habits we have been clinging to, and find the courage to change. And yet, attempting to avoid uncomfortable truths and pain in life only creates more heartache. Awakening asks us to embrace what mindfulness teacher and author Jon Kabat-Zinn calls the 'full catastrophe': an appreciation of the vastness and richness of life; an acceptance that, at some point, we will all experience deep love and great loss, blissful joy and dark despair, stunning success and spectacular failure.

Reflect on what you do to avoid facing uncomfortable truths. How do you distract yourself? How do you suppress these truths when they start arising? Do you reach for your phone? Do you plough your energy into your work? Do you put on your trainers and literally try to outrun them?

How do I habitually react to intense thoughts, urges and emotions?

Negative thoughts and unpleasant emotions are part of being human. We cannot stop them from arising or make them go away, but we can change how we relate to them. We can notice our thoughts without believing them. We can feel our urges without acting on them. We can experience our emotions without drowning in them. And yet, many of us believe that we cannot tolerate our reality moment by moment; that we need to escape it through people-pleasing and obsessive busyness. As we awaken, our task is to be aware when we leave the present moment, when we get lost in old patterns, and then to slowly and gently return to our bodies, welcoming whatever is present.

Reflect on how you habitually react to unpleasant thoughts, emotions and urges. What do you do when a self-critical thought arises? How do you respond to the urge to take something to the extreme? How do you express or suppress difficult feelings?

How often do I give myself space for my inner wisdom to emerge?

Sometimes we do not know what wisdom we carry until we give it space to come to consciousness. When we are caught up in the noise and chaos of daily life, this inner wisdom gets drowned out, and we find ourselves being pushed and pulled by the mental chatter of the 'monkey mind' and other people's opinions and expectations. By setting aside small moments of stillness throughout the day in which to be present, to focus on our breath and return to our bodies, we can create space for insight to crystallise.

Reflect on how often you pause throughout the day. How often do you carve out time for silence and stillness? Think back to when you last experienced an 'aha' moment that allowed you to see the world in a new way – what gave rise to that realisation?

What am I noticing right now?

Sometimes, awakening is sitting down and closing our eyes. Other times, it is staying right where we are and opening them. It is pausing. It is noticing. It is paying attention to the outer world at the same time as being aware of what is going on in our inner worlds. It is feeling the ground beneath us and the sky above us and the life force within us. It is witnessing and watching without trying to change anything. It is returning to our bodies and our breath and the beat of our hearts.

Pause and notice what is going on for you right now – without judgement, and without trying to change anything. What do you see? What do you hear? What do you feel? How is your mind? How is your body? How is your heart?

Awakening ego strength

Some forms of spirituality and pop psychology demonise the ego, but it can be a doorway to awakening rather than an obstacle. Instead of destroying the ego, we want to build it, to strengthen it, to integrate it. Ego strength is a psychoanalytic concept that describes our capacity to adapt to our environment, to stay connected to our values even when we are experiencing distress, and to balance our inner impulses with the demands of the external world. A strong ego is like an anchor for our healing and growth. It allows us to break free from our conditioning, learn from challenging experiences, set boundaries and pursue meaningful goals. When we have a strong ego, we can confidently say, 'This is me.'

Awakening is a process of integrating rather than eliminating the ego, and building ego strength is essential as we move deeper into the *Daily Awakening* journey. Use this section to explore your ego and how you can strengthen it.

What inner strengths and life skills do I already have?

Ego strength is something we develop over the course of our lives. According to psychologist Erik Erikson, we develop this strength as we resolve psychosocial conflicts in our development. Resolving these conflicts successfully leads to the development of inner strengths, such as hope, willpower, purpose, confidence and love. Through practice and life experience, we also build mental capacities called psychological skills (for example, focus, goal-setting, distraction resistance, arousal regulation and visualisation).

Reflect on the inner strengths and psychological skills you have already cultivated. Think about those listed above, as well as other ego functions, such as awareness, compassion, problem-solving, experiential acceptance (the capacity to be with difficult emotions), impulse control, abstract thinking, cognitive defusion (creating space between our thoughts and feelings so they no longer have such a hold over us), goal-setting, attentional control and arousal regulation. You might also like to include life skills, such as apologising, time-management, sticking to a budget, cooking nourishing meals and asking for help.

What ego strengths was I never taught when growing up?

If we lack certain ego strengths or skills, it's not because we are weak or because there is something wrong with us. It's because we were never taught how to set boundaries or deal with conflict or tolerate distress. It's because no one ever showed us how to express our anger or question our beliefs or regulate our emotions. Being aware that these are things we need to be taught allows us to treat ourselves with more compassion. If your inner critic calls you weak for eating an entire pack of cookies when you really only wanted one, you can respond compassionately: 'It's not because I'm weak. It's because no one ever taught me how to be with the discomfort of my emotions and impulses without acting on them.'

Reflect on the ego strengths you never learned growing up that you would like to work on and cultivate in the future. These can be anything from acceptance to stress tolerance and self-expression.

How can I cultivate these ego strengths now?

At school, we are taught about arithmetic, grammar and the periodic table. But no one teaches us how to set healthy boundaries. No one teaches us how to listen to our intuition. No one teaches us how to feel our feelings or communicate our needs or hold space for our pain. And yet, because the ego is continually evolving, if there are ego strengths and psychological skills that we were never taught as children, we can still learn them as adults.

Reflect on some practices you can use to help develop any unfamiliar ego strengths. For example, you might want to check in on your emotional state periodically throughout the day to strengthen your emotional awareness, while turning off notifications on your phone will allow you to strengthen your distraction resistance, and asking your partner to help you put together a list of rules for healthy arguing can strengthen your conflict-resolution skills. Be as creative as you can.

What makes me feel alive?

When we lack ego strength, we often lose touch with our own preferences and passions. Instead, we find ourselves wearing what our friends are wearing, watching the movies our partner likes watching, or following our parents' goals instead of our own. Sometimes what drives our actions can be traced back to childhood experiences. For example, if you used to love painting but were told you weren't good at it or wouldn't be able to make any money from it, you may have given it up, and so lost access to the energy and sense of being alive it gave you. You can strengthen your ego by reclaiming your right to like what *you* like, even if it's different to what everyone else likes.

Reflect on what you like and dislike. As a starting point, think about hobbies, food, music, movies, books, animals and places to visit. What are you passionate about? When in your life have you felt most alive?

What beliefs am I living by that are not my own?

Beliefs act as a filter through which we see ourselves and the world. If we believe success looks like having a lot of money and owning a lot of stuff, we will never be able to experience success in any other way. Untangling what we have been *conditioned* to believe from what we *choose* to believe strengthens the ego. As children, we are naturally influenced by the beliefs of our parents and peers, and those we are exposed to through education, religion and culture. As adults, we get to choose whether these beliefs are serving us and helping us be of service in the world. Because so many of our beliefs are unconscious, uncovering and understanding them is the work of a lifetime.

Reflect on some of your core beliefs and ask yourself whether each one is something you have been conditioned to believe or something you feel in your heart to be true. You might like to think about the beliefs you hold relating to your worth, your body, relationships, success, work, money, sex, God, time-management and rest.

What are my core values?

Our core values are the grounding forces that guide us through our lives. Knowing our values and honouring them strengthens our egos. However, unless we take the time to reflect on our own values, we tend to absorb the values of our families and culture. If the society we live in values productivity, physical attractiveness and material wealth, it's likely we will find ourselves valuing the same things unless we consciously reflect on them.

Reflect on your core values. These are not the values you feel you 'should' be living by, but those that live within you. You might find it helpful to read through this list and pick three to five values that resonate with you on an intuitive, embodied level: achievement, ambition, authenticity, balance, beauty, calmness, compassion, courage, creativity, dependability, discipline, empathy, ethical living, fame, family, freedom, friendship, fun, generosity, gratitude, hard work, health, hope, intuition, justice, kindness, logic, love, loyalty, motivation, openness, optimism, passion, peace, playfulness, power, presence, purpose, respect, selflessness, sensitivity, service, spirituality, status, thoughtfulness, trustworthiness, vitality, wealth, wisdom.

What challenges have I overcome in my life?

Sometimes, it's only when we reflect on our lives and everything we have overcome that we can see how strong we really are. Often, it's the most challenging situations that gift us our greatest strengths. This doesn't mean that these situations weren't painful or traumatic, or that we have to be grateful for having experienced them. Rather, it allows us to acknowledge the inner strength and resilience we have developed, even through our pain.

Reflect on the challenges you've overcome in your life. What have you learned from each obstacle, and what strengths have you gained from them?

How do I deal with difficult emotions?

As we strengthen our egos, we develop the capacity to feel our emotions without being overwhelmed by them. But there are times when it might not feel safe to experience the intensity of our emotions, especially as children. In these situations, we use psychological survival strategies to protect us from painful emotions and inner conflict. Although some of these coping mechanisms may appear self-destructive or frustrating to others (for example, passive aggressiveness), they are protective strategies that cushion us from the intensity of our pain until we feel safe enough to feel it.

Reflect on the coping mechanisms you use to deal with difficult emotions and consider whether they are life-enhancing or life-limiting. You might like to use this list of common psychological survival strategies as a guide: avoidance, denial, repression, suppression, projection, intellectualisation, humour, passive aggressiveness and acting out.

How would it feel to be someone with a strong ego?

Having a strong ego gives us a solid container that can hold the wild and creative energies that flow through us as we heal and awaken. As our egos get stronger, we are able to appreciate our uniqueness, accept our imperfections and hold ourselves with compassion when we get things wrong.

Reflect on how it would feel to have a strong ego. How would it feel to trust in your abilities, to be connected with a deep sense of purpose, and to feel able to balance your own needs with what the world demands of you? You might like to close your eyes and get a sense of how it would feel to be this awakened version of yourself. How would you speak? How would you move? How would you live? What would you be able to do that you don't feel able to do now?

What is one awakened action I can take to cultivate ego strength?

We build ego strength in the same way as we build physical strength: by training it. Reflect on something practical you can do to strengthen your ego. It might be pausing every evening to acknowledge your achievements and the strengths you have used. Or it could be reflecting on any reactive coping mechanisms you have used, and whether there was a more conscious, compassionate way you would have liked to respond. Or you might want to spend twenty minutes a day working on a long-term goal that has always fallen to the bottom of your to-do list, be it the book you've been trying to write or the business you've been longing to get off the ground.

Awakening authenticity

Self-reflection awakens us to the mystery of our own identity. We begin to wonder, 'Who am I?' We question who really lies behind the masks we wear, whether there is more to us than the person we allow the world to see, the version of us we've been told we should be. We feel called to dive deep within, to discover what is real in us, what is true. As we release the stories we tell ourselves about who we are and who we should be, we discover our true selves, waiting patiently within us in all their glory.

When do I feel most like myself?

There are moments in life when we stumble across something that feels *real* within us. Something unconditioned. Untamed. Unbreakable. Sometimes it's when we experience great joy, true love, overwhelming grief or deep despair. At other times, we might feel like our truest selves in seemingly ordinary, everyday moments, when the clouds of our conditioning begin to clear and the blazing presence that has been hidden behind them shines through.

Reflect on when you feel most like yourself. Who do you feel completely yourself with? Where do you feel most at peace? What are you doing when you feel most like yourself?

When I don't feel like myself, what is missing?

Sometimes we become strangers to ourselves. We lose touch with our essence, our aliveness. Things might look fine on the outside, but everything feels mechanical, and we become numb. It seems like we are observing our lives rather than living them. Without really knowing what's wrong, something essential appears to be missing. Often, it's difficult to work out exactly what we have lost during these periods of alienation, but, by taking the time to consider what is missing, we begin to make sense of what feels most real, and how we can stay connected to that part of ourselves.

Reflect on what is missing when you don't feel like yourself. Your energy? Your emotions? Your power? Your hope? Your trust? Your joy? Your confidence? Your worthiness? Your divinity? Once you have reflected on what is missing, think about how you can reconnect with those essential qualities and parts of yourself.

What does 'true self' mean to me?

Across cultures and traditions, there is a consensus that we have a true self, although it is called by many different names: essential self, authentic self, true nature, Buddha nature, inner compass, inner light, moral essence, universal consciousness, soul, spirit, spark of the divine, the still, small voice inside. Research has found that experiencing a connection with our true self, however we may perceive it, enhances our relationships, motivation and psychological wellbeing.

Reflect on what 'true self' means to you. Is it discovered or created? Is it unchanging and timeless or continually emerging? Is it connected to your values and morals? Does it feel separate from other parts of yourself, or more of a force that unites them all? Does it feel personal, universal or both?

What habits, traits and beliefs feel like part of my false self?

The 'false self' is born when we are not welcomed as we are: when we have to be someone other than ourselves in order to feel safe and loved. As we grow up, we begin to identify with this false self, to mistake conditioned behaviours and beliefs as part of who we really are. In his book *I Am That*, the spiritual teacher Sri Nisargadatta Maharaj writes, 'The false self must be abandoned before the true self can be found.' And leaving behind the false self can be painful. A stripping away of all that is not real. A necessary destruction that leaves nothing but what is true.

Reflect on the habits, traits and beliefs that feel like part of your false self. Who did you need to be in order to feel safe and loved as a child? A people-pleaser? A perfectionist? An over-achiever? What identities have you outgrown? How would it feel to release them?

When was the last time I listened to my true self?

Sometimes, we make decisions based on logic. We research the facts. We calculate the figures. We write lists of pros and cons. At other times, we might feel compelled to do something that doesn't make much sense and goes against other people's advice – and yet we do it anyway, because, intuitively, it feels like the right thing to do. Sometimes these are big things – changing jobs, leaving relationships, moving countries – and other times they are little, everyday things – what we fancy for lunch, which route we'll take on our walk, what book we want to read.

Reflect on the last time you listened to your true self. Think about how it felt and where it led you.

How does my true self communicate with me?

You need to learn the language your soul speaks: the way it communicates with you, how it whispers its wisdom in a way that is often beyond words. Most of us tend to miss the voices of our true selves, because they are drowned out by other people's beliefs and expectations, and because we have been encouraged to distrust anything not based on logic, facts or statistics.

Reflect on how your true self communicates with you. This might include strong gut feelings, random insights, unexplainable serendipities, symbols or visions in dreams or during meditation, finding yourself drawn towards certain myths, poems and archetypes, and sensing an inner voice that is softer and gentler than that of your inner critic.

When do I not feel able to be myself?

We often find ourselves in situations where we feel like we have to perform, to please, to pretend to be someone we are not. We become chameleons, adapting our personas to fit in. When it doesn't feel safe to be ourselves, we put on a mask, becoming who we think the world wants us to be, hiding the truth and beauty of who we are.

Reflect on some past situations where you didn't feel you could be your true self. Why did you feel that you had to hide who you are? When have you acted in ways that don't feel true to yourself? Who do you put on a mask with? Who do you feel you have to perform for?

When have I experienced inner conflict between my true self and another part of me?

We are multifaceted beings. Each of us contains different parts and subpersonalities that, alongside our true selves, make up who we are. Some of these parts feel nurturing – a loving parent, a playful child, a wise teacher – and other parts might seem to be in conflict with our true selves. We might know, deep down, that our drinking is becoming destructive, while an addictive part urges us to have another glass of wine. We might long to relax, and yet have a workaholic part that calls us lazy. We might know that our bodies are sacred, while an insecure part of us still criticises the size of our thighs.

Reflect on where you have experienced conflict between your true self and another part of you. Can you name the other part? How does it communicate differently from your true self?

In the depth of my heart, what do I truly want?

Our self-reflection often allows us to see that what we think we want is what we've been conditioned to want – the promotion, the big house, the pay rise. We realise that we have never allowed our true wants to reach the threshold of our awareness in case they are socially unacceptable. We fear that, unless we suppress our desires, they will overwhelm us. But the more we are aware of our wants, the less compulsive our actions become. As we become aware of what we need, both moment to moment and in the long term, we can align our actions with our truth.

Reflect on what you truly want. What do you long for right now? This week? This year? This lifetime?

What is one awakened action I can take to experience and embody my true self?

As we reflect more deeply on moments when we have felt most like ourselves, and times when we have felt alienated and estranged, we can get a sense of what distances us from our true selves and what unites us with the essence of our aliveness.

Reflect on one small, practical way you can begin to experience and embody your true self. Maybe when the urge to seek someone else's permission or approval arises, you can pause and tune into the wisdom of your own intuition. Perhaps you can take five minutes each day to sit in stillness, paying attention to any insights that arise. Or maybe you can keep a dream diary to explore what your true self is trying to communicate with you.

Awakening self-worth

If we believe we are unworthy, we tend to spend our lives striving to earn our worth through external things. And yet, some part of us knows that this scared, striving self is not who we truly are. That no matter how hard we work or how much we buy, we will never find our true worth in our appearance, achievements or accomplishments. Because our worth is rooted in something deeper, something indestructible and unbreakable. No matter how imperfect we judge ourselves to be, no matter how many mistakes we make or how many times we fail, we are, and always will be, worthy.

What conditions do I place on my own worth?

Self-worth is the feeling that we are enough just as we are, and that even if we've made mistakes and there are parts of ourselves we would like to change, we are still worthy and lovable. But in modern society, it's not easy to see our own worth, our own goodness. Instead, we tend to internalise the message that it is only through achieving external success and gaining the approval of others that we will be worthy.

Reflect on the conditions you place on your worth. For example, maybe you only feel worthy on the condition that you weigh less than a specific number on the scales, or if you earn more than a certain amount each month, or if you are in a romantic relationship. Usually, the conditions we place on our worth fall into six categories: approval, appearance, external achievement, family support, virtue and being loved by God or another supreme being.

What conditions do I place on other people's worth?

Often, the conditions we place on other people's worth are very different to those we place on our own. Sometimes, for example when we comfort someone who is in pain, there are no conditions at all. Their mistakes, their shame, their success – none of it matters. We see their inherent worthiness. We see that they are deserving. And, when they forget their worth, we are often the first ones to remind them of it, to show them their inner light. The Sanskrit word *namaste*, means, 'I honour the divine in you. I see that which is holy in you.' This captures our capacity to see another's inherent worthiness. And, when it is reflected back to us, it helps us to see our own.

Reflect on the conditions you place on other people's worth. How do they differ from the conditions you place on your own?

What beliefs, judgements and fears get in the way of me recognising my inherent worth?

Sometimes we get so caught up in our beliefs, fears and judgements that we forget who we really are. We can become so focused on fixing ourselves that we end up blind to our wholeness. Spiritual practices, like Mahayana Buddhism (which is one of the two major branches of Buddhism and is rooted in compassion) can teach us how to clear away the layers of limiting beliefs, ego desires and cultural conditioning that blind us to our worth, so that we can reconnect with our 'Buddha nature' – a state of being filled with compassion, wisdom and love.

Reflect on what is blinding you to your Buddha nature. What beliefs, judgements, fears and desires are getting in the way of you recognising your inherent worthiness? Where did you absorb these beliefs from? As you awaken, what do you choose to believe?

How is my self-worth based on how others perceive me?

Social media has made it easier than ever to base our self-worth on other people's approval. It opens the door to a world of comparing our bodies, our relationships and our lives with those of millions of strangers. The more we are exposed to idealised images of other people's lives, the vaster the discrepancy becomes between who we are and who we feel we need to be in order to be worthy.

Reflect on how much of your self-worth is based on what other people think of you. Do you need the approval of your friends and family? Does the number of followers you have on Instagram affect your self-worth? Does how people respond to your ideas at work affect your sense of worth?

What wounds of unworthiness need healing?

Our wounds of unworthiness are the past experiences that make us believe we are undeserving of love, happiness or fulfilment; that there is something wrong with us; that we need to fix a part of ourselves in order to be lovable. As children, and sometimes as adults, we are wounded each time we are criticised, rejected or punished for expressing our feelings or asking for what we need. This makes us believe we are flawed or 'bad', and, therefore, unlovable. We can be wounded unintentionally by those closest to us, and also intentionally, perhaps through bullying or due to cultural and religious attitudes.

Reflect on any wounds of unworthiness that need healing within you. Maybe you were wounded when you were called 'naughty' as a child and you internalised the belief you were 'bad'. Or perhaps you were wounded when a teacher made you feel that you weren't smart enough to go to college, or when a school friend commented on your weight.

What qualities of my true nature do I need to reconnect with?

In her book *A Return to Love*, Marianne Williamson writes: 'Our deepest fear is not that we are inadequate. Our deepest fear is that we are powerful beyond measure.' Growing up, we are taught to play small. To shrink ourselves. To be submissive, self-deprecating and tame. We learn to fear our inner light as much as our darkness. To be afraid of our true nature – the essence of who we are – and the wildness and wisdom it contains. Our true nature is not related to our appearance, identity, history, beliefs or opinions. Rather, it is the unconditioned 'soul qualities' we are born with: peace, truth, joy, compassion, strength, will, curiosity, presence and aliveness.

Using the list above, reflect on the parts of your true nature that you feel disconnected from. How can you reconnect with these essential qualities?

How does worthiness feel in my body?

Self-worth cannot be achieved or destroyed. It cannot be earned or diminished. No failure or flaw, no defeat or deficiency can take our worthiness away from us. It will always be within us, but we can lose touch with it – we can forget it exists. Then there are those moments when the storm clouds clear and we get a glimpse of our own sunlight, and we know, deep in our bones, we are sacred.

Reflect on how worthiness feels in your body. How does it feel when you are connected to your worth rather than disconnected from it? You might find it helpful to use the list of physical sensations on page 299 as a guide.

When do I feel most connected to my worth?

As we stop fixating on the parts of ourselves we've been led to believe are unlovable, our awareness expands beyond our perceived imperfections – not bypassing them, but *including* them – and we reconnect with our wholeness, our worthiness. As our wounds begin to heal, we experience more and more moments where we sense that we are enough, that we are sacred, where tender glimmers of our inner light glow through our self-criticism.

Reflect on those times when you feel most connected to your worthiness. Where are you? What are you doing? Who are you with?

Who treats me as sacred?

We internalise how we were loved as children as a reflection of our worth. Even as adults, if we only feel loved when we meet certain conditions, we can end up believing our worth is dependent on how we behave and what we achieve rather than simply who we are. By spending time with people who see our sacredness, we can unlearn our past conditioning. As we develop relationships where we can reveal ourselves fully and still be accepted, we rediscover that our worthiness has no conditions. Being truly seen and accepted by another reminds us that we are worthy for simply existing; that we do not have to do anything to earn it.

Reflect on who treats you as sacred. Can you remember a time when you felt truly seen and accepted? How might you develop and deepen relationships like this?

What is one awakened action I can take to reconnect with my inherent worthiness?

The idea of original sin – the idea that all human beings are born with some inherent badness due to the disobedience of Adam and Eve – pervades Western culture. As a result, many of us find ourselves living with a subtle sense that there is something wrong with us; something we need to atone for. However, as we reconnect with our inherent worthiness, we can begin to challenge the conditioning that has made us believe that our flaws and fears and failures – the very things that make us human – mean we are unworthy and unlovable.

Reflect on a practical way you can remind yourself that you are sacred. Perhaps you can arrange a weekly coffee date with someone who truly sees and accepts you, or maybe you can stick a photograph of yourself as a baby on the fridge as a reminder that you are worthy of love and devotion. Research has found that art, physical activity and being in nature can help to increase our self-worth, too.

Awakening self-trust

Society teaches us how to control ourselves – our bodies, our emotions, our desires – but not how to trust ourselves. As a result, many of us find ourselves second-guessing our decisions, valuing other people's opinions over our own, and doubting our capacity to handle the challenges we will inevitably face in life. This section will help you cultivate a relationship with yourself that is rooted in faith, trust and tenderness instead of control, doubt and betrayal.

Who do I trust and what makes these people trustworthy?

We learn both how to trust and that we can be trusted through our relationships. As children, when our needs are met by our parents or caregivers, we learn that our bodies, feelings and instincts can be trusted, that we have a right to feel what we feel and want what we want. As adults, we develop trusting relationships over time, when we learn that another person accepts us, cares about us and is there for us when we need them.

Reflect on the people that you trust. What qualities do they have? How have they shown they can be trusted? What makes you feel safe enough to be vulnerable or ask for their help? You might also like to think about people you don't trust and why.

How can I use the trusting relationships I have with others to help create a more trusting relationship with myself?

We build self-trust in the same way we build trust in any relationship: by being honest; by not making promises we can't keep; by honouring our feelings, desires, boundaries and time. If we have spent years overriding our bodies' needs, dismissing our emotions and sacrificing our true values in order to fit in, cultivating self-trust will take patience and practice.

Reflect on the qualities and behaviours you have identified in the people you trust. How can you begin treating yourself with the same compassion, acceptance and devotion they do? Are you making promises to yourself that you cannot keep? Are you setting goals that are impossible to reach? Are you honouring your hunger, your emotions, your core needs?

Where in my life am I struggling to trust myself?

When we are disconnected from our bodies, it is difficult to trust our instinctual needs for food, sleep and rest. When we are exhausted and overwhelmed, it is difficult to trust in our capacity to handle the pressures and demands of life. When we feel unworthy and afraid, it is difficult to trust the opinions we have and the decisions we make. By taking inventory of the areas in our lives where we do not trust ourselves, we can begin to understand why we lost that trust and how we can rebuild it.

Reflect on the parts of your life where you are struggling to trust yourself. Where do you feel out of control or feel the need to cling to it? Where do you doubt your abilities? Where do you seek constant reassurance?

What is preventing me from trusting myself?

To trust ourselves is to step into our own power, and also our own vulnerability. Self-trust requires a leap of faith, a loving surrender, a letting go of the need to figure everything out, to have all the answers, to be in control. Trusting ourselves also requires a feeling of safety. When we feel unsafe in our bodies, we tend to overestimate threats and underestimate our capacity to cope with challenges. We cannot trust ourselves until we feel safe within ourselves.

Reflect on what might be preventing you from trusting yourself in the areas you identified yesterday. Do you feel safe in your body? In your relationships? At work? Have you betrayed yourself in this area in the past? Has someone else made you doubt your abilities, or treated you as though your feelings, needs and boundaries do not matter?

What would it look like if I were to fully trust myself?

If we do not trust ourselves, what we feel and what we know, we tend to exhaust ourselves by following rigid schedules, keeping everything tightly controlled. We hide the cookies because we don't trust that we will only eat what our body needs. We write long to-do lists because we don't trust that everything will get done. We try to keep as busy as possible because we don't trust that we can cope with the stillness and silence of simply being. Re-establishing trust with ourselves involves honouring our feelings and needs, even if we do not understand why we feel hungrier or angrier or sleepier than usual.

Reflect on what it would be like to trust yourself in the areas where you are currently struggling to do so. How would trusting yourself change the way you eat? Work? Speak to yourself? Spend your time? Relate to others?

What skills do I need to learn so that I can trust myself and my ability to handle life's challenges?

What feels like a lack of trust in life is often a lack of trust in ourselves and our capacity to handle it. If we don't know how to cope with failure, we will spend our lives striving for perfection. If we have never been taught how to safely feel painful emotions, we might shrink our lives in an attempt to avoid experiencing them. If we've never learned how to have healthy conflict, we often stay quiet instead of speaking out. As we learn how to cope with failure, to sit with grief, to resolve conflict, we discover that we can cope with the world and all its beauty and suffering. That we can bear what we once thought was unbearable. That we can trust ourselves.

Reflect on the skills you need to practise so you can trust yourself. Maybe practising self-compassion will help you trust that you can cope with failure, and perhaps practising distress tolerance will allow you to trust in your capacity to experience intense emotions, while practising intuitive eating might allow you to trust your body so you can leave obsessive dieting behind.

What beliefs and behaviours erode my trust in myself?

We cannot trust someone we do not know. If we are busy all the time, if we never allow ourselves the time to get to know who we are beyond who we've been conditioned to be, we remain strangers to ourselves. Trusting ourselves requires knowing ourselves and knowing our own worthiness. It requires knowing that our feelings and needs matter. If we believe we are unworthy, if we gaslight ourselves by questioning our emotions, if we ignore our needs for food and nature and rest, our trust in ourselves begins to erode.

Reflect on what beliefs and behaviours may be destroying your trust in yourself. Where are you gaslighting yourself? How are you betraying yourself? What needs are you neglecting?

How has my conditioning made it more difficult to trust myself?

Trusting ourselves is often a process of deep unlearning, an untangling of our conditioned patterns and beliefs. If our basic needs were unmet as children, we will have learned to distrust our instincts. If we were told to stop crying, or that we had no right to be angry, we will have learned to distrust our emotions. If we live in a society that is dominated by science, where the opinion of external authorities matters most, we learn that our lived experiences cannot be trusted. If we allow ourselves to believe that, as human beings we are naturally inclined to behave badly, we learn not to trust ourselves.

Reflect on how your childhood and cultural conditioning has influenced your ability to trust yourself. Were your feelings welcomed when you were growing up? How have cultural beliefs around sin, goodness and human nature influenced you? How has living in Western society – which values logic over intuition, science over spirituality and the measurable over the mystical – affected your self-trust?

What feels different about making a decision from a place of trust rather than a place of fear?

We can feel trust viscerally in our bodies, in our heart rate, in our breath. While fear is a response to threat, trust is a response to safety. When we make a decision from a place of fear, our nervous systems are in a state of fight-or-flight, hijacking the networks in our brains that help us see clearly and think deeply. Being in a state of safety and trust expands our awareness, allowing us to see a situation from multiple perspectives so that we can make conscious, mindful decisions, allowing our inner wisdom to guide us.

Reflect on how it feels to make a decision from a place of trust rather than one of fear. How are trust-filled thoughts different from fear-filled ones? How does your body feel different? How does your breath change?

What is one promise I can make to myself to cultivate self-trust?

We cultivate self-trust by being with ourselves instead of busying ourselves. By honouring our emotions instead of burying them. By welcoming every facet of our beings rather than hiding the parts of ourselves we have been conditioned to believe are unacceptable. Cultivating this kind of self-trust is a slow and gentle process made up of honouring our needs and keeping the promises we make to ourselves.

Reflect on one small promise you can make to yourself. Start tiny. Maybe you can commit to meditating for two minutes each morning, or eating a piece of fruit at lunch, or reading a page of a book before bed.

Part one: Gentle reminders

* Often, what we most need to discover about ourselves will be found where we least want to look. Some of the questions in this book will shine light on our imperfections, anxieties and shame. Having self-compassion throughout this process is essential so that we can make space for these experiences in a safe, kind and loving way.

* We cannot make healing happen. We can only let it happen. It is always a by-product of being present. Of not running from our experience. Of embracing the wild mystery of being alive.

* Having a strong ego is not the same as being egotistical. A strong ego is a quiet ego. An integrated ego. An ego that serves your true self.

* It is not easy to stay true to ourselves in a world that can sometimes feel so fake. But, as we drop below the surface drama of our lives – below our judgements, comparisons and endless search for approval – we discover something deeper, something truer, something sacred.

- Recognising our own worth doesn't mean denying or neglecting the need for healing and inner work. Rather, it means recognising our shortcomings without attacking and shaming ourselves for having them.
- Self-acceptance expands our awareness so that we can say, 'I'm not where I want to be *and* I am still worthy', 'I have made mistakes *and* I am still worthy', and 'I'm sad and scared and struggling *and* I am still worthy.'
- Trusting ourselves doesn't mean that we will never fail or that everything in our lives will go smoothly. Rather, it means that we don't have to fear so much or cling so tightly because we know we have the capacity to deal with the full catastrophe of our lives.

PART TWO

Planting the Seeds

We hold the seeds of healing in our hands and in our hearts. We cannot keep planting seeds of self-hate and then wonder why love isn't growing. Hate grows hate. Only love blooms into love. If we are to create a world that is more loving, peaceful and kind, we must first plant loving seeds within ourselves.

This section of the book is about planting the seeds so that one day, slowly, softly, almost without noticing, love will bloom. Joy will bloom. *We* will bloom – into something wonderful and wild.

Awakening curiosity, courage and confidence

We need both gentle curiosity and fierce courage in order to face our inner demons, to walk away from the conditioned goals we have been taught are so important, and to be with the grief and loneliness that surface as we heal. By meeting our pain, fear and rage with curiosity instead of judgement, we can develop a new relationship with them. Rather than allowing them to close our minds and cramp our hearts, we can use them as opportunities to practise being more courageous, more vulnerable and more tender with ourselves and whatever arises in our minds, our bodies and our lives.

What am I curious about?

Awakening is not as much about finding answers or solving problems as it is about being okay with not knowing. It is a process largely driven by curiosity, acceptance and love. Curiosity offers us a more expansive way of being in the world, one where we feel safe enough to take risks, to tolerate the thrill of new experiences, and to explore the unfamiliar, unpredictable and unknown.

Reflect on what you are curious about. What has captured your attention lately? What questions have you been pondering? What do you find yourself wondering about?

How do fear and judgement get in the way of my curiosity?

Without curiosity, life stops feeling like an adventure and instead becomes a test to pass, with every decision filled with a fear of failure. We find ourselves agonising over the smallest decisions, seeking out guarantees before we dare begin. We become terrified of taking the 'wrong path', forgetting that we create the path as we walk it.

Reflect on how fear and judgement get in the way of your curiosity. Maybe you have a creative ambition that you'd like to pursue, but are too afraid to take the plunge because you're afraid you won't succeed. Perhaps you haven't started a meditation practice because there are no guarantees it will bring you the peace you seek. Or maybe you judge yourself each time you skip a workout, rather than being curious about what your lack of motivation could mean.

How would things be different if I replaced self-judgement with curiosity?

To replace our assumptions and expectations with curiosity and wonder is an act of vulnerability. We need to be brave enough to not know, to want to discover more, to fall in love with the questions. Moving curiously through the world, exploring new ideas and experiences, and shining light into the dark and dusty corners of our hearts opens us to risk and uncertainty, but also to healing and freedom.

Reflect on how things might be different if you brought curiosity and wonder to the situations currently filled with fear or judgement. Two phrases that might be helpful are, 'I wonder if ...' and 'Let's see what happens if ...'. For example, 'I wonder if I'm struggling to lose weight because this is actually where my body naturally wants to be,' or 'Let's see what happens if I meet up with a friend when I am feeling upset instead of scrolling through my phone.'

How have I been courageous in my life?

The French novelist Anaïs Nin once wrote: 'Life shrinks or expands in proportion to one's courage.' Courage is expansive. It allows us to live fuller, vaster, deeper lives. Without it, our lives remain cramped and constricted. Our doubts and anxieties become stop signs, preventing us from exploring new ways of being, rather than opportunities to slow down, pay attention and be curious about whether continuing in spite of our fears would allow us to live with greater freedom and joy.

Reflect on a time in your life when you have been courageous. This can include physical, moral or psychological courage. It might be a big, significant act, like leaving a toxic relationship even though you were afraid of being on your own, or a smaller step, like joining a new gym or setting a boundary with your colleagues around responding to work emails outside office hours.

Where is fear holding me back in my healing and awakening?

Anxiety doesn't mean something is wrong with us. Anxiety means something matters to us. The journey of healing and awakening can be one of anxiety as well as peace, because we are on a road we have never travelled before. It is uncertain, unfamiliar and beyond our control. It takes courage to enter the wild unknowns of our inner worlds. It takes courage to leave behind the seeming comfort of our addictions, phobias and harmful habits, and to feel the emotions we buried long ago. It takes courage to tell the truth about where we are hurting, remove the masks we've been wearing, and embrace who we dream of becoming.

Reflect on how fear is holding you back in your awakening. What are you scared of feeling? What are you afraid of discovering about yourself? In what ways would healing and awakening threaten your false self?

What would courage look like in my healing and awakening?

The practice of healing and awakening is one of both risk and choice, of courage and agency. It is a risk to dedicate time and energy to this journey when there is no guarantee of reward or applause. And it is a choice to return to our journals, our sacred spaces, day after day; to pay attention to each moment instead of drifting through our days on autopilot.

We do not need to be fearless on this journey. Rather, we need to hold our fears tenderly as we risk letting go of the beliefs and identities we have outgrown, as we move courageously into the wilderness of the unknown, so our lives become more aligned with our deepest values, with our higher purpose, with the calling of our souls. Reflect on what courage would look like in your healing.

Where do I doubt myself?

In Buddhism, doubt is considered one of the five hindrances, a mental energy that, along with sensual desire, anger, sloth and restlessness, obstructs our healing, freedom and awakening. When we experience this lack of confidence, it can be paralysing, and we might find ourselves trapped in a spiral of self-doubt. We might question our capacity to do a good job at work, to be a loving parent or committed partner, to make choices, to handle stress or to cope with the whole sacred messiness of life.

Reflect on where you are lacking self-confidence in your life. Where does self-doubt hold you back? Where do you lack trust in your own abilities? Where are you shying away from challenges and opportunities to grow?

What blocks my confidence?

Our confidence grows as we practise curiosity and courage in different areas of our lives. It is a by-product of our vulnerability, of our willingness to embrace discomfort, of our capacity to untangle ourselves from the 'can't-dos' and 'not-good-enoughs' that play on repeat in our minds.

Reflect on what is blocking your confidence in the situations where you doubt yourself. Do you believe self-confidence is something you are born with rather than something you can cultivate? Do you see failure as something to avoid rather than embrace? Do you find it difficult to tolerate the physiological signs of stress activation – rapid breathing, racing heart, sweaty palms – that often arises in situations that require courage?

What do I need to practise in order to feel more confident?

Self-confidence arises in the realm of the known. We build it as we gain experience in exploring the *unknown*, in practising curiosity and courage consistently. Our confidence increases slowly as we gently stretch our comfort zones so that, over time, they encompass those situations that once filled us with fear and self-doubt. Whether we want to feel more confident in social situations, to speak up at work or to confront situations head-on, we can, with practice, expand our windows of tolerance so we feel less anxiety doing these things. It's important to remember that self-confidence doesn't come from avoidance, nor from constantly exposing ourselves to the sources of our anxiety. Rather, it blossoms as we move in and out of our comfort zones, honouring our needs for both safety and stress in order to grow.

Reflect on what you need to practise to feel more confident. What small step could you take to stretch your comfort zone?

What awakened action could I take to cultivate curiosity, courage and confidence in my daily life?

Like juggling or speaking French or playing the piano, cultivating curiosity, courage and confidence takes practice. If we have spent years caught in patterns of judgement and avoidance, it will take conscious effort to rewire our brains, reprogramme our beliefs and recover trust in ourselves and our capacities. Much of this effort is about noticing when we are moving away from our goals and values because of doubts and anxieties – and then choosing curiosity and courage so that we can move towards them instead.

Reflect on one awakened action you can take to cultivate curiosity, courage and confidence in your daily life. Perhaps you can experiment with changing your posture when you experience self-doubt until you find one that feels more empowering, or maybe you can practise naming the feelings and thoughts that block your confidence when they arise – 'doubt', 'judgement', 'anxiety' – to stop you getting caught up in any mental chatter (this is known as developing 'witness consciousness' or cultivating the 'noticing self').

Awakening emotional awareness

As a society, we are encouraged to be positive all the time – to avoid the unpleasant emotions that are a deeply human reaction to the stresses and struggles of being alive. We learn that our painful emotions are bad, something to fear and so we suppress them, and they become trapped, subconsciously influencing our thoughts and behaviours, eventually exploding at the slightest trigger. As we become more aware of our emotions and learn to accept them and express them in healthy ways, we discover that letting our feelings breathe means they do not suffocate us.

What emotions do I feel on a day-to-day basis?

Emotions can be messy and confusing, especially when we are not fully aware of them. We are often taught to value thinking over feeling – and, as a result, our emotions tend to get pushed into the background. By paying attention to the emotions we experience daily, we can learn how to accept them, how to name them and how to express them. We can learn how to listen to them, trust them and let them be our guides.

Reflect on the emotions you feel each day. Be open to their nuances too (this is known as 'emotional granularity'). For example, joy, happiness, relief, pride, compassion and love are shades of a similar emotional experience, as are sadness, loneliness, grief, hopelessness and feeling lost. You can also make up names for emotions, such as feeling like 'it's-all-too-much', 'spread-too-thin' or 'connected-to-the-world'. There is a list of emotions on page 297 to help you.

How do different emotions feel in my body?

Emotions are embodied experiences. They arise in the body and call us back to it. In order to feel, in order to heal, we need to reconnect with our bodies, with our emotions, with the embodied experience of being alive.

Reflect on how different emotions feel in your body using the 'How to feel your feelings' practices on page 294. You might like to use the primary emotions (anger, sadness, fear, joy and shame) or explore the emotions you highlighted in the last question.

How does my childhood affect the way I experience and express emotions?

Many of the ways in which we experience and express emotions were learned during our childhoods. If, as children, we were called a cry-baby when we got upset, we may not feel safe to feel our sadness. Instead, it might manifest as frustration, irritability or fury. Or, if we never saw our parents expressing anger, our own rage as adults might show up as sadness, despair or shame.

Reflect on how your childhood has shaped the way you experience and express emotions. How did your caregivers express their emotions? How were you treated when you expressed sadness? How about anger? Excitement? Fear? Shame?

How does my sociocultural conditioning affect the way I experience and express emotions?

Emotions can be wild and unpredictable. They are potential threats to our productivity, and so Western culture encourages us to override our feelings, treating strong emotions as pathological and shaming us for feeling so deeply. But unless we are in touch with our emotions, everything tends to feel meaningless. As we honour our feelings, not as problems to solve or disruptions to our productivity, but as energies filled with wisdom, we rediscover the richness of being alive.

Reflect on how your sociocultural conditioning affects the way you experience and express emotions. How is your emotional expression limited by your gender? Race? Age? Religion? Are high-arousal emotions (e.g. feeling afraid, angry, distressed, excited) more or less acceptable than low-arousal emotions (e.g. feeling bored, calm, relaxed, tired) in your culture?

How do other people's emotions affect me?

We are wired for connection. Below our conscious awareness, our nervous systems are constantly scanning the world, simultaneously influencing and being influenced by the nervous systems of those around us, via a process Dr Stephen Porges terms 'neuroception'. If we are with someone who is grieving, we often find that we too can feel their pain. This shared emotional experience is at the root of compassion.

Reflect on how other people's emotions affect you. Can you differentiate other people's emotions from your own? When you are with someone who feels anxious, do you get pulled into their anxiety, or do they absorb your peace? Do you feel guilty for feeling happy when someone you love feels sad?

What is my relationship with big, painful emotions?

Most of us have never been taught how to safely feel intense emotions, or that these emotions are deeply human. Instead, we are often encouraged to believe there is a right way to feel (good, happy, peaceful) and a wrong way to feel (sad, anxious, angry). And so, when we do experience some kind of loss or threat, and these big, painful emotions naturally arise, we tend to create stories that are self-shaming and self-judging: 'I shouldn't be feeling this anxious. Something is wrong with me'; 'I need to make this grief go away'; 'If I was stronger and more resilient, I wouldn't get so upset'. The stories we tell about unpleasant emotions affect whether we are afraid of them or whether we can feel them, reflect on them, express them and find meaning in them.

Reflect on your relationship with big, painful emotions. What stories do you tell yourself about them? What emotions are you afraid of? What emotions do you try to avoid? What emotions feel stuck, trapped in your bodymind?

How can I turn towards intense emotions and feel them more intentionally?

We are often taught to run away from uncomfortable emotions. Posts on social media encourage us to write gratitude lists to get rid of our anxiety, or to meditate to overcome our rage. And, as helpful as these practices can be, they tend to offer us a temporary peace, bypassing the big, messy emotions that no amount of incense sticks and bubble baths can soothe. Turning towards our emotions and being curious about what it is we are feeling can stop us from feeling overwhelmed. Simply naming our emotions can help us begin to tame them.

Reflect on how you can begin turning towards your emotions. Maybe when you feel an intense wave of emotion, you could pause, place your hand on your heart, and ask yourself, 'What emotion is moving through me right now?' If you need a guide, you can use the list of emotions on page 297.

How can I practise expressing intense emotions?

If we don't know how to express our emotions in healthy ways, we tend to either 'act out' our emotions, by behaving impulsively and often aggressively, or 'act in' our emotions in a way that can be self-destructive, such as self-criticising and people-pleasing. We tend to 'act out' and 'act in' when we feel expressing our emotions would threaten our safety or cause rejection or abandonment. This means that in order to express our emotions, we need to feel safe: safe enough to notice what we are feeling, to explore the emotion with compassion, and to identify a healthy way to process it.

Reflect on how you currently express intense emotions and explore healthier alternatives you can practise. Could you express your anger by putting on loud music and letting your body move? Could you express your sadness by asking your partner to hold you while you cry? Could you express your anxiety by journaling, letting your fear spill out on the page?

What are my emotions telling me?

We evolved to feel. Our emotions allow us to navigate the world and connect to one another. They help us adapt to our environment. They bring meaning to our lives. They are our motivators and our guides. Love inspires kindness, compassion and connection. Fear readies us for fight-or-flight. Sadness pushes us to seek support, and calls us inward to integrate and heal. If we let ourselves feel emotions and express them, we will discover that even our big, painful, chaotic feelings have wisdom in them.

Reflect on what your emotions are telling you. What threats are they highlighting? What needs are they communicating? What adaptive actions are they signalling for you to take?

What is one awakened action I can take to practise emotional acceptance?

When we experience big, painful emotions, we can feel hijacked, as though our emotions are overwhelming our capacity to think clearly and making it difficult to tend to ourselves in the most compassionate way. By identifying practices and resources we can use in times of distress, and practising them when intense emotions arise, we learn to ride the waves of our emotions instead of drowning in them.

Reflect on an awakened action you can take when you feel threatened by your emotions. How can you make room for your feelings? How can you hold them gently? You might like to practise one of the 'How to feel your feelings' techniques on page 294.

Awakening relaxation

We are not designed to live in survival mode. Our bodies need safety. Our souls need rest. But, for many of us, living in this state of fight-or-flight has become the norm. We see rest and relaxation as something we have to earn, something we only allow ourselves when we've done all our chores and all our obligations have been met. And then, when we finally do allow ourselves to relax, we feel anxious. We start judging ourselves for being lazy, worrying that we are wasting time. Being in a constant state of stress overtaxes the nervous system and harms our wellbeing. It is only when we are in a state of safety and relaxation that our bodies can heal and restore.

Growing up, what was I taught to believe about work, productivity and rest?

Sometimes we find it hard to give ourselves permission to rest, even when we are exhausted. This is often the result of inherited norms and the way rest and relaxation were modelled to us growing up. If, as children, we were called lazy or shamed for not working hard enough, or if we never saw the adults around us relax, we may find it difficult to allow ourselves the rest we need now.

Reflect on the messages you received around rest and relaxation as a child. Did your parents have healthy boundaries between work and family life? How did they relax?

How do I feel about rest and relaxation now?

Allowing ourselves sufficient time for rest can protect us from burnout and stress-related illnesses. And yet, for many of us, rest is reserved for those rare moments when everything else is done – when our inboxes are empty and the house is clean and all the jobs on our to-do list are ticked off. Most of us live in a rest deficit. This is partly because of the machine pace of modern life, but also because, even though we yearn to rest, we feel guilty if we slow down.

Reflect on your relationship with rest and relaxation. Do you make it a priority in your life? Can you rest without guilt? How do you feel about intentionally being unproductive and consciously wasting time?

What are the signs I am stressed and need to relax?

Both stress and relaxation are embodied experiences – psycho-physiological states that influence our thoughts, emotions and behaviours, as well as the way we see ourselves and the world. Stress is a reaction to circumstances that require us to take action, shifting our nervous system into a state of fight-or-flight. Relaxation is the opposite. It is the 'off' switch to our stress response. We need to return to this state regularly in order for our bodymind – including our immune, muscular, neuroendocrine and nervous systems – to repair and restore.

Reflect on how it feels when you are stressed. How does it affect your digestion? Your breath? Your heart rate? Where do you feel pain or tension? How do your mental chatter and body image change when you're stressed?

What stops me from relaxing?

Modern life can make it challenging to rest. We've been conditioned to believe slowing down and stillness are a sign of weakness. We worry that if we rest, we will get left behind. It's also difficult to rest in a society that doesn't. Gyms, supermarkets and airports are often open twenty-four hours a day. When there is always something to do and somewhere to be, it makes it harder to relax.

Reflect on what stops you from relaxing. This could be external barriers, such as financial insecurity, caregiving commitments or work deadlines, or psychological barriers, such as worries about rest being a waste of time, or relaxation-induced anxiety (an increase in muscle tension or anxious thoughts when you try to rest – we'll explore this more in the next question).

How does relaxation-induced anxiety feel?

Relaxation is a practice: a skill we can develop through training. Sometimes, when we begin relaxing, we can actually feel more anxious. If we've been experiencing stress or anxiety on a daily basis for a long period of time, this tense, restless state can feel normal to us. Often, the experience of our nervous systems shifting from relaxed to alert can feel incredibly uncomfortable, so we might find ourselves living in a constant state of subtle anxiety in order to avoid this sharp surge in stress activation. This is known as contrast avoidance.

Reflect on whether you experience relaxation-induced anxiety, and think about what may be contributing to this. Does shifting from low to high arousal feel tolerable? Does relaxing make you feel vulnerable or out of control? Do the bodily sensations accompanying relaxation – heavier limbs, deeper breathing, looser muscles – feel unsafe?

How does my mental story change when I am relaxed?

Your physiological state shapes your psychological story. The state of your nervous system is like a lens that colours the way you experience yourself and the world. When the nervous system is in a heightened state of arousal, the stories we tell ourselves are dominated by danger, urgency and fear. By contrast, when our bodies are relaxed and our breathing is deep, the mental stories we tell ourselves about our safety and our worth shift – we experience self-compassion instead of self-criticism; we see our beauty as well as our flaws.

Reflect on how your mental stories change when you are stressed compared to when you are relaxed. How does the way you see yourself – and the world – change?

How does it feel in my body when I'm relaxed?

When we experience anxiety on a daily basis, feeling tense and jittery can become our baseline state and we can forget how it actually feels to be relaxed. Because relaxation is a skill, with practice, we can lower our baseline state of arousal so that anxiety is no longer our default.

Reflect on the last time you were deeply relaxed. Where were you? How did it feel in your body? (You might like to use the list of physical sensations on page 299 to help with this.) How often do you access this state of rest? If you're not sure how deep relaxation feels, the grounding and centring practices on pages 27–29 can often offer an embodied experience of relaxation.

What makes me feel safe enough to relax?

Relaxation is the capacity to be still without fear. To have a nap on the sofa. To sit and meditate. To surrender into the arms of someone we love. In order to relax, we need to feel safe. *Feeling* safe is not the same as intellectually *knowing* we are safe. *Feeling* safe is an embodied experience that we sense through neuroception (see page 85). This is the way our autonomic nervous system responds to cues of safety and threat in our environment. By paying attention to the things that make us feel safe, we can create a list of safety anchors to help us relax.

Reflect on what makes you feel safe enough to relax. Who makes you feel safe? Where do you feel safe? What makes you feel safe?

How do I currently practise relaxation?

The relaxation response occurs naturally when the nervous system senses that we are no longer in danger, allowing our bodies to return to a state that is optimal for health, growth and restoration. However, in modern life, we are triggered into a state of fight-or-flight many times a day – often by situations that aren't actually threatening to our survival, such as traffic jams, supermarket queues and work deadlines. Being constantly bombarded with these stressors means that, unless we consciously practise relaxation, our bodies might not have time to relax and restore before the next stressor occurs. When this happens chronically, we are more vulnerable to high blood pressure, reduced immunity, anxiety and burnout. Reflect on what you currently do to relax. How do you restore?

What is one relaxation technique or type of rest I would like to explore?

Relaxation doesn't have to be complicated or time-consuming. Something as simple as changing your posture, softening your jaw or sighing deeply can shift your physiological state away from fight-or-flight and towards safety and relaxation.

Reflect on a relaxation practice you'd like to explore over the next couple of weeks. This might be practising a guided relaxation, such as progressive muscle relaxation or yoga nidra (you can find these online), experimenting with incense sticks or aromatherapy oils, or carving out five minutes a day to listen to binaural beats while lying with your legs up the wall (this is a restorative yoga pose where you lie on your back with the backs of your legs and heels resting against a wall).

Awakening joy

We all have a right to live a joy-filled life. And yet, it can feel challenging to experience and prioritise joy when there seems to be so much fear and sadness within us and around us. But we cannot possibly face the suffering in the world without also delighting in the beauty of it. Joy provides us with the strength needed to hold our sorrows without crumbling under the weight of them. Even on this healing journey, we can find ourselves taking awakening terribly seriously, neglecting the joyful, the silly, the fun. And while it is important not to bypass our pain, it is just as important not to overlook our joy.

What does joy mean to me?

Joy has many different textures and many different flavours. It might blossom gently within us, offering an inner fullness, a wholeness. Or it might flow through us like a river in springtime, flooding us with energy, vitality and aliveness.

Reflect on your own personal definition of joy. Is it an emotion? A personality trait? A way of being? Is it fleeting, based on external conditions, or something deeper and more enduring? Is it the absence of suffering, or can it coexist with it? Do you resonate with how, in Buddhism, joy is seen as both a prerequisite for and fruit of awakening? (For a reminder of the attitudes for awakening, see page 19.)

Over the last month, when have I experienced true joy?

Most of us find it far easier to recall painful memories than to remember moments of joy. We may have developed this trait as part of evolution, as a way to protect us against future threats, but it means that, unless we consciously reflect on the happy and heart-warming moments in our lives, we can become blind to them.

Reflect on the moments of joy you have experienced over the past month. Think about excited joy as well as quiet delight. What pleasure-based joys have you experienced (e.g. an aromatherapy massage or a slice of carrot cake at your favourite café)? What passion-based joys have you felt (e.g. painting, running, dancing)? And what purpose-based joys have flowed through you (e.g. at work, as a parent, in spiritual practice)?

What simple, everyday things bring me joy?

If we believe joy needs to be reserved for the big things – birthdays, weddings, promotions, lottery wins – we miss it in the simple, everyday things. By slowing down and paying attention, we open our hearts to experiencing the joy that is always here, hiding in the present moment.

Reflect on the simple things that bring you joy: the ordinary moments that are deeply sacred. Maybe it's your morning coffee or a plate of perfectly scrambled eggs. Perhaps it's looking out of the kitchen window and seeing the wildflowers blooming. Maybe it's hearing bursts of laughter as your children play, or reading in bed each night.

How much of a priority is joy in my life?

There are often so many demands on our time that we don't make a conscious effort to experience joy. After all, when there are emails to send, errands to run and a planet that needs saving, how can we justify spending time having fun? And yet, without joy, it all feels empty. Prioritising joy doesn't mean disregarding the stressors in our lives or the injustices in the world. Rather, it means not treating life as a problem to be solved, not overlooking our happiness, and not forgetting to celebrate ourselves.

Reflect on how much of a priority joy is in your life. How much time do you dedicate to it? Is it more or less important than external achievement and social approval? If you were invited to a spontaneous morning out with friends but you still had chores to do, what would you choose?

What do I do purely for the joy of it?

We've been conditioned to believe that everything we do has to be productive, a step towards achieving a goal or completing a task, and that doing something purely for the love of it is childish, frivolous or irresponsible. Yet we need to remember to rest and return to a state of joy after stressful experiences so that our bodymind can recover. If we don't experience safety, rest and joy, we cannot restore.

Reflect on what you do purely for the joy of it. Do you dance? Do you sing? Do you read stories? Do you walk in nature? Do you swim in the sea? Do you bake? Do you create music?

How does joy feel in my body?

Joy can feel like a river flowing through us, or like champagne bubbles fizzing in our arms and legs. It can make colours seem brighter and our bodies feel lighter, our movements more fluid. It can expand our awareness, allowing us to zoom out from our flaws and fears so we can see ourselves and the world from a vaster, richer perspective.

Reflect on how joy feels in your body. Where do you feel it? What sensations do you notice? How does feeling joy change the way you breathe? The way you move? The way you see yourself and the world? How does superficial pleasure feel different from true joy?

What have I been conditioned to believe I need in order to experience joy?

Joy has been commodified in modern society. As a result, we may believe that joy can only be found through achievement and consumption. And, because the things we can achieve and consume are limited, it can feel as though joy is a finite resource – something we have to hoard, ration and compete for. As we begin to understand the way consumerist systems benefit from our underlying dissatisfaction, we can tap into a different type of joy: an unconditional joy that does not require us to buy anything or achieve anything or become anyone other than who we are. This inner spring of infinite joy is what Buddhism calls *mudita*. This doesn't mean we shouldn't enjoy material pleasures and little luxuries; it simply means releasing the belief that we can find happiness and self-worth in external things.

Reflect on what conditions you've placed on your joy. You might find it helpful to finish this sentence: 'I'll be happy when ...'.

What blocks my joy?

It is difficult to feel joy when we're exhausted, or stressed, or feeling unsafe. And no matter how unconditional our joy may be, there are some very real socioeconomic situations, inequalities and injustices that make it more challenging to tap into the river of joy flowing within us. When we don't feel safe – regardless of whether the threat is real or perceived, personal or collective, in the present or in the past – we go into survival mode, and all we can focus on is staying alive. Feeling safe creates a neural platform that shifts our nervous systems from survival to aliveness, from protection to connection, from fear to joy.

Reflect on what is blocking your joy. What threats are you experiencing? What injustices are you facing? What forms of inequality are shifting your nervous system to focus on survival rather than aliveness?

How do I hold myself back from experiencing joy?

For some of us, the possibility of experiencing joy is met with ambivalence and fear. Sometimes, we convince ourselves we can't be happy until we lose the weight or buy the car or get the promotion. At other times, our anxiety has kept us safe in the past, and lowering our defences feels like it would make us too vulnerable. If we're used to feeling stressed or depressed, joy can feel so unfamiliar that we might subconsciously sabotage joyful experiences, like holidays and relationships. And, if we are perfectionists, we might struggle to let ourselves feel joy for fear it will make us unproductive and lazy.

Reflect on how you might be holding yourself back from experiencing joy. Does anxiety feel safe? Do you sabotage your joy? Do you feel worthy of happiness? Is your heart open to experiencing the 'ten thousand sorrows and ten thousand joys' we all encounter in this lifetime (according to Buddhist and Daoist teachings)? Or have you closed your heart in an attempt to avoid the pain of life, and, as a result, find yourself missing out on the joy too?

What is one awakened action I can take to welcome and cultivate joy in my life?

We cannot force ourselves to feel happier, but we can create the conditions in which joy can blossom. We can surround ourselves with people who feel good to our nervous systems, because joy is contagious. We can pay attention to the little things we are thankful for, because gratitude and joy reinforce each other in a beautiful upward spiral of healing. And we can make space for our emotions, allowing ourselves to enter the darkness of our pain so we do not dim the brightness of our joy. Reflect on one small thing you can do to welcome joy in your life.

Awakening success

The way we define success shapes the way we see ourselves, how we spend our time and what we dedicate our lives to. Without pausing to reflect on what success means to us, we tend to adopt the white, Western, middle-class standards of success that dominate modern culture: achievement, status, wealth, power and beauty. By exploring our relationship with success, we can become aware of the goals we are chasing that were never really our own, and instead dedicate our lives to what truly matters to us.

What does success mean to me?

The way we define success is both individual and collective, influenced by our parents, peers and the culture in which we grew up. If, as children, we were rewarded for our academic achievements, we might pursue qualification after qualification without any sense of true fulfilment. Or, if we live in a society that equates money with success, we might stay in a high-paying job that we hate, even if our relationships and wellbeing are suffering.

Reflect on what success means to you. This might include broader things, like meaningful work, time for family and friends, being healthy, contributing to society, financial freedom, material possessions, leaving a legacy, feeling at peace with yourself and living in harmony with the earth, as well as more specific things, such as visiting two new countries a year, picking your kids up from school every day or reaching a managerial position at work.

How does my definition of success differ from society's standards of success?

If we live in an individualist society, success tends to be defined in terms of wealth, innovation, status, personal achievement, independence and ownership of property and possessions, while we tend to undervalue caregiving, community, contribution and collective goals.

Reflect on how your own sense of success differs from how success is defined in the society you live in. You might like to think about income, job, parenting choices, education, relationship status, possessions, appearance and work–life balance.

How am I currently chasing society's definition of success instead of my own?

Sometimes, cultural standards of success have become so deeply embedded within us that we find ourselves chasing society's goals instead of our own. Even if we know, deep down, that spending time with our family brings us more meaning and joy than our career does, we might still find ourselves chasing promotions and higher salaries. Even if we know in our hearts that success means being at peace with our bodies, we might still try diet after diet in an attempt to fit in with society's standards of beauty and success.

Reflect on areas of your life where you are chasing a definition of success that is not your own. Where do you feel pressured to live out of alignment with your values in order to be successful? Where are you prioritising society's definition of success over your own?

When have I felt successful in the past?

It's easy to overlook the successes we have accomplished and the challenges we have overcome. We tend to forget our achievements in pursuit of the next goal, to overlook our small wins because we're so focused on the big ones, and to remember the times we have failed but not those when we've succeeded. And yet, if we don't celebrate our past successes, our future ones will feel empty.

Reflect on times in your life when you have felt successful. Where were you? What were you doing? How did it feel in your body? How did you celebrate? What small, weekly wins have you been ignoring? How can you celebrate them?

When have I felt like a failure in the past?

As humans, we make mistakes, we underperform, we don't always achieve what we set out to do. And often, these failures fill us with shame. Instead of seeing our defeats, mistakes and heartbreaks as a natural part of life, we internalise them. Rather than treating our failures as momentary events, they become part of our identity.

Reflect on times in your life when you have felt like a failure. How have these failures shaped you? What have you learned from them? For example, maybe you felt like a failure when a romantic relationship broke down – and yet it taught you the qualities you need in a potential partner. Or maybe you felt like a failure when you couldn't give up an addictive habit – and yet it gave you deep compassion for others who are trying to make healthy lifestyle changes.

What is my relationship with failure?

So often, we forget that we are human. Imperfect. Messy. Unfinished. We expect ourselves never to mess up, never to break down. We judge ourselves when we come across a problem we can't solve, a goal we can't achieve, an obstacle we don't know how to overcome. Our fear of failure stops us from taking risks, opening our hearts and going after our dreams. We procrastinate, give up, or sabotage our goals in order to protect ourselves from the possibility of experiencing the pain of failure. And yet, as we accept that defeat and adversity are a natural part of life, we discover that what at first looks like failure is actually a stepping stone. We feel how we are always failing forwards into vaster awareness, greater resilience and a deeper capacity to love.

Reflect on your relationship with failure. Do you fear it or embrace it? Do you see it as empowering or embarrassing? Where did your beliefs around failure come from?

If I weren't afraid of failing, what would I do?

When we give ourselves the freedom to fail, we give ourselves the freedom to live. Realising that failure is part of being human, instead of a reflection of our worth, allows us to embrace it rather than fear it. Accepting that when we do experience failure, it might hurt for a little while, stops us playing small in an attempt to avoid the pain of it.

Reflect on what you would do differently if you weren't afraid of failing. What goals would you attempt? What dreams would you chase?

In what ways am I afraid of success?

Many of us fear success as much as we strive for it. We might worry that if we're successful, we'll be abandoned by our friends, alienated from our communities and judged as arrogant or self-important. If our failures have become our identity, we might fear who we will be if we succeed. If it is through our struggles that we have found connection and community, we might be afraid of being ostracised if we succeed in overcoming these struggles. And if we have experienced extreme stress or adversity, the excitement that accompanies success can feel similar to the heightened arousal of our original trauma.

Reflect on your fear of success. How is it holding you back? What negative consequences of success are you afraid of? What self-defeating strategies do you use as you get closer to your goal?

Who do I see as successful?

Finding people we admire awakens us to our own potential for success. It shows our subconscious what is possible. These people are our awakeners. Whatever it is that inspires us about them, we can also find within ourselves.

Reflect on who you see as successful (in your personal life and in the media). Who inspires you? What about them do you feel makes them successful? Their career? Their relationship? Their confidence? Their compassion? Their contribution to the world? What can you learn from them?

What is one awakened action I can take to begin living more in alignment with my own definition of success?

Every step on the path to success is a success, even if it is a failure. Honouring failure as a source of wisdom allows us to embrace it instead of fearing it. Celebrating our small wins enables us to delight in the process as well as the end goal. Expanding our definition of success beyond wealth, status and achievement means we can stop striving for the pot of gold and simply enjoy the rainbow.

Reflect on one small, practical thing you can do to live more in alignment with your own definition of success. For example, if success to you is being fully present with your family, maybe you could turn off your work emails when you get home. Or if, to you, success means growing your own food, maybe you could plant some strawberries on your kitchen windowsill.

Awakening meaning and purpose

What is the meaning of life? This is a question many of us grapple with. We yearn for meaning, for purpose, for our lives to be significant. And yet, so often, we find ourselves living a life of conformity and compliance instead of listening to the true calling of our souls. We often find ourselves stuck in a spiral of stress and struggle as we strive unsuccessfully to find meaning in things that leave us feeling empty. And yet, if we can slow down and listen inwardly, our souls will begin to speak, sharing the truth and wisdom that we seek.

What does living a meaningful life look like to me?

When we begin pondering the meaning of life, we can find ourselves in a kind of existential crisis, wondering what the point of all this is. By recognising that *we* as individuals get to decide what it is to live a meaningful life, we free ourselves from the existential angst that there is some grand objective we have to find.

Reflect on what living a meaningful life looks like for you. Does it include living with fulfilment and joy? Does it involve dedicating your life to something you care about deeply? Does it encompass any specific goals?

What brings meaning to my daily life?

Living a meaningful life asks us to pay attention to what breaks our hearts, to what brings us joy, to what our souls are calling us to do – and then to make a conscious decision each day to do the things that will make us feel alive, and walk away from those that do not. We can experience meaning in different ways: through feelings of fulfilment and significance; by contributing and being of service; by having a sense of direction; through living by our deepest values; and through feeling that our lives make sense, that there is coherence amongst the chaos.

Reflect on what brings meaning to your life. What daily experiences bring you joy? When do you feel most of service? What values do you live your life by?

What makes me lose track of time?

Meaning often feels mysterious, something that ebbs and flows throughout different periods of our lives. And yet, it is also something we can only find in the present, something we stumble upon by giving ourselves fully to the moment we are in. Paying attention to what we are doing in those moments when we are so immersed in the present that we lose track of time (a state often referred to as 'flow') can serve as a doorway to discovering the deeper meaning and purpose of our lives.

Reflect on what makes you lose track of time. What do you become so enthralled in that you stop worrying about the future or ruminating on the past? What are the qualities behind these activities (e.g. adventure, teamwork, leadership, learning, caregiving), and can this guide you towards living a more meaningful life?

What breaks my heart?

One of the reasons many of us struggle to find meaning in our lives is because we have closed our hearts to the suffering of the world. We pretend we don't care in order to protect our hearts from breaking. But in doing so, we have turned away from what truly matters. If we are to live a meaningful life, we have to fill our lives with things that matter – things that matter to us (even if they don't matter to anyone else) and things that we know matter to others (even if they don't matter to us). We have to walk away from our superficial goals and let our grief guide us towards our deeper purpose. We have to let our hearts break, trusting this is one way in which our soul speaks.

Reflect on what breaks your heart. What really matters to you? How can you let your heartbreak guide you?

Would my ten-year-old self be proud of the life I am living?

We are hardwired to seek meaning in our lives. Without it, we suffer. Cardiovascular disease, suicide and psychological distress are all related to lack of purpose. And yet, for many of us, at some point during our childhood or adolescence, other people's voices, demands and expectations begin to drown out the quiet calling of our souls. Instead of spending our days doing things that matter deeply to us like we did as children, we find ourselves living by 'shoulds' and 'musts' and 'ought-tos'. The dreams and passions we once had get buried beneath limiting beliefs and the pressures and cost of living. But it is never too late – those dreams are still there, planted like seeds, waiting for us to shine the sunlight of our awareness on them and begin nurturing them.

Reflect on whether your ten-year-old self would be happy to see the life you are living. What would they be proud of? What would make them cry? What childhood dreams and aspirations would they want you to nurture?

What has been missing when my life has felt meaningless?

External success will always feel hollow if we've had to sacrifice our souls to achieve it. Meaning is something that emerges from our souls as a deep calling, and yet this so often gets drowned out by the stresses of daily life, by our superficial goals, and by ethical values that are not truly our own. When there is a lack of meaning, we might achieve the goals we've been striving for, only for the expected elation to be eclipsed by a feeling of emptiness, or we might burn out because the standards we are trying to live up to are coming from external expectations rather than the truth of our souls.

Reflect on periods of your life when you have experienced a sense of meaninglessness. What was missing? Joy? Awe? Self-trust? Deep purpose? Authentic service? Acceptance of your limitations? Belonging? Spiritual connection? Honouring your intuition?

What do I feel called to do?

Our purpose does not come from striving for goals or conforming to values that are not our own simply because we think that's what a meaningful life should look like. Rather, it comes from doing something we feel called to do, something we cannot *not* do, often for reasons we can't explain or understand. Meaning comes not from what we feel we *should* be doing, but from living in a way that is true to our deepest values.

Reflect on how the life you are living is different from the life you feel called to live. Where are you striving instead of listening? Where are you living by 'shoulds' instead of your own deepest values? What heart callings have you been ignoring? What does your soul say when it speaks?

What does society want from me, and what does my soul want from me?

Sometimes what society demands from us is very different to what our souls truly need, and it often feels like a fragile and frustrating task to balance the needs of our inner worlds with the demands of the outer world. This is especially true when the demands of daily life seem to differ so vastly from the needs of our souls; when we are forced to live in a way that requires us to sacrifice our basic needs – for sleep and stillness, nature and community – in order to make ends meet.

Reflect on how society's expectations differ from your soul's calling. How can you serve the world without sacrificing your soul? Where have you betrayed your purpose for social approval? What socioeconomic inequalities stop you from being able to honour your true calling?

What unique gifts and talents do I have?

Theologian Frederick Buechner speaks of purpose as 'the place where your deep gladness and the world's hunger meet'. This combination of joy and service is what ripples through the research on living a meaningful life. This means embracing your true nature, both in terms of the gifts you have been given to share with the world and the limits you need to honour so that you don't burn out from trying to give what you do not have.

Reflect on your gifts as well as your limits. What energises you and what exhausts you? What fulfils you and what drains you? Where does your joy and the world's hunger meet?

What is one awakened action I can take to live a more meaningful life?

Meaning does not come through force. It comes through listening. Through connecting our inner purpose – to be our whole, authentic selves – with our outer purpose. Through allowing our love and care to flow into everything we do. We achieve the big things by paying attention to the little things. We are most of service when we are honest about the things that matter to us, when we honour our limits, and when we live from the inside out, from the values and truths we find in our hearts instead of those that are imposed on us.

Reflect on one awakened action you can take to live a more meaningful life. This could be something like taking photos of meaningful moments each day and looking for patterns to help you discover what truly matters to you, devoting ten minutes a day to something that makes you lose track of time, or using moments of ambition-induced anxiety as a cue that you have lost your connection with your true purpose.

Part two: Gentle reminders

- Awakening is beautiful and ugly and grief-filled and glorious, much like life. Curiosity and courage give us the confidence to remain open to ourselves and the world, enabling us to experience the fullness and richness and vastness of being alive.
- Sometimes, when it feels like our hearts are breaking, they are actually stretching, opening, expanding. As we awaken, we discover that our hearts can hold it all. We can feel both grief and gratitude, both bliss and despair, and both anger at the unfairness of life and awe at being alive to experience it.
- Our emotions are not something we need to fear. Rather, letting our hearts be filled by anger and love, joy and fear, deep pain and great passion is what makes us fully human, fully divine, fully alive.
- Experiential acceptance is about accepting and honouring our emotions and inner experiences. It is not about passively accepting and adapting to toxic relationships, destructive life situations and unjust societies.
- Awakening joy isn't about bypassing our pain. Rather, it is about opening our hearts and allowing joy to exist alongside our pain.

- If we are living in survival mode due to stress, trauma or a neuroception of threat, our nervous systems will prioritise survival rather than joy. We need to feel safe in order to feel joy.

- Learning to relax – to be still without anxiety or shame – often takes conscious practice. But, as we reshape our nervous systems and rewire our brains to counteract the idea that our worth is found in our productivity, we discover that relaxation is not a luxury, something we get to do once everything else is done, but an essential part of creating a rich, authentic, meaningful life.

- If we can see success as more than wealth, prestige and power – if we can embrace it as multidimensional and deeply personal – we will find that it is not something we have to strive for. Rather, success is something that happens, a by-product of living a life in line with our own values, something we discover when we listen to the tiny, tender voice of our soul.

- There will be times when we lose connection with why we are here; times when our lives feel meaningless, and we feel lost and alone. In these moments, we are being called to slow down, to let ourselves care completely about what matters to us, and to listen inwardly to what our hearts have to say.

PART THREE

Pulling the Weeds

For plants, the motivation towards growth is innate. The same is true for humans. And yet there are weeds that starve us and strangle us and stop us from thriving. Weeds of self-doubt. Weeds of shame. Weeds of people-pleasing and perfectionism and compulsive productivity.

This section is about uprooting the conditioning that stops us from living a rich and meaningful life, unblocking the beliefs that keep us small, scared and shame-filled, and untangling ourselves from the thoughts and feelings that suffocate our aliveness.

Awakening from limiting beliefs

Our beliefs can empower us to live brilliant, beautiful lives, or they can hold us hostage. They can help us grow or keep us small. As we pay attention to the underlying beliefs that drive our thoughts, emotions and behaviours, we can begin to question whether they are what we truly believe or simply what we have been conditioned to believe. We often discover that many of our beliefs are not our own, or that they are echoes from the past that we have since outgrown. With awareness and compassion, we discover that we can rewire our brains and reprogramme our beliefs so that we can do the things we long to do, be the people we yearn to be and create the kind of world we want to live in.

What are three things I believe about myself that hold me back?

Our limiting beliefs are the fear-based stories we tell ourselves about who we are, the relationships we have and what is possible in our lives. They colour the way we see the world and restrict what we think we are capable and worthy of. Many of these beliefs are either instilled during childhood, or internalised when we attribute the external qualities of a situation to ourselves. For example, failing an exam becomes 'I am a failure'; going through a relationship break-up becomes 'I am unlovable'; and comparing ourselves to airbrushed models in magazines becomes 'I am ugly'.

Reflect on three beliefs that are currently holding you back.

What do you believe is wrong with you? What do you believe you can't do or don't deserve? How do these beliefs stop you from doing what you want to do and being who you want to be?

Where did I absorb these limiting beliefs from?

We are not born with our beliefs. Every belief we have is learned – either from our family, peers, education, religion or the media, or directly, through our personal experiences. Because our brains are so malleable when we are children, the beliefs that limit us the most are often those we have internalised growing up. By bringing our awareness to where our beliefs come from – to the people, places and painful experiences that have determined the stories we tell ourselves about who we are and who we have the potential to be – we discover that we are more powerful, more beautiful, more magical than we have been conditioned to believe.

For each of the limiting beliefs you have identified, reflect on where or who you learned it from. Did you absorb it from a person or group, or from wider society? How old were you when you started believing it? Does it still feel true for you now?

How have these beliefs changed over time?

The core beliefs we develop as children become hardwired as synaptic pathways in our brains. The more we repeat these beliefs through our thoughts, emotions and actions, the stronger these neural pathways become. While some beliefs and their neural pathways will strengthen over time due to repetition and reinforcement, others may have changed as we've encountered new experiences, developed new relationships and been exposed to new ideas.

For each of the limiting beliefs you've identified, reflect on how it has evolved over time. Did you believe the same thing when you were a child or teenager as you do now? If not, what did you believe back then? What happened to bring about this change in belief? Did any specific person, group or experience inspire this change?

How do these limiting beliefs colour the way I see myself and the world?

Our beliefs are like tinted glasses, colouring everything we see. They act like filters, blocking out any information that doesn't support what we already believe. For example, if we have been taught to believe that being beautiful means being lean, tanned and wrinkle-free, we will never be able to see, honour or enjoy beauty as anything other than that.

Reflect on the ways in which your limiting beliefs colour how you see yourself and the world. What are they highlighting? What are they filtering out? What are they stopping you from seeing? What alternative things are they preventing you from believing?

How have these limiting beliefs protected me in the past?

At some point in our lives, even the most limiting of our beliefs will have served a purpose. Growing up, they might have protected us from rejection, abandonment or emotional overwhelm.

And yet the beliefs that helped us navigate our childhoods may no longer serve us in the adult world. In the same way that it would be painful if we walked around all day with our adult feet squeezed into our childhood shoes, we can outgrow our beliefs too.

For each of the limiting beliefs you have identified, reflect on how it has served you (and how it may still be serving you). How has it protected you in the past? How is it stopping you from living a rich and meaningful life in the present?

What emotions are bound up in these limiting beliefs?

Emotional memories are at the core of our limiting beliefs, and the more intense the emotion that preceded the belief formation, the more challenging the belief can be to change. Often, our limiting beliefs formed because, as children, we didn't have the capacity to process these intense emotions. But as adults, we can ground ourselves in the safety of the present moment and open ourselves up to the emotional energy bound up in our limiting beliefs. By giving ourselves space to experience and express these emotions in a conscious, compassionate way, our limiting beliefs begin to lose their power.

Reflect on the emotions underpinning your limiting beliefs. What emotions arise as you think about each belief? What feeling states tend to make each belief louder or stronger? For example, feeling guilty may trigger the belief 'I am unworthy', or feeling lonely may trigger the belief 'I am unlovable'. You might like to use the feelings list on page 297 as a guide.

How do these limiting beliefs shift when I feel safe, seen and supported?

Our autonomic and emotional states influence the stories we tell ourselves. When we sense we are in danger and our bodyminds have shifted into survival mode, what we believe about ourselves and the world tends to be very different to what we believe when we feel safe. For example, if a relationship feels unstable and uncertain, we might interpret this as a sign that there is something wrong with us. But if we are in a relationship where we feel safe, seen and supported, how we see ourselves begins to change. Through experiencing the safety of a loving relationship, we can begin to see ourselves from the perspective of a loving other – as beautiful, lovable and worthy.

Reflect on how your beliefs change depending on your autonomic and emotional state. You might like to use the following sentence openers: 'When I'm feeling safe, I believe ... ' and 'When I'm feeling unsafe, I believe ... '.

How have these limiting beliefs become part of my identity?

The more invested you are in a certain belief, the more it becomes part of your identity. As we begin exploring and questioning our deeply held beliefs, it can feel like a threat to who we are. By separating what we believe from our true selves, we create space for our beliefs to change and evolve while staying connected to our essence.

Reflect on how your limiting beliefs have become part of your identity. You might find it helpful to replace 'I am ... ' with 'I feel …'. For example, when we replace 'I am unworthy' with 'I feel unworthy', or 'I am too old to start a degree' with 'I feel too old to start a degree', we can begin to see how our limiting beliefs are driven by feelings rather than truths, and by culturally conditioned judgements rather than who we truly are.

What alternative beliefs would help me to live a richer, fuller, more meaningful life?

As we become more aware of our limiting beliefs – how they were formed and how they hold us back – we get to choose whether we want to continue living by them, or if we want to explore new beliefs that would support us in being the kind of people we would like to be and creating the kind of world we would like to live in.

Reflect on your limiting beliefs and, for each one, identify a couple of alternative beliefs that would be more empowering and expansive. Try on each new perspective like a pair of glasses and see how the world looks and feels through that lens. For example, how would it feel to replace the belief, 'I don't deserve to rest' with 'Rest is a requirement, not a reward'? Or to replace 'I am a failure' with 'I am a human being who sometimes fails and sometimes succeeds – and is always worthy'?

What is one awakened action I can take to embody these more empowering, expansive beliefs?

Changing our beliefs doesn't happen overnight. Instead, it is a slow evolution. Our beliefs change bit by bit as we dismiss our intrusive thoughts instead of getting lost in them, let our

deepest values guide our actions and expose ourselves to opportunities and experiences that support a new, more empowered
way of seeing ourselves and the world. We can change what we
believe through what we do. Awareness and awakened action
can literally rewire our brains (this is known as 'self-directed
neuroplasticity').

The more evidence we have for a belief, the more we will
believe it. For each new belief you wish to adopt, reflect on one
small, practical habit you can create that will embody it. For
example, being in bed by 10pm each night might be a way to
show that you are worthy of rest, while moisturising your arms
each morning might be a way of reminding yourself that your
body is sacred.

Awakening from perfectionism

Perfectionism is a combination of having excessively high standards and being overly critical of ourselves (and sometimes of others). It often comes with a sense of never feeling good enough, worrying about what other people think and obsessing over perceived flaws. Believing that who we are is not enough, we find ourselves caught in a cycle of perfectionism and shame – desperate to perfect ourselves, but disappointed when we fail to live up to our own unrealistic expectations. Pursuing perfectionism often leaves us feeling empty. By striving to achieve as much as possible and constantly seeking the approval of our peers, we neglect our rich inner worlds, and, eventually, we burn out.

In what ways did I feel the pressure to be perfect when I was growing up?

We aren't born perfectionists. Perfectionism is a learned behaviour. Expecting perfection of ourselves is often rooted in someone else's excessively high expectations of us. For example, if, as children, we felt we had to get straight As at school, somewhere along the way we might have begun to believe that we have to be overachievers in every area of our life in order to be worthy. Or, if we're a member of a stigmatised group and were told growing up that we needed to work twice as hard to get half as far, we might burn ourselves out by striving for perfection.

Reflect on any ways you felt the pressure to be perfect growing up. Were you shamed for making mistakes? Were there expectations for you to overachieve academically? Were you ever told your best wasn't enough?

In what areas of my life do I feel the pressure to be perfect now?

Being a perfectionist doesn't mean that we're always perfect. It means that we experience shame and distress when we're not perfect – which is always, because perfection is unachievable. And so, we find ourselves in a vicious cycle of setting ourselves impossible standards, only to feel shame when we are unable to meet them. To escape the feelings of unworthiness, we then set our standards even higher.

Reflect on areas of your life where you are caught in this perfectionism–shame cycle. As a starting point, you might want to think about: work, food, exercise, body, money, relationships, parenthood, home life, spiritual practices and social media. Be mindful that healthy striving is different from perfectionism. There is nothing wrong with working hard towards our goals; the problem comes when we base our self-worth on achieving them.

What would 'good enough' look like in these areas?

In the 1950s, the psychoanalyst Donald Winnicott termed the phrase 'good-enough parent' after realising how much distress his patients were experiencing when they failed to meet their own unrealistically high expectations of parenthood. He discovered that we don't need to be perfect parents. A 'good-enough parent' *is* enough. We can apply this idea of 'good enough' to other areas of our lives, too. Our bodies can be 'good enough', even if they don't look like the airbrushed pictures in magazines. Our jobs can be 'good enough', even if we find them boring sometimes. Our relationships can be 'good enough', even if we have disagreements.

Reflect on what would be 'good enough' in the following areas: work, food, exercise, body, income, savings, relationships, parenthood, home life, spiritual practices and social media. You might like to take it further and ask yourself: what would beautiful look like in these areas? What would awake and alive and wild look like?

Who do I feel the need to be perfect for?

When we are under the spell of what researchers Paul Hewitt and Gordon Flett termed 'socially prescribed perfectionism', we feel that we need to be perfect in order to be accepted, valued and loved. We only feel worthy if others approve of us. We believe that if we look and behave a certain way, we can avoid rejection. As children, being rejected and abandoned can be life-threatening, so perfectionism can be a powerful coping strategy that ensures we get our basic needs met. However, as adults, we can meet these needs for ourselves – we no longer have to be perfect in order to survive.

Reflect on where the pressure to be perfect comes from. Is it internal or external? Who do you feel the need to impress? Where do you feel you have to hide parts of yourself that might be judged as unacceptable? How do you try to edit out your imperfections?

How does perfectionism help me and how does it harm me?

Ultimately, perfectionism is an attempt to feel safe, worthy and lovable, but it can hold us back from living as fully and freely as we would like. By striving for perfection, we are trying to protect ourselves from feeling the shame that often comes with failure. And yet experiencing failure, pain and shame is an inevitable part of being human, and something none of us can avoid.

Reflect on how perfectionism has helped you and protected you in the past, and then reflect on how it is now harming you, holding you back, and preventing you from trying new things, reaching your potential and feeling fully alive.

How does my idea of the 'perfect self' differ from my true, authentic self?

Perfectionism robs us of our authentic selves. When we believe we are not good enough as we are, we subconsciously create a false self that we believe will make us more acceptable and lovable. As we get more in touch with our true selves, an inner conflict between who we have been taught we need to be in order to be worthy (the perfect self) and who we truly are can arise.

For today's self-reflection, you might like to create two columns – one titled 'perfect self' and one titled 'true self'. Under each heading, write down the qualities and values you associate with them. Think about what each self cares about, what they enjoy, how they spend their time and money, and how it feels in your body when you're striving to become the 'perfect self' rather than being your true self.

Which parts of myself am I hiding because I am afraid they are imperfect?

Perfectionism is rooted in the messages we have internalised from family, schooling, religion, media and our wider culture. When we absorb the message that only parts of ourselves are wanted and welcome, we tend to hide the parts we see as imperfect and unlovable. As we get to know the parts of ourselves we have rejected, we can befriend them and integrate them, so we feel confident in letting our whole messy, imperfect selves be seen.

Reflect on the parts of yourself you are hiding. What behaviours were you shamed for as a child? What are you afraid someone might find out about you? What parts of yourself do you judge to be unacceptable?

How might my life be richer and more meaningful if I stop striving to be perfect and let people see the real me?

Perfectionism is exhausting. We are constantly striving towards goals we cannot reach and living with a voice in our heads that is critical and mean. Plus, if we believe we have to keep parts of ourselves hidden, we can never relax, for fear that our masks will slip and our imperfect parts will be exposed. However, as we begin to reveal our hidden parts – our fragilities and vulnerabilities and flaws – we can finally relax, because we have nothing to hide anymore. Nothing to defend. Nothing to protect. By neutralising the threat of our whole, imperfect selves being seen, we allow our nervous systems to shift out of fight-or-flight mode, and we can begin to enjoy our lives instead of simply enduring them.

Reflect on how your life might change if you were to stop striving for perfection and instead allow your whole self to be seen.

In what ways do I expect other people to be perfect?

The unrealistic expectations and harsh criticisms we impose on ourselves are often far greater than those we would inflict on family, friends and colleagues, but sometimes we might find ourselves holding others to our own perfectionistic standards. This is known as 'other-orientated perfectionism' and manifests as an intolerance of imperfection in others. It can be destructive for relationships, because, by holding others to impossibly high standards, we will inevitably be disappointed when they cannot reach them.

Reflect on where you are expecting perfection from others. Maybe you expect your children to never argue, your partner to always agree with you or your friends to reply to your texts immediately. How would it feel to release these expectations and let others be their full, flawed, authentic selves?

What is one awakened action I can take to practise releasing perfectionism?

As we release perfectionism, we discover something better: authenticity, vulnerability and deep inner joy. But if we have spent years setting unrealistic expectations, then allowing ourselves to make mistakes and softening our self-criticism takes practice. Reflect on a practical way you can release yourself from perfectionism. Maybe you could try something new and accept you aren't going to be immediately good at it. Or perhaps you could give yourself a time limit for a task you would usually spend an excessive number of hours trying to perfect. Or maybe you can focus on embracing other people's imperfections – for example, staying calm when your partner doesn't clean the shower after using it, or not pointing out the grammatical errors in a colleague's email.

Awakening from people-pleasing

We are social creatures. We are wired to love, to give, to be aware of one another's feelings and needs. But pleasing is different from loving. At its core, people-pleasing is an attempt to feel safe, loved, wanted. It's based on the belief that if we are nice and quiet and well-behaved, if we don't speak up, if we prioritise everyone else's needs over our own, we will not be rejected. That if we give others everything they want, we will gain their approval. Deep down, we desperately hope that if we take care of other people, they will take care of us too.

How does people-pleasing feel different from being loving, generous and kind?

Pleasing comes from a place of fear rather than love. When we are scared of rejection or terrified that we are unlovable, we exhaust ourselves trying to make others happy, hiding our opinions and bypassing our own needs in an attempt to avoid abandonment and earn approval. The truth is, acting from a place of love means we might sometimes displease people. For example, maintaining a personal boundary for our own wellbeing might upset someone. Expressing our anger might cause conflict. Putting our own needs first might be met with judgement. But as we shift from pleasing to loving, our relationships deepen. Our generosity no longer comes from a need for approval or a fear of rejection, but from a place of deep authenticity and abundance.

Reflect on how people-pleasing feels different to loving. How does an authentic 'yes' differ from an obligatory 'yes'?

In what ways do I seek other people's approval?

When we are struggling to accept ourselves, we tend to look for external approval. We become nice and compliant and agreeable. We overcommit. We find it difficult to set boundaries. We hide our true feelings and sacrifice our own needs.

Reflect on the ways in which you habitually seek other people's approval. Where do you stay quiet in order to avoid possible conflict or rejection? Where do you neglect your own needs? What do you put up with in order to seem like a nice person? From whom do you seek praise or validation – both online and in person? How often do you apologise for things that aren't your fault?

How does it feel when I set a boundary?

As we awaken from people-pleasing, we learn the power of the sacred 'no'. We learn to say, 'No, I can't take on any extra work right now', 'No, I haven't got time to bake cupcakes for the school fair', 'No, it's someone else's turn to do the washing-up tonight'. We learn that setting boundaries can be uncomfortable, that we might feel guilty – even if we set our boundaries compassionately, with the intention of creating more authentic, intimate relationships – and that our boundaries might be met with resistance as we step out of our role as people-pleasers and the dynamics in our relationships begin to shift.

Reflect on how it feels to set a boundary. How does it feel in your body? What emotions arise? Where do you avoid setting boundaries because it feels uncomfortable?

What thoughts and feelings drive my people-pleasing?

The things that drive our people-pleasing as adults are often the things we needed as children but did not receive. We might people-please because the only way for us to feel safe as a child was by being helpful, by hiding our emotions, by always doing as we were told. We might have started to believe that we were only lovable if we were useful; only worthy if we put everyone else's needs before our own. Alternatively, we might people-please because there are certain psychological skills we have never been taught – for example, how to have healthy conflict, how to cope with rejection and how to handle the guilt that often arises when we set a boundary.

Reflect on the thoughts and feelings that drive your people-pleasing. Maybe you believe people only care about you when you do something for them, or that you're less likely to be rejected if others need you. Or maybe you notice yourself people-pleasing in relationships or situations where you feel anxious and unsafe.

How have sociocultural norms influenced my people-pleasing?

In patriarchal societies, there is an expectation for women to be nice, to please others, to forfeit their own needs, while men are encouraged to suppress their emotions to meet cultural expectations of masculinity. In collectivist cultures, altruism and self-sacrifice are highly valued. Racism may make people-pleasing a necessity for members of oppressed groups in order to avoid discrimination. And in certain religions, we can be encouraged to repress our needs and follow rigid rules in order to please God, a divine power or spiritual guru.

Reflect on how cultural norms have influenced your people-pleasing. How do race- and gender-based expectations affect you? Have you been part of a religious or spiritual community that promoted self-sacrifice as a virtue? How does your socioeconomic background influence your need to please others?

How is people-pleasing preventing me from living a rich and meaningful life?

As children, people-pleasing can be a protective strategy. Much like perfectionism (see page 125), it can be the only way for us to get our dependency needs met. As adults, we might continue using the same strategies even though the threat has passed and we can now meet these survival needs ourselves.

As honourable as self-sacrifice might appear on the surface, over time, people-pleasing can leave us burned out and with a lower capacity for love. Reflect on how people-pleasing is harming you or holding you back. What are you sacrificing by always prioritising other people's needs? Does people-pleasing leave you feeling more connected to or more resentful of those you love? Does it move you towards or away from the person you want to be and the life you want to create?

How might my people-pleasing be limiting or disempowering others?

People-pleasing is a conditioned response. We are taught that it is good to be a martyr, that it is our responsibility to make other people happy. But our people-pleasing can be disempowering to the people we love. By constantly coming to the rescue, we might be taking away another's agency, pushing them into the role of victim. By trying to make the people we care about happy all the time, we may be preventing them from feeling and processing their disappointment, grief or rage.

Reflect on how your people-pleasing might be disempowering others. How might it be preventing them from taking responsibility in their own lives? How would it feel to let someone you love be angry? What would happen if you didn't always rush to the rescue?

What am I afraid will happen if I start prioritising my own feelings and needs?

As people-pleasers, we find our worth in helping others. We worry that if we are not putting everyone else first – if we eat when we are hungry and rest when we are tired and say 'no' when we are overstretched – then we are selfish, unworthy and unlovable. Deep down, we hope that if we take care of everyone else, that at some point someone will take care of us too. We forget that *we* are the ones who need to take care of ourselves. We are the ones who need to give ourselves permission to rest, to heal, to grieve. We are the ones who need to prioritise fun, relaxation and joy in our lives. We are the ones who need to speak up, to express our feelings and ask for what we need.

Reflect on what you are afraid will happen if you stop people-pleasing and start prioritising your own needs. Are there relationships you're afraid might change? Or feelings you might have to face? Or outgrown identities you might need to release?

How would my life be different if I stopped people-pleasing?

By spending our lives pleasing others, we become alienated from ourselves. We feel lost and empty, fragmented instead of whole. In *Women Who Run With the Wolves*, psychoanalyst Clarissa Pinkola Estés writes: 'To be ourselves causes us to be exiled by many others, and yet to comply with what others want causes us to be exiled from ourselves.' And this is the choice we face multiple times a day: to please others or to be ourselves. We can let our fear of abandonment and our longing for approval drive us to please and fix and rescue, or we can be present with our fears and our longings and practise more compassionate, empowering ways of responding to them.

Reflect on how your life would be different if you didn't people-please. How would you express your feelings and needs? How would you eat? How would you dress? How would you spend your free time?

What is one boundary I can set this week?

As we awaken from people-pleasing, it's normal to feel guilty for setting boundaries, to feel cruel for expressing our anger, to fear rejection when we ask for what we need. But just because something feels unfamiliar or uncomfortable, or someone disagrees with us or expresses their frustration, it doesn't mean we've done anything wrong. It takes practice to unlearn the habits of people-pleasing, to experience what loving and giving from a place of abundance feels like, and to trust that we are still worthy when we prioritise our own needs.

Reflect on one loving boundary you can set this week. Can you give less in one area of your life? Does someone need to hear your sacred 'no'? Is there an internal boundary you need to set – to rest more, to check your emails less, to stop trying to control things that are beyond your control?

Awakening from burnout

Burnout is your body's way of telling you that you are doing too much and that you need to rest. We burn out when we experience too much stress with too little recovery for too long. This chronic stress may be the result of heavy workloads, caregiving commitments, relationship issues, financial burdens or an ever-present pressure to be productive. It's often experienced as overwhelming exhaustion, feeling disconnected, negativity towards others, a sense of incompetency and not being able to cope.

This section will help you explore how to recover and restore from exhaustion and protect you from burnout in the future.

What are the signs I might be heading towards burnout?

Feeling exhausted is often the first sign that we're heading towards burnout. This exhaustion can be physical, psychological, emotional, creative, spiritual or sensory – or a combination of these things. As we become aware of the signs, we can be more compassionate towards ourselves. We can tenderly remind ourselves, 'You are not crazy or lazy or broken. You are exhausted.'

Reflect on what exhaustion feels like for you. Common signs include: intense physical and emotional fatigue; heart palpitations; difficulty sleeping; forgetfulness; trouble concentrating; feelings of overwhelm, emptiness and disconnection; changes in appetite; feeling like a robot; living on autopilot; anger and irritability; dread of the day ahead; and feeling like nothing matters, like you have nothing left to give.

Do I feel close to burnout now? What is my past experience of burnout?

In a world that values productivity about all else, being busy all the time has become a badge of honour. For many of us, it's the norm to work long hours, be selfless and put everyone else's needs before our own.

Reflect on whether you are close to burnout now and think about any episodes of burnout you might have experienced in the past. Think about the three dimensions of burnout: physical and emotional exhaustion; a sense of disconnection from work, family or life in general; and a lack of trust in your own abilities.

What external stressors are putting me at risk of burnout?

There is a lot we can do personally to reduce our risk of burnout, but social inequalities and productivity culture can make it more challenging to access the resources we need to restore. As we become aware of how our upbringing, demographics and wider culture limits us, we can begin holding our experiences with less judgement and more compassion.

Reflect on what external stressors are putting you at risk of burnout. This could include both systemic factors – for example, the gender pay gap – and more personal factors, such as working in an office where there is an unspoken expectation that employees should respond to emails in the evenings and at weekends. External stressors include: a high workload; lack of social support; exam pressure; being a caregiver; chronic illness; low income; lack of autonomy at work; being a member of an oppressed group; mental health stigma; and lack of access to education.

What internal stressors are putting me at risk of burnout?

Sometimes it's the pressure we put on ourselves – for example, to be the perfect parent or straight-A student or overachieving employee – that puts us at risk of burnout. By setting more realistic expectations for our work, our parenting and our lives, we can balance the needs of our bodyminds and souls with what our families, workplaces and communities need from us.

Reflect on what internal stressors could be putting you at risk of burnout. This might include things like saying yes to too many projects, not setting clear work and family boundaries, striving for perfection, negative self-talk, fear of failure and neglecting your body's need for rest.

What boundaries do I need to put in place to prevent burnout?

Lack of boundaries is one of the biggest contributors to burnout. Boundaries act like interpersonal fences that protect our health, our energy and our time. They can be physical (for example, if you don't want to be adjusted in a yoga class, or don't want alcohol being drunk in your home), material (for example, letting a friend borrow your car only if they refill the petrol afterwards) or emotional (for example, stating that you won't accept being spoken to in a certain way). Our boundaries may also be intellectual, sexual and time-based. We can also set internal boundaries with ourselves, such as pausing when we feel triggered instead of reacting immediately, and not making any major life decisions when we are feeling exhausted or are in a state of fight-or-flight.

Reflect on what boundaries you need to put in place to protect you from burnout. Think about boundaries at work and with friends and family as well as internal boundaries.

What resources do I have to help me recover from stress and exhaustion?

Protecting ourselves and recovering from burnout is about replenishing lost resources and gaining new ones. Often, we have more resources at our disposal than we realise, but we may struggle to access them or be reluctant to use them for fear of being judged. For example, we might be surrounded by support-ive family members who have no idea how exhausted we are. Or we might have inner resources – such as courage, creativity, curiosity and compassion – that are locked away inside us.

Reflect on what restorative resources you have access to and whether you need to explore other resources to balance your cur-rent life stressors. These could include social support, hobbies, exercise and self-care tools like journaling and meditating, as well as coping skills like time-management, and psychological resources, such as compassion, gratitude and hope.

Who can I ask for help when I'm feeling exhausted and overwhelmed?

Burnout can often feel incredibly isolating. A common sign is that we feel disconnected from our partners, children, friends, colleagues – and even ourselves. This sense of aloneness can make it really difficult to ask for help, which is usually exactly what we need to do. As humans, we are wired for togetherness.

We have core needs that we cannot meet on our own. There will be times when we need to do the holding, and times we need others to hold us.

Reflect on who you can turn to if you're feeling exhausted. This might include a partner or parent, a friend or colleague, or professional support, such as a therapist or doctor.

How can I ensure I am using my non-work time to support my recovery from stress?

Sometimes we aren't able to reduce our workloads or take time off, even if we are exhausted. But we can use any downtime we do have to help us recover from the stressors in our lives. One of the biggest barriers to recovering from stress is our fear of 'wasting time', which can see us filling our evenings and weekends with the pursuit of goals – training for a marathon, starting a side hustle, writing a blog – and never truly allowing our bodies and minds the restoration they need.

Reflect on how you currently spend your non-work time and whether it is adding to your stress or helping you restore. For example, many of us mindlessly scroll through social media in our free time, which rarely leaves us feeling rested or restored (researchers are now studying 'social media burnout' because of the way it can exhaust our cognitive capacities through information overload). Be mindful that what we find restorative will be personal to each of us. For some, restful activity might be reading, napping and meditating, and for others it might be something more active, like dancing, cycling and hiking in nature.

How will I know when I'm ready to take on more in my professional and personal life?

Healing from burnout takes more than a few days of rest. It takes time to reshape our nervous systems, rebalance our hormones and restore our energy. To prevent us from taking on too much too soon, it's helpful to reflect on how we feel when we have a balance between stressors and resources, when we have the capacity to take on a new challenge, and when we feel relaxed, refreshed and restored.

Reflect on how you feel when you are truly rested and ready to set a new goal or start a new project. How do you feel in your body, in terms of energy, pain and tension? How is your sleep, digestion and mental chatter? How are your relationships with family, friends and colleagues – and with yourself?

What is one awakened action I can take to help me recover from stress, support my emotional balance and prevent burnout?

Sometimes the most powerful opportunities for rest show up in the micro-moments of everyday life – the tiny spaces that open up between one action and the next. If we're waiting in line at the supermarket, we can focus on being present instead of reaching for our phones. We can turn off the radio in the car to give our minds a rest from sensory overload. We can take five deep breaths at the end of our work days as a boundary ritual, marking the transition from work to home.

Reflect on one thing you can do to help protect yourself from burnout. This could be a bigger thing, like changing your work patterns, starting therapy or booking a holiday, or a smaller, everyday habit, like going to bed five minutes earlier or having a daily check-in with a friend to share how you're feeling.

Awakening from shame

Shame is an existential feeling of unworthiness. It is a universal human emotion, and yet it is something we are afraid to talk about. And because we don't talk about it, shame often becomes a hidden emotion, showing up in our lives as anxiety, perfectionism, addiction, aggression and emotional distress. By exploring, recognising and understanding our shame, we can shift from a place of secrecy, silence and self-judgement to one of connection, empathy and compassion. Make sure you are grounded and centred before exploring these questions (see pages 27–29 for techniques).

What is my earliest memory of feeling shame?

Shame researcher and bestselling author Brené Brown defines shame as: 'the intensely painful feeling or experience of believing that we are flawed and therefore unworthy of love and belonging'. When we're shamed as children – often unintentionally – we grow up feeling there is something inherently wrong with us. If our emotional needs are dismissed, or we're criticised for expressing our feelings, we assume that our feelings and needs are wrong – and shameful. As adults, we might yearn to relax, but we don't, because we were punished for daydreaming as a child. We might long to dance, but we stop ourselves, because we were once called a show-off. We might hide our sadness when we are filled with grief, because we were told to 'stop being such a baby' whenever we cried.

Reflect on your earliest memory of feeling shame. How old

were you? Where were you? Who were you with? Do you still carry this shame with you? How is this experience of shame affecting your life now?

When do I experience shame now?

We experience shame when the way we see ourselves is different from the way we think we should be, or when we believe someone else views us negatively. Unlike guilt, which we tend to feel in relation to a specific action where we have acted against our values, shame is the agonising feeling that who we are is fundamentally flawed, bad and unworthy. Shame can feel like we are being suffocated by expectations and are powerless to meet them, or it can manifest as feelings of worthlessness, anxiety, depression and burnout.

Reflect on the areas of your life where you experience shame now. Although each of our shame triggers will be personal, there are some common triggers, including appearance and body image, sex and sexuality, parenting, careers, religion, mental and physical health, aging, trauma and stereotypes. Emotions may also be bound with shame. For example, feeling depressed can trigger feelings of shame, as can feeling happy. Shame itself might also trigger more shame.

In what ways do I shame myself?

We shame ourselves in the same ways we have been shamed by others or by society. If we were bullied as children about the size of our bodies, we may have a lot of negative self-talk around our weight. If we were criticised for being too emotional, we may beat ourselves up for being oversensitive. Over time, shame trickles into our belief systems, trapping us in a painful loop of negative self-talk and ever-intensifying shame.

Reflect on the ways in which you shame yourself. What are your core shame-triggered beliefs? How could you meet these beliefs with compassion? For example, if a shame-triggered belief is, 'I shouldn't be feeling so anxious,' maybe you could meet it with compassionate self-talk, such as, 'I feel anxious today and it's really draining, so I'm going to slow down and take care of myself.'

How does shame feel in my body?

Shame lives in our bodies, in our nervous systems, in our breath. It is an embodied experience, shifting our nervous systems into a state of fight-or-flight, making us want to run and hide or rage and attack. Our brains register the pain of shame in the same way they register physical pain. Shame is often so uncomfortable to experience that we subconsciously substitute it with other emotions, like anger, guilt, depression or excessive pride. Or, because being in connection with our bodies means being in touch with our shame, we might find ourselves stuck in our heads, viewing our bodies with disgust and hatred for the shame they contain. As we reconnect with the embodied experience of shame and discover we can sit with it without it overwhelming us, we can escape the cycle of emotional avoidance and emotional distress that traps us in an ever-deepening shame spiral.

Reflect on how shame feels in your body. You might like to use the 'How to feel your feelings' techniques on page 294 to help you.

How does shame show up in my life?

Shame can show up in our lives as a number of things: perfectionism, insomnia, drinking or eating too much, substance misuse and excessive productivity. Because it's difficult to let someone get close to us when we believe we are inherently flawed, shame may shut us down and stop us from developing intimate relationships. Like other forms of chronic stress, which can cause immunological and hormonal dysregulation, shame may also show up through exhaustion, burnout and physical illness.

Reflect on how shame shows up in your life. How does it affect your work? Your relationships? Your physical and mental health? Your sleep? Your inner dialogue?

How are my feelings of shame influenced by sociocultural stereotypes?

Chronic shame is often rooted in sociocultural inequalities and expectations. When an aspect of our identities – race, gender, body size, sexuality, socioeconomic status or neurodiversity – is stigmatised, shame becomes a constant background noise in our daily lives. By awakening to the influence of sociocultural forces on our personal experiences, we can release some of the shame that traps us.

Reflect on how your feelings of shame are influenced by sociocultural expectations. Maybe you live in a larger body in a society that values thinness. Perhaps you identify as non-binary in a culture that pigeonholes people into binary genders. Maybe you are an introvert in a society that is biased towards extraversion.

What do I habitually do when I feel shame?

According to humiliation and resilience researcher Dr Linda Hartling, when we experience shame, we generally do one of three things: move towards, move away or move against. These strategies protect us from feeling the pain of our shame in the moment, but may also hold us back from living rich, meaningful lives in the long term. By identifying the strategies we use to avoid feeling our shame, we can begin to catch ourselves when we turn to them, giving us space to name our shame and respond to it in a more compassionate, healing way.

Reflect on how you habitually react when you feel shame. Moving towards it might look like people-pleasing, gift-giving and saying yes when we want to say no. Moving away from it might look like numbing with food or alcohol, isolating ourselves and keeping secrets from those we love. Moving against it might look like lashing out, being sarcastic or blaming or shaming others.

How would I like to respond to feelings of shame?

Shame isn't something we can avoid, but shame resilience is something we can cultivate. By becoming aware of our shame, recognising the early life experiences and sociocultural expectations that fuel it, and sharing our stories with a compassionate listener, we can begin to escape the webs of chronic shame we have been trapped in and respond consciously whenever shame arises.

Reflect on how you would like to respond to shame. Who would you reach out to? What grounding technique could you explore? How could you practise self-compassion?

Who can I trust with my shame?

Shame thrives in silence and secrecy. And, as Brené Brown writes in her book *Daring Greatly*: 'If we can share our story with someone who responds with empathy and understanding, shame can't survive.' By having the courage to speak about our shame with people who can hold space for our pain, we develop resilience and discover a deeper meaning in our feelings.

Reflect on who you can share your shame with. Who deserves to hear your story? Who can hold space for you without judgement? Who can be with your pain without trying to fix it? Who makes you feel safe, seen and soothed?

What is one awakened action I can take to cultivate shame resilience?

We cultivate shame resilience by repeated experiences of compassion and connection. Over time, we begin to see more clearly the webs of shame that trap us and to discover the power we have to free ourselves from them: the power to question our conditioning, to reject harmful social expectations and to feel our shame fully, respond to it mindfully and share it vulnerably with people who truly see us.

Reflect on one awakened action you can take to cultivate shame resilience. Maybe you can remove the phrase 'I'm fine' from your vocabulary, and instead be open with friends about how you really feel. Perhaps you could join a support group so you can share your shame with people who can say 'me too'. Or maybe you can practise self-compassion when you would usually self-shame.

Awakening self-forgiveness

We are imperfect, flawed human beings. We mess up. We make mistakes. We betray people. We say things that are cruel. We act in ways that are harmful to ourselves and others. And then we struggle to forgive ourselves for our humanness – sometimes, because we expect eternal perfection of ourselves, and sometimes because the mistakes we have made have become so entangled with who we are that we have forgotten that we can screw up and still be worthy.

What does self-forgiveness mean to me?

We live in a culture that knows little of forgiveness. Instead, we meet mistakes and wrongdoings with judgement and shame. Acknowledging the people we have hurt and the suffering we have caused often comes with fierce waves of guilt, and so instead of letting ourselves feel the depth of our regret, we often blame ourselves and others in an attempt to avoid our pain. Sometimes we resist self-forgiveness because we've internalised the idea that we can only atone for our transgressions through shame and punishment. We can also mistake self-forgiveness with letting ourselves off the hook, rather than seeing it as a way of accepting responsibility while releasing self-resentment, untangling our self-worth from our wrongdoings and taking restorative action instead of being paralysed by our shame.

Reflect on what self-forgiveness means to you. How does it feel? What actions would it involve? Is it a single decision or something that requires regular practice?

What do I need to forgive myself for?

Unforgiveness is heavy. It shackles us to our pasts instead of allowing us to be fully alive in the present. It keeps us at war with ourselves when what we need, what we deserve, is peace. Taking inventory of the pain we have caused allows us to untangle who we are from the mistakes we have made, to make amends where we can, to learn from our pain and to accept ourselves as imperfect, fallible humans.

Make a list of things you are struggling to forgive yourself for. What mistakes have you made? What promises have you broken? Who have you hurt? Who have you betrayed? Where are you still at war with yourself? What are you blaming yourself for that was never your fault? (Remember, when you are the victim, you have done nothing wrong, so there is nothing to forgive yourself for.)

Why did I act in the way that I did?

Pain breeds pain. We hurt others when we are hurting, when we are re-enacting patterns from our pasts, when we are coping with our pain mindlessly instead of with awareness. Understanding why we have behaved in a way that caused suffering to ourselves or others does not mean condoning our actions. Rather, it allows us to turn towards our mistakes, to accept responsibility for them, to hold them with compassion. Seeing the suffering within us that caused us to act in ways that weren't in alignment with our values helps us to release the self-condemnation that imprisons us, the self-shaming that keeps us trapped in our pain.

Look through the list of things you are struggling to forgive yourself for, and, for each one, reflect on what contributed to your behaviour. What need were you trying to meet? What survival strategy were you using? Were you under stress? Were you in pain? Were you afraid? Were you on autopilot? Were you doing the best you could with the tools you had available?

How is not forgiving myself causing me to suffer?

Self-forgiveness can be messy and complicated. Sometimes, we are both the victim and the perpetrator, the prisoner and the guard, the transgressor and the transgressed against. Avoidance can be a healthy coping strategy when another has wronged you, but it is impossible to avoid the one who has caused harm when that person is yourself. The only way to escape yourself is through self-alienation or self-destruction. Self-forgiveness protects us from abandoning ourselves. As we learn to forgive, we reunite with each glorious, terrifying, ugly part of ourselves.

Reflect on how your refusing to forgive yourself is causing you to suffer. Are you stuck in a spiral of shame? Do you ruminate on what you should have done differently? Is the stress of your self-condemnation causing you illness and pain?

How would it feel to take responsibility for the pain I have caused to myself and others?

Self-forgiveness involves two processes. The first is accepting responsibility for our behaviour, so that in the future we can act in accordance with our deepest values. The second is replacing self-condemnation with self-compassion. Both of these processes take conscious practice. It takes practice to own our mistakes, to accept the role we have played in someone else's pain, to hold ourselves with compassion and let our remorse move through us, allowing it to inspire loving, conscious action instead of pushing us more deeply into our shame.

Reflect on how it would feel to take responsibility for the mistakes you have made. How would it feel to say, 'I deeply regret that my actions caused pain *and* I still love myself', 'I acted in a way that was not in alignment with my values *and* I still accept myself', 'I hurt someone *and* I am still worthy'.

What would making amends look like?

Often, what we want most from someone who has harmed us is an apology, an acknowledgement they know how much they have hurt us and that they feel regret for what they have done. The five Rs of forgiveness offer us a framework to follow: *remembering* we are human (and that all humans make mistakes); accepting *responsibility* for the hurt we have caused; feeling *remorse*; taking *restorative* action by making amends or apologising; and learning from our wrongdoings and experiencing *renewal*.

Reflect on what you can do to make amends for your mistakes. How can you express your regret to those you have hurt? What can you do to make amends if it is yourself you have betrayed?

How would I act differently knowing what I know now?

Unless we forgive ourselves, we tend to live with a deep ache of shame. Refusing to forgive is stressful. Criticising ourselves and ruminating on our transgressions, day after day, increases the levels of our stress hormones, and puts us at risk of deeper distress, depression and burnout. By forgiving ourselves, recognising what we have learned from our mistakes, and committing to changing our behaviour so it is in alignment with our values, we can make peace with ourselves and escape the cycle of shame.

Reflect on each mistake or wrongdoing you have identified. How would you act differently knowing what you know now?

What would I say to someone else who had made similar mistakes?

Often, we find it easier to forgive others than we do ourselves. By looking at our mistakes as if it was someone we love who made them, we awaken compassion and forgiveness. When we stop holding ourselves to account as if we are superhuman, without fragilities and flaws, and stop treating ourselves as if we are sub-human because we have erred, we can begin to embrace being fully human.

Reflect on the mistakes you have made and what you would say to someone else if they had made them. How would you comfort them? What would you say to remind them their transgressions do not define who they are – that just because they've hurt someone, it does not mean they should suffer forever?

How does forgiveness feel in my body?

In *An Essay on Criticism*, poet Alexander Pope famously wrote: 'To err is human, to forgive, divine.' And that's how forgiveness can feel. Divine. Sacred. Holy. By forgiving ourselves, we are both embracing our humanity and embodying our divinity. Both unforgiveness and forgiveness are embodied experiences. They affect our nervous systems, our hormones, our neurochemicals, our posture, our breath. As we practise forgiveness, we often experience our bodies opening, softening, releasing – becoming free to relax now that they no longer have to carry the weight of our shame.

Reflect on how forgiveness feels in your body. You might like to use the 'How to feel your feelings' practice as a guide (page 294).

What is one awakened action I can take to practise self-forgiveness this week?

Self-forgiveness is a practice. If we have spent decades berating ourselves for causing ourselves or another pain, it is going to take practice and patience to trust in the beauty and power of forgiveness.

Reflect on one small, practical way you can practise self-forgiveness. You might like to practise a one-minute body scan, bringing your awareness to different parts of your body and its physical sensations, starting at the top of your head and moving to the tips of your toes. You could do this before getting out of bed each morning, mentally scanning your body for any feelings of shame and visualising a healing white light of forgiveness radiating through this space. Or, when you catch yourself stewing over a past mistake, you might like to repeat to yourself, 'I forgive you. I forgive you. I forgive you.'

Part three: Gentle reminders

- It's very difficult to reach our goals if we don't believe we deserve to. The beliefs we learn early in our lives are hardwired into our brains, and we have to make a conscious effort to reprogramme them. As the psychoanalyst Carl Jung famously said, 'Until you make the unconscious conscious, it will direct your life and you will call it fate.'

- When we are no longer striving for perfection, we can welcome the fullness of each moment with all its joy and beauty and uncertainty, and we can embrace the fullness and fragility and freedom of who we truly are. This is captured beautifully in the Sanskrit word *purnatva*, which means 'perfect fullness'.

- Awakening from people-pleasing teaches us the difference between pleasing and loving, obeying and respecting, and being nice and being true to ourselves.

- When we are no longer striving for other people's approval, we give ourselves the freedom to discover who we are, where we belong and what truly matters in our lives.

- We cannot heal our exhaustion after one weekend of resting. Healing takes time. Recovery from burnout means the psychophysiological systems that were activated during our exposure to stress – autonomic, hormonal and neurochemical – need to return to healthy levels.

- Reframing our exhaustion not as weakness, but as our body's way of warning us that we are under too much pressure, can help us remember we are not superhuman:

we are fully human, with innate needs for sleep, play and rest.

- We cannot shame people – ourselves or others – into changing. We need to feel safe if we are going to take the risk of changing. Shame creates the opposite of safety. It triggers danger, dysregulating our nervous systems and pushing us further into our pain.

- As we become aware of our shame triggers and recognise how external factors have influenced them, and as we find people who remind us of our worth when we are blinded by our own shame, we can move away from pain, blame and shame, and towards connection, compassion and courage.

- As you move through this book and reflect more deeply on yourself, shame may arise. If it does, meet it with compassion and reach out for connection so you can process it, integrate it and awaken from it.

- True self-forgiveness consists of accepting responsibility in such a way that it heals us. That it changes us. That it empowers us. By gathering our mistakes, by telling the truth about the pain we have caused and the people we have hurt, and by making amends where we can, we free ourselves from the prison of our own condemnation.

- By honouring our humanness, our unfinishedness, we give ourselves permission not only to mess up, but to learn from the times we have stumbled, to let our mistakes and misdeeds and missteps carve us into more conscious, loving humans.

PART FOUR

Embracing the Bees

If our planet is to thrive, we need bees to pollinate our plants. If we are to thrive, we need emotions to pollinate our lives. Without them, everything becomes dry and dead and empty. And yet, so often, we fight our emotions and we fear them. We fear their wildness and their unpredictability. We fear the way they can sting and throb and ache. We fear the way they disrupt our productivity, our achievement, our tightly controlled lives.

This section is about allowing emotions to re-pollinate our lives, creating an inner garden where it is safe for our deepest feelings to arise, harnessing our emotional energy as a powerful force that communicates, illuminates and motivates us to create rich, meaningful and beautiful lives.

Awakening bodymind healing

Healing is an embodied process. In the same way we experience distress through the physical sensations in our bodies, through pain and fatigue and heartbreaking, gut-wrenching emotions, we find healing through the body too. The outdated philosophy of mind–body dualism (seeing the mind and body as separate), combined with Western culture's 'push through' mentality, means that many of us devalue the stress and trauma our bodyminds experience – sometimes on a daily basis. And, because we dismiss it, we tend to neglect the recovery time we need to heal. In giving our bodyminds the recovery they need, we can begin thriving rather than simply surviving.

(Gentle reminder: I use the term 'bodymind' to refer to the whole psychophysiological system, including our immune, muscular, digestive, cardiovascular, neuroendocrine and nervous systems, as well as the ways in which our thoughts, emotions and environment influence these systems.)

What sources of stress am I currently facing?

Stress can come from internal or external sources. It can be acute or chronic, physical or psychological. It can be rooted in the present, rekindled from the past or triggered by the anticipation of something in the future. Many of us downplay the stressors we are experiencing – convincing ourselves 'it's not that bad' or reframing our experiences by thinking positively. Becoming aware of the stressors in our lives allows us to truly appreciate how much our bodyminds have been through so we can give ourselves the time we need to recover and restore.

Reflect on the stressors in your life, both in the past and in the present. What adversity did you experience growing up? What shock traumas have you experienced? What chronic, everyday stressors are you experiencing now?

How does stress arousal feel in my body?

A traumatised person lives in a traumatised body. An anxious person lives in an anxious body. An exhausted person lives in an exhausted body. We cannot separate our inner, emotional worlds from our physical one. Whenever we experience a threat – perceived or real – our bodyminds respond, shifting our energy to focus on dealing with our immediate safety at the expense of recovery processes. This means that, while stress arousal is protective in the short term, if our stress is chronic, our bodyminds never get the opportunity to fully restore, making us vulnerable to stress-related illness. Being aware of how stress arousal feels in our bodies is often the first step towards healing. The more awareness we have, the more agency we have in our lives.

Reflect on how stress arousal feels for you. How does your breathing change? How does your posture shift? Do any areas of your body become tense? How do your thinking and focus change? What emotions arise?

How much of a priority is bodymind healing in my life?

Healing involves learning to take care of ourselves in ways we may not have been taken care of growing up. Many of us have simply never been taught about the impact chronic stress has on us physiologically, and so we often find ourselves overlooking our basic needs – working long hours, trading sleep for productivity and juggling multiple stressors without giving our bodyminds the time they need for restoration and repair. Without adequate recovery time, the chronic stress of everyday life builds 'allostatic load' (wear and tear on our bodies and brains).

Reflect on how much of a priority healing and recovery are in your life. You might like to think about the different ways in which you can reduce allostatic load, and consider how much you prioritise these things: sleep and non-sleep deep rest (e.g. yoga nidra), nourishing food, spending time in nature, physical activity and social connection.

What stops me from making bodymind healing a priority in my life?

Chronic stress creates pain in every area of our lives. It colours the way we see ourselves, each other and the world around us. When we are stressed, everything feels like a threat or a trigger. We might struggle to sleep, eat, concentrate or make decisions. We might feel anxious, irritable or depressed. Over time, we might experience stress-related health problems – high blood pressure, type 2 diabetes, irritable bowel syndrome and auto-immune diseases. And yet, even when we know the harmful effects of stress, we often struggle to make recovery a priority in our increasingly over-scheduled lives.

Reflect on what holds you back from giving your bodymind the recovery it needs. What beliefs drive you to push through when you are exhausted? Do you have techniques to help turn off your stress response? Are there socioeconomic factors that mean you simply do not have the resources to allow your bodymind to recover?

What are the warning signs that my bodymind is becoming dysregulated?

Many of us spend much of our lives outside what professor of psychiatry Dr Dan Siegel terms our 'window of tolerance' – the zone of stress arousal where we can regulate our emotions and cope with the demands of everyday life. When we are chronically outside this window, our allostatic load builds and, over time, we begin to experience dysregulation, which may manifest physically, emotionally, cognitively, spiritually and behaviourally. By knowing the signs that our bodyminds are becoming dysregulated, we can use them as cues showing that we need to move back inside our window of tolerance by prioritising recovery.

Reflect on how dysregulation manifests for you. Think about physiological symptoms (e.g. muscle tension, headaches, bloating, fatigue), cognitive symptoms (e.g. brain fog, catastrophising, forgetfulness), emotional symptoms (e.g. mood swings, panic attacks, withdrawal), behavioural symptoms (e.g. procrastination, excessive use of caffeine or alcohol, emotional eating) and spiritual symptoms (e.g. loss of meaning and identity).

What pseudo-regulators do I use?

Sometimes we try to cope with stress by using substances, habits and behaviours that might soothe, suppress or distract us from our distress in the moment, but actually increase stress in our bodyminds in the long term. These coping strategies may have served us at times in our lives when we didn't have any other resources available, but may now be preventing true healing. In her book, *Widen the Window*, Dr Elizabeth Stanley calls these habits 'pseudo-regulators'. Because we often feel the urge to use one of these pseudo-regulators when our bodyminds are already experiencing dysregulation, we can use these urges as another sign that we need to prioritise recovery.

Without judgement, reflect on what pseudo-regulators you use. Common pseudo-regulators include self-criticism, self-harm, obsessive thoughts and behaviours and any of the following in excess: caffeine, sugary foods, alcohol, work, social media, gaming, television and gambling.

What purpose do these pseudo-regulators serve?

Our habits always serve a purpose, no matter how irrational or destructive they appear on the surface. By exploring and honouring the ways in which our pseudo-regulators have served us in the past – and may still be serving us in the present – we can begin to release any shame we have around them and explore alternative ways to meet our needs that will support our long-term healing.

Reflect on what function your pseudo-regulators are serving. What do they distract you from? What uncomfortable emotions do they protect you from feeling? How do they soothe you?

What alternative resources could I explore that would allow true healing?

There is no cookie-cutter approach to healing. The tools and resources that will allow you to return to your window of tolerance, so that your nervous system feels safe enough to turn off your defences and dedicate energy to recovery, restoration and growth, will be personal to you.

Reflect on alternative resources you could explore when you feel the pull to use one of your pseudo-regulators. If you're feeling anxious, angry or irritable, you might try soothing strategies, such as meditation – this is known as 'downregulating' stress arousal. You could also try something like going for a run or dancing in the kitchen in order to expend any excess stress activation (our stress response readies our body for immediate action – to fight or flee – so exercise provides an outlet for the physical action it was preparing for). If you're experiencing shame, depression or procrastination, you could try playful tools to gently bring energy into your system and upregulate joy, such as creating a playlist of happy tunes.

What does healing feel like for me?

Healing doesn't always feel like healing, especially in the beginning. When we live in a culture that tends to promote healing as bubble baths and scented candles, we can ignore the reality that healing comes with its own kind of pain. If we have experienced years, or even decades, of stress without full recovery, the stress we have suppressed often comes to the surface for release as we begin to give our minds and bodies opportunities for rest. Much like thunder and lightning, we might cry, yawn, sigh, shake, shiver and tingle as our emotional storm clouds pass through us and clear away.

Reflect on what the process of healing feels like for you. How do you feel as you release the stress stored in your bodymind? What does healing feel like in the long term?

What is one awakened action I can take to support my bodymind healing?

We cannot hack our healing. There are no shortcuts. No magic pills. No quick fixes. Healing has its own rhythms, its own seasons. We cannot make healing happen more quickly or with less pain. In fact, we cannot *make* healing happen at all. But we can create the conditions that *allow* our healing to happen. We can acknowledge the stress we are experiencing rather than dismissing it. We can recognise the ways in which we are overriding our body's needs, and choose to honour them instead. We can explore practices, techniques and relationships that regulate our nervous systems, rewire our brains and allow us to discharge the stress we have been carrying. All of this takes time. Reducing our allostatic load, rebalancing our endocrine system and reprogramming our habits takes time. Seeing our healing as a practice, a process, allows us to be patient rather than striving towards healing as some kind of finish line. Reflect on a healing resource you can explore using this week.

Awakening from anxiety

Many of us live with an ever-present sense of anxiety humming beneath the surface. Sometimes, we feel anxious in specific situations – in the dark, on aeroplanes, when public speaking – and other times we might feel anxious without knowing why we're afraid. We might experience anxiety as a feeling of dread or foreboding, a sense of unease without any specific source. Alternatively, it may manifest as constant hypervigilance, a belief that we aren't safe, that things will never be okay. Rather than trying to get rid of our anxiety, this section focuses on becoming curious about it, turning towards it, listening to what the anxious part of you has to say.

What makes me feel safe?

Anxiety arises when we feel unsafe inside our bodies, when our nervous systems are being bombarded by warnings of threat. These can be real-world threats, or may be due to our threat-perception systems becoming oversensitive due to chronic stress and past adversity. With our brains on high alert, we see danger where other people see safety. Discovering the people, places and practices that make us feel safe allows us to move out of this anxious state of hyperarousal so we can see things more clearly, think more deeply and feel more empowered in our lives.

Reflect on what makes you feel safe. Where do you feel safe? What everyday rituals and practices give you a sense of safety? With whom do you feel physically and emotionally safe? How can you make these safety anchors a priority in your life?

What resources can I use to shift my nervous system towards safety and connection?

By learning how to navigate our nervous systems – to move fluidly between states of self-protection and states of safety and connection – we can take effective action against a threat or stressor when we need to, and enjoy experiences of play, intimacy and relaxation when we don't.

Reflect on what resources you can use to move your nervous system towards a state of safety and connection. What can you do on your own (e.g. listen to soothing music, lengthen your exhales, walk barefoot on grass)? What can you do with others (e.g. phone a friend, get a massage, play cards)?

How does anxiety feel in my body?

Like all emotions, anxiety is an embodied experience. By paying attention to what is going on in our bodies and befriending whatever sensations we find, we can escape the spiral of anxiety we often get lost in when we're sucked into the worries racing through our minds. As we focus on our inner experiences, we discover that our physical sensations ebb and flow, arise and pass away. And, knowing they are impermanent, we discover we can sit with them. We notice how subtle changes in the way we breathe, the way we hold ourselves and the way we move can ground us, calm us and free us.

Reflect on how anxiety feels in your body. You might like to use the 'How to feel your feelings' techniques on page 294, noticing how anxiety feels different to safety, peace and joy.

What triggers feelings of anxiety?

Understanding *why* we feel anxious doesn't always change *how* we feel, but it allows us to be with our experiences with more compassion and less judgement. Some of the things that trigger anxiety are unique, based on our personal experiences, while others tend to be more universal, innate fears that once served an evolutionary purpose. For example, feeling anxious in social situations is thought to have helped our ancestors as it meant they stayed alert to social threats within their tribes, helping them avoid being ostracised (which in prehistoric times could have been fatal).

Reflect on what makes you feel anxious. What situations trigger anxiety for you? Who do you feel anxious around? Does what you eat and drink affect how anxious you feel? When you feel anxious, what is being threatened (e.g. your safety, certainty, belonging, beliefs, values, identity)?

In what ways do I experience status anxiety?

With the rise of social media, status anxiety has become pervasive in modern life. Many of us find ourselves worrying about being perceived as unsuccessful, living with a fear of not achieving enough, not having enough, not being enough in other people's eyes. Advertisements and marketing campaigns tap into our vulnerabilities by creating a sense of unease – that our armpits are too hairy, that our faces are too wrinkled, that our phones are too slow – and then convincing us that our anxiety can only be relieved by purchasing their product.

Reflect on how you experience status anxiety. Maybe you feel ashamed because your salary is lower and your house is smaller than your friends'. Perhaps you feel humiliated when you scroll through Instagram and see strangers posting photos of exotic holidays. Or maybe you impulse-buy, spending money on luxury goods in an attempt to boost your social status.

How do sociocultural forces contribute to my feelings of anxiety?

Anxiety is a deeply human reaction to the oppression, prejudice and stigma that exist in society. If we are part of an oppressed group, discrimination is an ever-present threat to our safety. For example, if you are a woman living in a patriarchal society, your anxiety may be a natural reaction to potential workplace harassment, the threat of sexual violence and exposure to sexually degrading language. As we identify the oppressive systems and cultural forces that threaten our safety, our anxiety becomes contextualised. It begins to make sense. Instead of pathologising it, we can honour it and even embrace it as a force for change.

Reflect on how sociocultural forces could be contributing to your feelings of anxiety. For example, maybe you feel trapped in a low-paying job. Perhaps you live in an area with a high crime rate. Maybe you work in an office where women are routinely degraded. Or perhaps you are Black in a society built for White people, and you carry the trauma of your ancestors in your bones. What do you have control over in these situations? Who can you reach out to for support? How can you harness your anxiety as a force for social change?

How do I usually cope with feelings of anxiety?

Sometimes we can sit with our anxiety. At other times, it can feel overwhelming. When it feels unbearable, we might find ourselves using coping strategies that, while reducing our distress in the moment, may not be health-enhancing in the long term (you might find it helpful to reflect back on the question on 'pseudo-regulators' on page 163 as a reminder of these common coping strategies).

Reflect on what you usually do when you feel anxious. What is your habitual reaction? How do you act on it or react to it? How do you try to get rid of it? How do you try to avoid it?

What do I usually worry about when I feel anxious?

We are storytellers. If we are feeling afraid and there is no obvious threat, our brains will make up a story in an attempt to make sense of what is going on in our nervous systems. When we're in a state of fight-or-flight, our brains will tell very different stories to those they tell when we feel safe and connected. Our stories become habitual and predictable, with negative thoughts playing on repeat. Registering the themes of these thoughts helps us to identify them when they arise, so we know which thoughts we can trust, and which are the result of outdated neurological wiring and outgrown conditioning.

Reflect on the things you worry about when you feel anxious. What stories play on repeat? What are the themes?

What message could my feelings of anxiety be giving me?

Sometimes our anxiety has a biological cause – hyperthyroidism, hormonal imbalances, dysregulated neurotransmitters – but it can also be a meaningful, functional response to what's going on in our lives. By being curious about our anxiety and listening to that part of ourselves, we can learn from what it has to say. Some people find it helpful to personify their anxiety as a subpersonality, a member of the family of inner selves that lives within each of us.

Reflect on what the anxious part of you might be trying to tell you. Where in your body do you notice this part of you? What does it look like? What does it want you to know? What is it protecting you from? What is it afraid of?

When I am feeling anxious, what is one awakened action I can take to help me feel safe?

As we become more aware of what triggers us to feel anxious, it's important to identify the things that help us feel safe when anxiety arises. This means that when we notice our nervous systems shifting, we have a range of resources we can use to navigate back to a state of safety.

Reflect on one practical tool you can use in times of anxiety over the next few days. You might want to pick one of the resources you identified in response to the question 'What resources can I use to shift my nervous system towards safety and connection?' on page 168. Alternatively, you might like to explore simple breathing techniques to use in moments of high anxiety, such as intentional sighing (taking a short inhale through your nose followed by a long sigh through your mouth) or doing a pretend yawn (opening your mouth, flaring your nostrils and exhaling). These work as a kind of psychophysiological reset button to help bring your bodymind back into balance. The grounding and centring practices on pages 27–29 can also be helpful for high-anxiety moments.

Awakening to love

Our quest for progress and perfection often leaves little room for love. And yet, in spite of everything, that's all most of us want. The journey of awakening is less about learning information and more about deepening our capacity to love. To open our hearts. To let the world touch us deeply. To let our lives become an expression of our love. To let love be the guiding force behind everything we do.

How do I experience true love?

Love is both within us and beyond us. It is both an act of great power and one of deep surrender. Like grief and God and truth, love is transrational – far vaster than our rational minds can understand. It is something to be felt, witnessed and held in wonderment. Love has many shades, many colours: platonic, romantic, parental, universal. And yet, throughout each, there runs a common thread. Love is the bridge that both separates and unites – mother with child, human with earth, lover with beloved.

Reflect on how you experience true love. What are its qualities? Is it a feeling – a tenderness, a longing, a sense of being seen? Or an action – kindness, devotion, giving? Or more of a way of being present, an intimacy with life? As psychologist Erich Fromm, author of *The Art of Loving* says, perhaps for you love consists of care, responsibility, respect and knowledge. Or, as psychotherapist David Richo writes in *How to Be an Adult in Relationships*, perhaps you experience love as the five As: Attention, Acceptance, Appreciation, Affection and Allowing.

When and with whom do I feel deep love?

Love is rooted in feeling safe and seen by another. Physiologically, the experience of being loved changes us – our heart rates, our nervous systems and even our hormones. Being loved creates a neural platform that, in turn, allows us to love ourselves, each other and the world around us. This creates an ever-deepening spiral of safety, tenderness and connection.

Reflect on when and with whom you feel deep love and deeply loved. Remember, love comes in many forms – spiritual love, erotic love, parental love, and love for places and poems and passions.

What is blocking my love?

Every day, we are given an abundance of opportunities to love and be loved, and yet, so often, we miss them. Usually, it's because we're too busy, or we don't believe we deserve to be loved, or we're too afraid to open our hearts in case they get broken. Our beliefs and busyness block our love, like a boulder blocks a stream. The protective walls we build around our hearts eventually get so high they stop love from entering or leaving.

Reflect on what could be blocking your love. In what ways does being busy blind you to its presence? What beliefs get in the way of you experiencing and expressing love? What barriers have you built that now imprison you instead of protecting you?

What do I use as a substitute for love?

When the river of love is blocked within us, we are left with a thirst that we try to quench with external things. We might feel there are things that are more deserving of our time, that are more important than love, such as achievement, money and power. We give so much energy to the productive, the profitable and the prestigious that love often gets pushed into the background of our lives. And yet, once we feel love, we often discover that we never needed the praise or power or perfection we desired. It was love that we were seeking all along.

Reflect on what you prioritise over love and what you use as a substitute for it. Looking at how you spend your days, what comes before love? What do you turn to when you are feeling unloved – work, food, TV, shopping, social media, achievement?

Where am I living from a place of fear instead of love?

Love colours the way we see the world. As we become more aware of what love feels like and the way it alters our perceptions of ourselves and the world, we can begin to notice when our actions and beliefs are inspired by love, and when we are driven by fear.

Reflect on where in your life you are inspired by love and where you are driven by fear (remember that fear can be a healthy response to real-life threat). What decisions have you made recently that were driven by fear? Where does fear creep into your daily choices about what to eat, what to wear and what to say? What actions have you taken as a way to express love, and what actions have been motivated by an attempt to earn it?

Where do I judge instead of love?

In every moment, we choose, whether consciously or unconsciously, to love or to judge. We can look in the mirror and tear apart the figure staring back at us, or we can feel awe and tenderness for the body we see. We can belittle the human sleeping in a doorway, or we can open our hearts to our shared humanity. If we find ourselves judging instead of loving, it is often because we have felt judged. However, as we remove the obstacles blocking our love, as we open our hearts and allow more love into our lives, the activity in our brain circuits associated with judgement are downregulated. Loving stops us from judging.

Reflect on the areas of your life where you judge instead of love. How do you judge others? How do you judge yourself? What would love look like in these areas?

When has love caused me pain?

Anyone who has experienced great loss or deep grief knows that love is not the absence of pain, but an opening to it. It is an acceptance that if we are to love, at some point our hearts will get battered, bruised and broken. And yet, the other option – to close our hearts and lock them away – leaves them unreachable. As we awaken, what emerges is a love that is not the opposite of grief or hate or pain, but one that embraces them. We discover that love works both ways – it can cause pain, and it can heal it. Early research suggests that holding hands with your romantic partner, or simply being in their presence or looking at photographs of them, can buffer your response to pain.

Reflect on how love has hurt you and how it has healed you. When has your heart been broken? What other emotions does love contain? In what ways has protecting yourself from pain also walled you off from love?

In what ways do I believe I am unlovable?

Healing involves grieving for the love we needed but did not receive in the past, and also offering ourselves the love we need in the present. If our caregivers were unable to love us in the way we needed to be loved, if we have been in relationships that are toxic, or if we live in a society that profits from our self-hate, learning to love ourselves is fierce and challenging work. But it is one of the most worthwhile things we will ever do, because when we know all parts of ourselves are lovable, including the parts we have been conditioned to believe are unwanted and unworthy, we no longer have to hide who we are.

Reflect on the ways in which you believe you are unlovable. Where did you learn these parts of yourself were not worthy of love? How would it feel to hold these parts of yourself with love and compassion?

How would my life be different if my love for myself was unconditional?

Nothing heals us more than being loved by someone who loves themselves. And yet, so often we see self-love as narcissistic and selfish. However, as we learn to love ourselves unconditionally, along with our mistakes and flaws and darkness, we learn how to love and accept the darkness in others too. Self-love gives us an experience of being both lover and beloved, of giving love, receiving love and being love.

Reflect on how your life might be different if you treated yourself with unconditional love. When do you withdraw love from yourself? How might you offer yourself David Richo's five

As of love (Attention, Acceptance, Appreciation, Affection and Allowing)?

What is one awakened action I can take to embody love more deeply?

Love is energy. It can ignite us and inspire us and burn away anything that does not serve us or the world. If we can take the risk to open our hearts, to let love flow through us, we can harness this energy, this fire, for healing, for awakening, for creating a more beautiful world.

Reflect on a practical way in which you can embody love more deeply. How can you translate love into action? What is love asking you to do? What can love burn away? Maybe love is asking you to turn off your phone in the evenings. Perhaps love looks like making the effort to see an old friend. Or maybe you can remind yourself to keep your heart open to love through a daily mantra, such as, 'Love flows through me like water. My task is to keep unblocking the stream.'

Awakening to grief

None of us can escape loss, pain, illness and death. Nor can we outrun our grief. But we can learn to carry it. We can let it soften us and deepen us. We can let our hearts be stretched wider by it. Awakening to grief is not about overcoming it or transforming it. Rather, it is about honouring it. Turning towards it. Giving ourselves permission to hurt. It is about learning how to be with our pain, so we don't drown in it or exhaust ourselves by constantly trying to outrun it.

What are my beliefs around loss and grief?

We live in a culture that treats grief as a problem to be solved instead of an experience to be witnessed. We are encouraged to control our despair, to hide our heartache. We are told that our sorrow is pathological, that if we can't get over a loss in a few weeks, there is something wrong with us.

Reflect on your beliefs around grief. Is it something that needs to be fixed or something that needs to be honoured? Is grief an interference in normal life or an essential part of being human? Is it something shameful that needs to be hidden or a healthy response to loss – something deeply human that calls us to pause, slow down and rest?

Who and what have I lost?

Losses come in many forms, some of which we will never be done grieving. We can experience loss for someone or something we once loved but is no longer in our lives, and also for the things we needed or hoped for but did not receive. Acknowledging and accepting these losses allows us to begin grieving and healing.

Reflect on the losses you have experienced. This may include: the deaths of loved ones, relationships that have ended, infertility, illness, missed opportunities, loss of independence, loss of identity, financial loss, the loss of a happy childhood, or not having your needs met as you were growing up. Loss can also come from changes in your life that are positive or celebrated. For example, having children can come with a loss of freedom, and retirement can be accompanied by a loss of meaningful work. Loss can also be collective, such as the loss of landscapes and species, as well as a loss of justice and equality in the world.

How have these losses affected me?

In his book, *The Wild Edge of Sorrow*, psychotherapist Francis Weller speaks of how it is easy to dismiss the pain of our losses if we compare them to situations we judge as worse than our own. But there is no hierarchy to grief. Every loss changes us. Shapes us. Breaks us and remakes us. Our lives are forever altered. Grief calls us back to our pain, not so we can fix it, but so we can accept our losses and honour how they have shaped us, so we can stop exhausting ourselves by pretending that we're fine, that it doesn't matter, that it didn't hurt.

Reflect on how your losses have affected you. How have they altered the path of your life? How have they changed the way you see yourself and the world?

Where am I in the process of grieving these losses?

Grief is a wild, messy emotion. It cannot be controlled or predicted. It doesn't follow a neat set of stages. We can move backwards and forwards between denial and acceptance. We can feel okay one minute and find ourselves falling to our knees and weeping the next. We can busy ourselves to avoid experiencing the full force of our losses, until one day we wake up to find ourselves buried in the deep, earthy darkness of our grief. But, with support, tenderness and compassion, we discover that, although we might never get over our grief, we can hold it. We can be with it. And we learn that our love can coexist with our pain.

Reflect on where you are in the process of grieving. Have you experienced periods of denial? Anger? Acceptance? Have you ever felt safe enough to descend into the depths of your sorrow? Is there space for love and joy alongside your grief and pain?

How does grief feel in my body?

Grief calls us back to our bodies, and through our bodies we are brought into a deeper connection with the world. Sometimes grief comes in waves, breaking our hearts open, causing tears to stream down our faces. Sometimes it clings to the walls of our lungs, making every breath ache. And sometimes it weighs down on us, a heavy, squeezing presence.

Reflect on how grief feels in your body. Where do you feel it? What sensations do you experience? How does it manifest itself physiologically (e.g. loss of appetite, fatigue, nausea, headache)? How does it shift and change over time?

What have I discovered about myself and the world through the grieving process?

Loss is not always transformational. Sometimes there is no silver lining. No spiritual growth. No deep meaning or profound realisation. Sometimes, loss simply teaches us that love is painful. That being human is hard. That not everything can be fixed. That life is cruel and full of suffering, and also glorious and beautiful and divine.

Reflect on what you have discovered about life through your grief. Maybe you've learned that love doesn't end when life does – that it lives on. Perhaps you've realised that it's okay to be angry, that you don't need to be positive all the time. Or maybe grief has reminded you of just how fragile it all is; how precious it is to be alive.

In what ways have I felt shamed or judged for my grief?

Sometimes we feel shamed for our grief by the people who love us most. Instead of holding us in our pain, they try to fix us or save us, and although it can come from a good place, that doesn't mean we don't feel the weight of their judgement.

When we are grieving, people try their best to stop us hurting. They might say things like: 'Everything happens for a reason', 'It was God's plan', 'They are in a better place now'. Or we might be told that they find it tough seeing us so sad, that we've been grieving too long, that we should be over it by now, and that we need to start 'living' again. Reflect on how you have felt shamed or judged for your grief, and how this impacted the way you came to terms with it.

How do I avoid feelings of grief and loss?

Trying to stay busy and distracted in the face of grief can be a coping mechanism for dealing with the pain we feel, but if we close our hearts to grief, our hearts are simultaneously closed to love, beauty and joy. While we need to balance the pain of our grief with permission to set it aside for a time, we also need a safe place to take our grief.

Reflect on habits and behaviours you use to avoid feeling your grief. What do you do when waves of sorrow wash over you? How do you distract yourself when a loss comes to mind? Where is a safe place to take your grief?

Who can support me when I am experiencing grief?

Grief is too heavy to be carried alone. As we grieve, we need others to see us, to soothe us, to hold space for our sorrow. We need to be able to tell the truth about how much we are hurting, to reminisce and remember, to keep our love alive, even inside our pain. But not everyone has the capacity to hear us, to hold us, to be with us when our hearts are breaking.

Reflect on who can support you when you are grieving. Who do you feel safe with? Who won't criticise you, or give you advice, or try to fix you? Who can hold space for your pain?

What is one awakened action I can take to care for myself when my grief feels heavy?

Practices and rituals can deepen our capacity to be with our grief, to be gentle with ourselves in the midst of our pain. By cultivating a safe space, a daily ritual of meditation, yoga or prayer, or of writing, dancing or painting, we create a place where our grief can breathe, where we can tend to it, honour it and allow it to flow through us and beyond us.

Reflect on how you can care for yourself while grieving. Perhaps you can write a poem about your love and your loss. Or maybe you can give yourself daily 'cry time' where you put on some beautiful music and let yourself weep.

Awakening to belonging

Belonging is part of our biology. Like food and shelter, belonging is an innate human need. Without this deep connection with ourselves, each other and the planet we live on, we feel restless and empty. We yearn to be part of something greater than ourselves. We long to belong. And yet, despite the world becoming increasingly connected through technology and social media, many of us feel lonelier than ever. This section focuses on exploring our feelings of belonging and unbelonging, allowing us to cultivate a deeper connection with our bodies, our souls, our communities and the places we call home.

What does belonging mean to me?

One of our deepest needs is to belong. To love and be loved. To share ourselves and our lives with those who value us. Belonging comes in many shades. We can belong publicly through our familial and social circles. We can feel a sense of belonging with those who share our values, views and characteristics (for example, religious, political and cultural). And yet, anyone who has ever felt lonely when they are surrounded by people knows that belonging is about more than shared identities and being part of a group. It is deeply emotional, primal and sacred.

Reflect on what belonging means to you. Is it based on members of a group accepting and approving of you or is it something you feel within you? Does it depend on common characteristics and shared interests or is it rooted in something deeper?

Where do I feel I truly belong?

Sometimes, belonging is something we feel when we connect with something outside ourselves – a lover, a place of great natural beauty, a line in a song. At other times, belonging blossoms in our hearts when we connect with something within us, when we stumble upon our own sacredness and feel safe enough to share our authentic selves with the world.

Reflect on where you feel you truly belong. What places and spaces feel like home to you? Who do you feel you belong with? What spiritual practices give you a sense of belonging to something larger than yourself?

How does 'fitting in' feel different to true belonging?

Our need to belong is so primal, and our fear of revealing our whole, imperfect selves is so huge, that we often sacrifice true belonging for social approval. We smother our uniqueness in order to fit in. We withhold our truths in order to avoid conflict. We form pseudo-communities – pleasant and functioning on the surface, but lacking the intimacy, honesty and vulnerability required for deep connection and true belonging.

Reflect on how 'fitting in' feels different to true belonging. Where do you feel you have to water yourself down to fit in? What pseudo-communities are you part of, and how do these make you feel? Where are you seeking social approval as a substitute for true belonging?

When and where have I felt like I don't belong?

At some point in our lives, many of us will have experienced a subtle but uneasy sense that we don't truly belong. This could be in our families, workplaces or social circles, or we might struggle to find a sense of belonging in our own bodies, in the places where we live or in the wider world around us. The increasing divisiveness in society – political, economical and ideological – has blinded us to our shared humanity. And, even in the communities where we think we belong, we often worry about saying or doing the wrong thing and being shamed or excluded. Our belongingness often comes with conditions.

Reflect on when and where you have felt like you don't belong – either in the past or in the present, acutely or chronically. When have you felt like an outsider? When have you felt excluded? What made you feel this way?

What are my habitual coping strategies when I feel like I don't belong?

As humans, we have an evolutionary need to live in close communities, to be part of a tribe, to cooperate towards shared goals. But the rugged individualism of modern life has meant that many of us live with a feeling of unbelonging – an emptiness, a loneliness, a sense that no one really cares. And so, we find ourselves trying to fill this emptiness with the things we believe will bring us meaning and make us happy.

Reflect on how you cope when you feel as though you don't belong. How do you deal with feelings of loneliness, rejection and isolation? Do you blame yourself? Do you suppress your feelings? Do you use social media as a substitute for belonging? Do you seek superficial connections rather than building deeper relationships? Are you able to reach out for true connection?

How has my conditioning impacted my sense of belonging?

To feel a sense of belonging, we need to feel seen, to feel wanted, to feel held in love. If, growing up, we were excluded based on certain qualities, or shamed for our quirks and vulnerabilities, we learn to reject certain parts of ourselves in order to survive. And because other people are hiding these unique, afraid parts of themselves too, we all end up feeling alone. Our sense of unbelonging is heightened further if we are socially excluded based on our age, race, sexuality, gender identity, disability or socioeconomic status.

Reflect on how your childhood and cultural conditioning has impacted your sense of belonging. What parts of yourself make you feel as though you don't belong? What qualities were you led to believe were unacceptable? What societal norms have left you feeling excluded? How can you begin to embrace the parts you have rejected?

What beliefs limit my sense of belonging?

Limiting beliefs stop us from taking risks, from reaching out, from trying something new. They will have been adaptive at some point in our lives, protecting us from experiencing pain we didn't have the resources to deal with. But often these beliefs outlive their usefulness – trapping us in too-small lives when we have the capacity to live in a way that is richer and deeper, with more beauty, intimacy and togetherness than we can imagine.

Reflect on any beliefs that limit your sense of belonging. What beliefs stop you from reaching out when you are feeling lonely? What beliefs hold you back from forming new relationships? What beliefs drive you to sacrifice your truth to fit in?

How much do I prioritise community and connection in my life?

Living in a world that values individualism above community means that many of us strive for self-reliance at the expense of meaningful relationships. Instead of cooperating as a society to achieve shared aspirations of equality, we often find ourselves prioritising our personal goals, because we no longer trust that if we fall, we will be caught in the loving arms of a community. The pressure to be constantly productive and work longer hours means that many of us don't have the time to invest in relationships and community, even though social connection is essential for our wellbeing.

Reflect on how much you prioritise community and connection in your life. How often do you see friends? How well do you know your neighbours? How much effort do you make with your colleagues?

What does belonging to myself feel like?

In the sixteenth century, philosopher Michel de Montaigne wrote, 'The greatest thing in the world is to know how to belong to oneself.' In many ways, our belonging is rooted in the relationships we have with ourselves. In not hiding from ourselves. In making a home within our bodies. In embracing every part of ourselves with loving acceptance. Belonging to ourselves is a practice, a remembering of our sacredness, a rediscovery of our courage to both stand alone and be part of a greater whole.

Reflect on what it feels like to belong to yourself. Does your body feel like a home? Do you feel a sense of belonging when you are alone? In those moments when you don't feel like you belong to yourself, who do you belong to? Your parents? Your partner? Your boss? Your past?

What is one awakened action I can take to cultivate belonging?

Chronic loneliness leaves a scar. If our needs for relationship, community and belonging are not met, our bodymind starts to alert us that something is wrong, that our survival is under threat. Over time, our loneliness affects our stress hormones, immune function and emotional regulation, which can then make us more likely to isolate ourselves and push away the relationships we crave. Cultivating belonging takes courage. It asks us to reach out, even when we are afraid to reveal our true selves.

Reflect on one way in which you can cultivate belonging. What could you do at work? At home? With friends? In your community?

Awakening to uncertainty

Life is full of uncertainty. No matter how much we plan, or how much care we take, there are many things in life that we cannot control, many things that we cannot predict, many things that we cannot know. Awakening to uncertainty means waking up from the illusion of certainty and control, realising that no matter how hard we try, we cannot make our lives risk-free. But we can make friends with uncertainty. We can learn to accept the truth of not knowing, to embrace the unknowable, the unplannable and the unpredictable as part of the beauty and mystery of being alive.

What is my earliest memory of feeling uncertain?

If we experienced a level of uncertainty growing up that we didn't have the tools to cope with, as adults we may experience the same level of intense anxiety whenever we feel uncertain. Discovering that our intolerance for uncertainty is rooted in the past offers us insight into why we feel the way we do, and what tools and resources we need to develop so that we can be with uncertainty without it overwhelming us.

Reflect on your earliest memory of uncertainty. What did you feel uncertain about? Who was there to offer reassurance? How has this affected your relationship with uncertainty as an adult?

What feels uncertain in my life right now?

A vast amount of our lives is unknown and unpredictable. No matter how hard we try, we cannot predict exactly where we will be this time next year, how our career will pan out, or who we will love. Some of the uncertainties we live with are shared – the weather, the traffic, or when the next global pandemic will hit – and some are more personal, such as whether we'll get the job we applied for, if we'll find love on the dating app we downloaded, or how long it will take for an injury to heal.

Reflect on what feels uncertain in your life right now. This might include issues surrounding your relationships, your career, your health and your finances.

How does uncertainty feel in my body?

The less we know, the more threatened we tend to feel. Uncertainty triggers our autonomic nervous system to shift into a state of hypervigilance so that we can protect ourselves from potential dangers. This is a healthy, adaptive response in the short term, but we aren't designed to live in survival mode in the long term. When we do, we tend to misinterpret our bodily sensations as threatening, overestimating the chances of bad things happening and underestimating our capacity to cope if they do. As we befriend our uncertainty, as we get to know how it feels viscerally, we can learn to accept it, to stay grounded, to embrace it as part of being alive.

Reflect on how uncertainty feels in your body. You might like to bring to mind a situation you feel uncertain about and use the 'How to feel your feelings' techniques on page 294.

What do I believe about uncertainty?

The beliefs we have about uncertainty mediate the stress response we have to it. If we believe that uncertainty is unacceptable and unfair, that we should be able to plan everything in advance and have a guaranteed outcome before we begin, we are likely to feel far more anxious than if we accept that much of life is unknowable and unplannable.

Reflect on your beliefs about uncertainty. How do these beliefs affect your stress response? What would be a more expansive, empowering belief that would allow you to see uncertainty as a doorway to creativity, possibility and aliveness?

How do I usually react to uncertainty?

Uncertainty is unavoidable. Not knowing is part of the adventure of being alive. However, many of us resist uncertainty. We try to control the uncontrollable and predict the unpredictable. We ruminate and overthink and run through every possible scenario in our heads so we don't get caught off guard. Or we try to escape the discomfort of uncertainty by avoiding situations that aren't familiar or within our control.

Reflect on how you usually react to uncertainty. Common reactions include avoiding new experiences, procrastinating, ruminating about the future, seeking excessive reassurance from others, double- and triple-checking emails, refusing to delegate and obsessively making lists.

How is uncertainty keeping me stuck?

Uncertainty can paralyse us. We might long to write the book or leave the relationship or start the business, and yet find ourselves continually counting to three and never beginning. Instead, we find ourselves researching alternatives, making lists and creating back-up plans. We obsessively doubt ourselves: 'What if it doesn't work out? What if I can't do it? What if I fail?'. We long for change, and yet the uncertainty that accompanies it feels unbearable.

Reflect on how uncertainty paralyses you. Where do you feel stuck? How would you like things to be different? What do you need in order to feel safe enough to risk change?

Where do I try to control the uncontrollable?

Our tolerance for uncertainty – our perceived capacity to be with and cope with the unknown – determines whether we can rest in the uncertainty of the present moment or attempt to control the uncontrollable. This might manifest as people-pleasing in an attempt to control what other people think about us, or obsessing over our cellulite and wrinkles in an attempt to control the way our bodies naturally change as they age. As we awaken to uncertainty, we learn what we have control over and what needs our attention and acceptance. Acceptance does not mean passive resignation; rather, it means seeing the reality of our situations, acknowledging how we feel and identifying where we have agency.

Reflect on where you try to control the uncontrollable. How would it feel to accept that you don't have control over these things? To rest in the uncertainty?

What can I control amidst my current uncertainty?

As we awaken to the inherent uncertainty of life, we can begin to disentangle those things we can control from those things asking for our acceptance. We discover anchors to steady us in the ocean of impermanence, uncertainty and change. We learn that we can be grounded in the groundlessness.

Reflect on what you can control in your current situation. Can you control your breath? Your self-talk? What you're paying attention to in each moment? What books you read? How you respond to your emotions? How you nourish yourself? What time you go to bed?

What psychological skills do I need to cultivate so I can cope with uncertainty?

If we've never been taught the skills we need to deal with uncertainty, we might find ourselves feeling anxious when there is a lot that is unknown in our lives. But rather than attempting to avoid or escape uncertainty, or trying to cling on to control by our fingertips, we can develop psychological resources that help us to tolerate uncertainty, to be with it calmly and compassionately instead of being overwhelmed by it.

Reflect on what psychological skills you need to cultivate so that you can ride the waves of uncertainty instead of drowning in them. These might include acceptance, curiosity, persistence, trust, emotional regulation, gratitude, hope and compassion.

What is one awakened action I can take to embrace uncertainty?

Uncertainty is rarely comfortable, but it can be tolerable – and, with practice, even enjoyable. We read crime novels because we don't know what twists and turns might happen on the next page. We watch television dramas because, when we feel safe, suspense can be thrilling. Opening presents on our birthdays is fun because there is an element of surprise.

Reflect on one practical thing you can do to practise embracing uncertainty. Maybe you can watch a film without first looking at the reviews. Perhaps you can let your friend pick the restaurant next time you go out for dinner. Or maybe you can start a painting without knowing what the finished picture will be.

Part four: Gentle reminders

- There is a great gulf between what society wants from us and what we truly need. Many of us learn how to work hard. How to hustle. How to achieve. But we don't learn how to relax. How to restore. How to give our minds and bodies the care and compassion they deeply need.

- Prioritising our health, our bodies and our souls over society's goals often means making sacrifices that don't make sense to the outside world. There is no award for sleeping an extra hour every night. No pay rise for getting out on a walk on your lunch break. No prize for turning down that promotion so you can live a quieter life. But making choices like this may be the only way we can find inner peace and deep healing; the only way to give our minds and bodies the rest and recovery they long for.

- By becoming curious about our anxiety, by contextualising it and looking at the sociocultural forces that contribute to it, we can begin to understand it instead of fearing it or judging it. By befriending our nervous systems, becoming aware of our triggers and identifying resources and practices that make us feel safe, we can work with our anxiety instead of fighting against it. We can honour it. We can listen to it. We can learn from it.

- Healing does not come through force, but through love. If we want to help someone heal or change or awaken, we have to love them as they are. We have to hold them in our hearts with acceptance, awe and appreciation. And if *we* want to change – to eat more healthily or go to bed earlier or stop drinking – we first have to love ourselves – and let ourselves be loved – exactly as we are. This is the power and paradox of love.

- Life is full of great loss and deep love. Learning to carry these two truths is incredibly healing. As we grieve, we discover that loss, grief and pain can coexist with love, peace and joy. That, even though we might never be able to get over our grief, it doesn't have to destroy us. Instead, it can be a reminder of our love, of how fragile it all is: part of this precious adventure of being alive.

- Belonging is at the heart of every mystic tradition, of every spiritual practice, of what it means to be human. And yet, the more we awaken to it, the more we discover that it is something of a paradox. Our belonging lies in both our uniqueness and our shared humanity, in knowing we are both the wave and the ocean, in our courage to stand alone and our awareness that we are part of a vaster, deeper, richer whole.

- Uncertainty can be so painful that many of us will choose unhappiness over the unknown. By accepting uncertainty as a natural part of life – something we can't escape or control – we discover there is a joy and beauty in the things we cannot plan and do not know. We begin to see that if everything was certain, if we knew how the story went in advance, life would be empty of its richness, its abundance, its aliveness.

PART FIVE

Fertilising the Earth

As we awaken, we realise there is nothing to fix because nothing is broken, and nowhere to go because we are already home. We stop striving for a different body or a different life. Instead, we make *this* body, *this* life, *this* earth our home. And, being home, we begin taking care of ourselves, nourishing ourselves, getting to know what drains us and what replenishes us, what restores us and what exhausts us, what helps keep our bodies healthy, our hearts open and our love strong.

Our daily habits can contribute to our suffering, or they can lead us to healing and awakening. This section explores our relationship with everyday things like food, money and time so that we can eat the food that nourishes us, practise the habits that restore us and make conscious choices to create authentic, abundant and awakened lives.

Awakening health

We have access to more health information than ever before, and yet many of us have forgotten how it actually feels to be healthy. To wake up with energy and vitality each morning. To sleep deeply, eat slowly and move without pain. To care for our bodies instead of judging them. To prioritise our mental health over our productivity. To experience deep spiritual joy. Our health is an ever-evolving state of wellbeing that encompasses many intertwined elements, including the physical, psychosocial and spiritual. This section will help you to explore what being healthy means to you, and any lifestyle changes you might like to make so you can experience more energy, vitality and aliveness.

How do I feel when I'm physically healthy?

Although there are many objective measures of physical health – such as blood pressure, cholesterol levels and cardiovascular capacity – it's also helpful to get in touch with how being physically healthy feels for each of us individually. Your subjective experience is important because there is so much conflicting information online, in the media and even among health experts (for example, some professionals use Body Mass Index or BMI as a measure of health, while others advocate for a Health at Every Size approach).

Reflect on how you feel when you are physically healthy. This might be something general, like having a body that can sleep, poop, and move without pain, or it might be more specific, such as being able to deadlift your bodyweight or comfortably run a 5k.

How do I feel when I'm mentally healthy?

After decades of being a taboo topic, mental health is finally being spoken about openly. Collectively, we are realising that we need to look after our mental health in the same way we take care of our physical health in order to cope with the stressors and pressures of life.

Reflect on what being mentally healthy means to you. This might include: experiencing and expressing a range of emotions, using compassionate self-talk, feeling a sense of meaning and worth, being able to focus and pursue goals, having the capacity to regulate stress levels, and not overusing addictive substances like caffeine or alcohol.

How do I feel when I'm socially healthy?

We are born with an innate need for connection and belonging. Relationships are a physiological necessity for our health. Our nervous systems learn how to self-regulate through co-regulation, by being in connection with people who make us feel safe, seen and soothed. But in our modern, individualistic society, over half of us report feeling lonely and isolated much of the time. Our social health is something we can cultivate by prioritising it – and doing so will have a ripple effect, enhancing other areas of wellbeing.

Reflect on what being socially healthy means to you. This might include things like having a supportive group of family and friends, feeling comfortable in a wide range of social situations, being able to balance solitude with social commitments, feeling a sense of community and being able to be yourself when you are with others.

How does it feel when I'm spiritually healthy?

In her book *A Simple Path*, Mother Teresa writes of the spiritual poverty we experience in the Western world. This spiritual poverty leaves us with a feeling of emptiness and deep disconnection, a hunger for something we cannot name. We often find ourselves neglecting our spiritual health because we don't really know what it is or how to nourish it. Emerging research by Dr Neera Dhar, Suresh Chaturvedi and Dr Deoki Nandan at Santosh University has identified three elements of spiritual health: self-evolution (growing, awakening and becoming more conscious), self-actualisation (realising our full potential), and transcendence (connecting with a deep happiness within ourselves and also a universal love beyond ourselves).

Reflect on what being spiritually healthy means to you and how it feels when you take time to nourish your spirit.

How has my health changed over my lifetime?

Our health is a result of biological, psychological, relational and cultural factors that change over time. By reflecting on our health in the past, we might be able to find patterns that will help us to optimise our health in the present and take care of it for the future.

You might find it helpful to draw a timeline for each area of your health – physical, mental, social and spiritual – as a visual representation of how your health has changed over time. Place age along the horizontal axis and health up the vertical axis with 'flourishing' at the top and 'languishing' at the bottom. Map out how your health has changed using dots, then connect the dots and reflect on the interconnection between the different elements of health.

What am I currently doing to support each area of my health?

It's easy to treat our health like a constant self-improvement project. But if we are constantly aiming to do more and be healthier – to sleep better or run faster or feel calmer – it's easy to forget how far we have come, and we can become disheartened and unmotivated.

Reflect on everything you are currently doing to support each area of your health. Are you making time for regular nourishing meals? Are you moving your body regularly? Are you making time for friends and family? Are you journaling, meditating or practising yoga?

What areas of my health am I neglecting?

In the modern world, health is often reduced to a numbers game – weight, BMI, step count, calories. And yet, by obsessing over the quantifiable, we often find ourselves neglecting other areas of our health. Ultimately, health is about wholeness. Being healthy means paying attention to the whole of life – mind, body, spirit, relationships, society and the earth on which we live.

Reflect on any areas of your health that need a little more attention. What have you been neglecting? What thoughts, behaviours or habits are you engaging in that are harmful to your wellbeing?

In what ways do I judge or shame myself in relation to my health?

Many of us have been taught to believe that self-criticism will motivate us to eat more healthily, work out harder and push through when we are exhausted. This harsh judgement is often absorbed from our parents, peers and the media. We might have been bullied about our weight or shamed for being 'greedy' when we were growing up. Or we might constantly compare ourselves to the extreme diets and the filtered and retouched bodies we see on social media.

Reflect on the ways in which you judge or shame yourself when it comes to your health. Do you judge the size of your thighs, the depth of your grief, the number on the scales? Do you shame yourself when you need to cry, when you need to eat, when you need to rest?

What health inequalities make it more challenging for me to optimise my wellbeing?

Looking after our health is about more than discipline and will-power. There are developmental and sociocultural inequalities that can limit our abilities to access resources that would support our health and wellbeing. All areas of our health are influenced by both our early life circumstances and our current social, economic and cultural situation.

Reflect on any health inequalities you have experienced, both now and during your childhood. Were you brought up adhering to a strict diet? Do financial pressures mean you can't afford to see a therapist? Does systemic oppression mean you have to work twice as hard to get a promotion? Is it impossible for you to get enough sleep because you need to work three jobs to make ends meet? Do you live in a society that offers little financial or emotional support for parents?

What is one awakened action I can take to support my health and wellbeing?

There is no such thing as perfect health – and striving for it will only leave us feeling exhausted. And yet, by creating small, health-enhancing habits, we can nudge our bodies, minds and spirits in the direction of healing, health and aliveness. Reflect back on what each element of health means to you, as well as any health-limiting behaviours you have developed. From this, create a list of simple, practical habits you could cultivate to bring you more energy, vitality and joy. Once you've made your list, choose one to practise this week and keep working your way through the list, one item at a time, integrating a new habit once the previous one feels more natural and effortless.

Awakening body kindness

Making peace with our bodies can be hard, but it's not nearly as difficult as spending our lives at war with them. When we live in a culture that worships being thin and treats physical perfection as the path to happiness, our bodies become problems to solve and objects to control. They feel like prisons instead of homes. As we reconnect with our bodies – not as something to look at, but as something to live in – and reawaken to the energy and emotions they contain, we rediscover our beauty, our power, our aliveness.

What do I appreciate about my body?

'This is your body, your greatest gift, pregnant with wisdom you do not hear, grief you thought was forgotten and joy you have never known,' writes psychoanalyst Marion Woodman in her book *Coming Home to Myself*. So many of us have lost touch with the gifts of the body: our sensations, emotions and intuitions; the messages hidden in our breath, in our tired eyes, in our tight muscles and aching hearts. Western culture objectifies the body, and encourages us to treat our bodies as machines to exploit for productivity, progress and profit. But when our bodies become objects to control, we lose touch with the visceral experience of living in a body, with all its gifts, its rawness.

Reflect on what you appreciate about your body. You might like to create a timeline of everything your body has survived.

When do I feel most beautiful? Most sensual? Most alive?

It is through our bodies that we experience beauty, pleasure and joy. The moments when we feel most alive are those when we are most embodied, when we get out of our heads and let ourselves be touched by the raw sensations of life. When we are disconnected from our bodies – when we judge them from the outside instead of experiencing life from within them – we become numb and empty. So, we turn to food, shopping, social media, alcohol, achievement, constant busyness – anything that will give us some kind of rush. As we become more fully embodied, even the most mundane moments will have a fullness to them, so we will no longer need to overstimulate our senses as substitutes for our lack of aliveness.

Reflect on when you feel most beautiful and most alive. Where are you? Who are you with? What are you doing?

How embodied am I?

Awakening means returning to our bodies, not avoiding them. Honouring them, not abandoning them. Loving them, not judging them. Being fully embodied means being at one with who we are, embracing every part of ourselves without judgement. But many of us spend most of our lives disembodied, stuck in our heads, judging, analysing and worrying instead of experiencing the raw sensations of life. Because it is within our bodies that our emotions reside, our disembodiment protects us from feeling pain, shame and unworthiness. But it also stops us from experiencing joy, excitement and awe, from feeling fully awake and fully alive.

Reflect on how embodied you are. Are there parts of your body you feel connected with? Parts that feel numb? Parts that you judge? You might like to close your eyes and ask yourself, 'How much am I living in my body?' and then wait for your body to offer an indication in the form of a phrase or percentage.

What negative beliefs do I have about my body?

We are constantly barraged with messages that tell us we are only worthy if our bodies look a certain way. We absorb these messages from parents, peers and people in power, such as celebrities, social media influencers and patriarchal systems that benefit from us spending so much energy worrying about our weight that we are too exhausted to fight for social justice and systemic change.

Reflect on the negative beliefs you hold about your body. Who did you learn them from? How have these beliefs changed over time? Who profits from you believing them?

What were my parents' or caregivers' relationships with their bodies like when I was growing up?

Many of the negative beliefs we have about our bodies are learned in childhood. If our mothers don't love their bodies, we do not learn how to love our own. If our fathers use their muscularity to express their masculinity, we learn to use the size of our bodies to communicate rather than expressing ourselves through our values, actions and words.

Reflect on your parents' or caregivers' relationship with their bodies. Did they criticise their own size or shape? Did they take care of their bodies? Did they comment on other people's bodies? How has this influenced your relationship with your body?

If my body could speak, what would it say?

Our bodies are always communicating with us. When our shoulders hunch and our jaws tense, our bodies are speaking to us. When our tummies bloat and we can't go to the toilet, our bodies are telling us something. When our muscles hurt and we are exhausted, our bodies are calling for our attention. However, much of the time, we don't listen. This is partly because the violent pace of modern life makes it challenging to be present enough to listen to what our bodies have to say, but it's also because we've lost confidence in our bodies. Instead of approaching them with curiosity, we judge them. Instead of trusting them, we fear them.

Reflect on what your body is trying to communicate to you. What would your tight muscles say? What would your aching shoulders say? What would your breath say? What would your belly say? What would your heart say?

What would a love note to my body say?

Like any relationship, developing a relationship with our bodies takes time and isn't always easy. As we begin communicating with our bodies, we often realise how much we have neglected them, how often we have abandoned them and how much pain is enfolded in them, patiently waiting to be accepted and integrated. As you open a conversation with your body, you will discover it is not a battleground. It is sacred ground. Wise. Beautiful. And worthy of your deepest devotion.

Write a letter to your body. This could be a love note, a letter of apology or a poem expressing your deep gratitude. It doesn't need to be long. It could be as simple as this: *Dear body, I'm sorry for all the times I forgot to treat you as sacred.*

What do I blame my body for?

Our bodies often take the blame for whatever we feel is going wrong in our lives. Much of the time, it is easier to blame our unhappiness on the size of our thighs than it is to face the struggles in our marriages, or the stress of our job, or the emptiness in our souls. Diet culture has convinced us that by achieving the 'perfect' body, all our other problems will go away. As we awaken from the illusion that we can find happiness by perfecting our bodies, that our life purpose is weight loss, we free up energy to face the true source of our distress and to discover what really matters in our lives.

Reflect on what you blame your body for. What expectations do you place on it? How do your body goals distract you from deeper distress? How do you think your life would be different if you had your idea of the perfect body?

What does my body like to eat? When does my body like to sleep? How does my body like to move?

Our bodies have their own rhythms, their own seasons. Some of us are early birds, others are night owls. Some of us thrive when we eat fresh, crunchy salads, while others feel energised when we nourish ourselves with creamy curries and spicy soups. Some of us love hiking in nature, and others feel most alive when we're lifting weights in the gym. Because we live in a culture of disembodiment, it takes conscious effort to tune into our bodies' needs. In fact, we are often encouraged to ignore the rhythms of our bodies – to down caffeine so we can work longer hours, to starve ourselves in order to conform to socially constructed beauty ideals, to sit behind desks when our bodies yearn to move.

Reflect on the rhythms and needs of your body. How much sleep do you need? How does your body like to move? How does your body like to relax? Which foods leave you feeling energised and which ones leave you feeling sluggish?

What is one awakened action I can take to help me reconnect with my body?

If we have spent years neglecting, abandoning or trying to dominate our bodies, reconnecting with them takes practice, patience and gentleness.

Reflect on one simple way you can reconnect with your body. This could be as simple as placing your hand on your heart in moments of distress and asking yourself, 'What is the kindest thing I can do for my body right now?' Alternatively, you might like to check in with your body throughout the day, naming the sensations and emotions moving through it (you can find a list of feelings and sensations on pages 297–300).

Awakening nourishment

For many of us, food is no longer just food. Instead, it is a reward, a punishment, a comfort, a measurement of our worth. It has become a way to suppress our emotions, to ease our boredom, to express our distress. Many of us live with a subtle but ever-present food anxiety that hums beneath the surface. For some of us, our eating habits – dieting, bingeing, starving – dominate our lives. In a culture that promotes dieting as not only the path to the perfect body but also the perfect life, having a healthy relationship with food takes awareness, gentleness and compassion.

What role does food play in my life?

Many of us spend a lifetime struggling with food. We ping-pong from one restrictive diet to the next. We follow rigid rules about which foods are good and which are bad. We count carbs or points or calories. We struggle to eat a cookie without feeling a wave of guilt or shame.

Without judgement, reflect on your relationship with food and what function food has in your life. You might find it helpful to finish the sentence 'I use food as a . . .', using the following list of words and phrases as a guide. Pay attention to whether any of them cause you discomfort or emotional shifts as you read them: reward, punishment, comfort, distraction, celebration, way to connect with people, form of nourishment, tool to regulate difficult emotions, substitute for my real needs, coping strategy when I'm stressed, way to reduce boredom, form of self-soothing.

What were conversations around food like when I was growing up?

Many of the eating habits and dietary patterns we have now were absorbed during childhood from our parents, peers and the media. If, as children, we were forced to clear our plates before leaving the table, we may find it hard to leave anything on our plates now – even when our bodies are telling us that we've had enough. If our mothers were constantly dieting, we may believe restricting our food is normal, and that dieting is a girl's rite of passage into womanhood.

Reflect on how food was talked about when you were growing up. What was your parents' relationship with food like? Did you have enough to eat? Were you expected to clean your plate? Were you allowed to have seconds? Were you ever shamed for eating, or put on a diet? How might these things still be influencing your relationship with food now?

What emotions arise when I think about food?

Food can trigger feelings of great fear and deep pleasure, immense shame and gentle joy. We can eat as a sacred act of nourishment, or we can imbue food with so much emotion and expectation that our eating is filled with anxiety and guilt. Our eating habits can become so intricately intertwined with our sense of worth that something as simple as eating an ice cream can fill us with shame.

Reflect on what emotions and judgements arise when you think of the following foods: blueberries, peanut butter, cake, cheese, kale, brownies, carrots, bread, cauliflower, quinoa, chocolate, potatoes, celery, pizza, butter, eggs, salad, ice cream.

How would I like my relationship with food to be different?

Sometimes the eating habits that served us in the past stop us from feeling fully alive in the present. Rather than judging our dieting or starving or bingeing, healing our relationship with food means honouring the ways in which our eating behaviours have previously served us, while acknowledging the ways in which they are also limiting our health and happiness.

Reflect on how you would like your relationship with food to be different. What eating habits are no longer serving you? How are these habits impacting your health and happiness? How would life feel without these food struggles?

What food rules do I follow?

Living in a Western, patriarchal culture, we are taught to value masculine principles – quantities, plans, rules, weights, calorie counts – over the feminine qualities of awareness, intuition and emotion. Instead of trusting our bodies to tell us what, when and how much to eat (through a process known as interoception), we outsource our power to diet books, meal plans and calorie calculators.

Reflect on your food rules. Are there any 'forbidden foods' you don't allow yourself to eat? Do you keep certain foods out of the house? Do you stick to a certain calorie intake even if you're hungry? Where did these food rules come from? Do they move you towards or away from the person you would like to be and the life you would like to create?

What is getting in the way of me eating intuitively?

As children, we eat when we are hungry and stop when we are full. However, at some point, usually around puberty, we start doubting the wisdom of our bodies and ignoring the intuitive messages they send. Surrounded by diet culture, we learn that in order to be attractive, worthy and lovable, we need to control our hunger, suppress our appetites, override our bodies' signals and reject our biological needs. Socioeconomic barriers can also prevent us from eating intuitively – we simply may not be able to afford the nourishing food our bodies need.

Reflect on what is getting in the way of you eating intuitively. What stops you from trusting your body to tell you what, when and how much to eat? How in touch with your hunger and satiety signals are you? How do your food rules get in the way of you listening to your body? Can you afford to buy the food your body craves?

How would I eat if I loved myself unconditionally?

The way we eat is an expression of our self-worth or our self-disgust, our self-compassion or our self-loathing. Our love for ourselves often comes with food- and weight-based conditions. We might believe we are only worthy when we stick to our diets, go to the gym and hit our weight-loss goals. Having a slice of cake at a friend's birthday or stepping on the scales and seeing the number go up can fill us with shame.

Reflect on how you would eat if you loved yourself unconditionally. What foods would you allow yourself to enjoy? What recipes would you try? What restaurants would you explore? Would you eat at different times, or in a different room, or with different people? Would you stop when you were full and have seconds when you were hungry? Would you eat more slowly? More mindfully? With more pleasure and less fear?

What triggers me to eat in a way that is not in alignment with my values?

Sometimes we find ourselves eating in a way that is in conflict with what we know in our hearts to be true. In her book *Eating in the Light of the Moon*, clinical psychologist Anita Johnston writes: 'We must be willing to go beyond the food itself to discover the presence of the real hunger.' We must be willing to face the deeper pains in our lives instead of counting calories and obsessing over every gram of fat to distract us from these pains. We must be willing to acknowledge our other hungers – for connection, meaning, self-expression and spiritual fulfilment – so we can eat in a way that is in alignment with who we want to be and the world we want to create.

Reflect on the things that trigger you to eat in a way that is not in alignment with your values. This might include physiological triggers, such as being over-hungry or having low blood sugar; environmental triggers, including buffets, food adverts and diet talk; and emotional triggers, like stress, loneliness, body-image anxiety and boredom.

How does my relationship with food reflect my relationship with life?

Our relationship with food is often a microcosm of our relationship with life. For many of us, healing our relationship with food can offer a doorway into our inner worlds, a step on our paths of spiritual growth and maturation. As we begin to explore our relationship with food, we often find it echoed in our relationships with everything else – money, work, rest, pleasure, sex, God.

Reflect on how your relationship with food reflects your relationship with other areas of your life. Perhaps you binge on social media the same way you binge on pizza. Maybe you obsess over money the same way you obsess over calories. Or maybe you suppress your feelings in the same way you suppress your appetite.

What is one awakened action I can take to heal my relationship with food?

Western culture teaches us to ignore our intuition and override our bodies' needs. Truly nourishing ourselves means reconnecting with our bodies, honouring our hunger and eating in a way that meets our psychophysiological needs. Learning to listen to the whispers of our body is a practice, especially if we have spent years ignoring them. But, as we practise listening, as we learn to eat when we're hungry and stop when we're full, we discover that our intuition can be trusted – not just in our relationship with food, but in other areas of our lives too.

Reflect on one practical thing you can do to nurture your relationship with food. This could be anything from unfollowing people on social media who encourage extreme diets to truly enjoying a meal without worrying about the calories.

Awakening abundance

Abundance comes in many forms, from having an abundance of money to feeling an abundance of vitality, love and joy. Abundance can also be a way of being in the world, one where we feel safe, where we feel held, where we trust there is enough to go round.

This section focuses on financial abundance and your relationship with money. As you answer these questions, be mindful that you may have beliefs around money that are preventing you from experiencing financial abundance. There may also be some very real socioeconomic inequalities that affect your access to financial resources.

How would it feel to live abundantly?

Living a rich and abundant life will mean something different to each of us. Living abundantly might mean earning a certain amount of money each month, or being able to travel abroad each year. It might mean having the financial freedom to jump in a taxi if we get caught in the rain, or being able to afford organic food. It might mean having control over when and how much we work, or it may simply mean having no debt.

Reflect on what living an abundant life means to you. Be as specific as you can. How would it feel to have this freedom and embody this life?

What does money mean to me?

Many of us grow up learning that money is something we shouldn't talk about. It's hard to cultivate a healthy relationship with money when it is treated as such a taboo. Because we don't talk about money, we often worry about whether we have enough of it or avoid thinking about it altogether.

Reflect on your relationship with money. Do you hoard it? Are you always in debt? Do you feel guilty for spending it? Do you worry about it? Do you avoid looking at your bank statements? You might find it helpful to think of a few words that capture your relationship with money, using this list as a guide: freedom, power, survival, shame, greed, guilt, status, success, validation, joy, control, fear, privilege, luxury, envy, anxiety.

What was my parents' or caregivers' relationship with money like when I was growing up?

The way money was talked about and modelled for us as children often impacts our relationship with money as adults. If our parents worked long hours for a low wage, we may now believe earning money has to be a struggle. If we were given financial rewards for good behaviour or academic achievement, we now may believe that financial success is a reflection of our worth.

Reflect on your parents' or caregivers' relationship with money as you were growing up. How was money spoken about? What was it used for? How has this affected your relationship with money now?

How have socioeconomic inequalities affected my relationship with money?

Awakening abundance is not just about shifting our mindsets around money. It is also about becoming aware of how socio-economic inequalities have influenced our access to financial resources. For example, there are still pay gaps when it comes to race and gender, and if our ancestors experienced financial hardship, it can have intergenerational consequences.

Without judgement, reflect on your socioeconomic advantages and disadvantages, and consider how they have affected your access to financial resources as well as your attitude towards money. Were you born into a flourishing economy or into war or poverty? Could you afford higher education, or did you need to leave school and get a job at a young age? Were you gifted money to help buy a house? Do you live in an area where there is mort-gage discrimination based on your race?

What beliefs have I absorbed around money from family, friends, religion and society?

Our beliefs around money can influence how we earn it, how we spend it and how open we are to attracting more of it into our lives. Many of these limiting beliefs are absorbed from our par-ents, peers and the society in which we grew up. Exploring these beliefs allows us to rewrite the limiting stories we tell ourselves so that we can be open to a more abundant way of being alive.

Reflect on your current beliefs around money. Where did they come from? Are these beliefs life-enhancing or life-limiting? What would be a more expansive, empowering belief? For example, if you believe that it's not spiritual to want money, you might like to replace this belief with something like, 'Financial abundance allows me to live a generous, spiritual life.' Or if you find yourself caught up in an inherited story that you're from a working-class family, you might explore replacing it with the belief, 'I can be financially successful without forgetting my roots.'

What shameful experiences have I had surrounding money?

When we don't talk about money, we can end up carrying shame-filled secrets about our finances. We may experience this shame because of our spending habits, or because we're in debt, or because we have financial freedom when other people are struggling to make ends meet.

Reflect on any shame you carry around money, and the experiences that might have contributed to this shame. These experiences could be anything from being bullied as a child because you couldn't afford designer trainers, to being called names because you went to a private school; from losing your job and having to move back home with your parents, to having generational wealth that allowed you to buy your own house mortgage-free.

In what ways do I base my self-worth on my financial success?

There is nothing wrong with having money or aspiring to a more financially abundant life, but when we base our self-worth on financial success, we can start to suffer. When our sense of worthiness becomes entangled with money, we struggle to separate our financial successes and insecurities from who we really are. We might find ourselves on a financial treadmill, constantly striving to earn more money in the hope it will stop us feeling unworthy. Or we might find ourselves pursuing financial goals at the expense of looking after our health and spending time with the people we love.

Reflect on your experience of what's known as 'financially contingent self-worth'. Does how much you earn affect how much you accept yourself? What financial conditions do you place on your worthiness?

Is the way I spend my money in alignment with my values?

Money is just a stand-in for whatever it is we really want. Perhaps we need it in order to buy a house, because we want to feel safe. Or maybe we want it to buy designer clothes, because we long to feel like we belong. Maybe we want it so that we can go on holiday, because we yearn to feel relaxed.

Reflect on how you spend your disposable income. Are your spending habits in line with your values? Are there areas where you can spend less so you can invest in things that really matter to you?

How would I live differently if money was no object?

Money – how we earn it and what we spend it on – can be a distraction from more existential issues, such as the meaning of life and the fear of death. But what if money was no object? What if we didn't have to spend the majority of our lives working just to make ends meet? How would we live then?

Reflect on how you would live differently if money was no object. This can help you discover what really matters to you. Would you still work if you didn't need the money? What would an ideal day look like? What would you do for fun? What would you dedicate your life to?

What is one awakened action I can take to help me live more abundantly?

Living abundantly is a practice. If we, or our ancestors, have experienced poverty or been through financial hardship, we can find ourselves living with a sense of scarcity years after the threat has passed. The mere feeling of not having enough money, even when we're out of financial danger, keeps our attention so focused on our finances that we become blind to what is most meaningful and beautiful in our lives.

Reflect on one action you can take to heal your relationship with money. There are lots of things you could consider: asking for a raise at work; making a donation to your favourite charity; treating yourself to a punnet of fresh raspberries; cancelling your gym membership because you never use it, and instead investing in a decent pair of hiking boots because you love exploring the outdoors.

Awakening slowness

In a culture that values progress, productivity and continuous self-improvement, it's difficult to honour slowness. Busyness has become a status symbol. We find ourselves overloading our to-do lists, rushing through our days, and skimming the surface of our lives instead of fully and fiercely living them. As we awaken slowness, we discover what has been hiding beneath our busyness: the simple joys and everyday miracles that have been here all along. We just had to slow down enough to notice them.

How do I currently spend my time?

We tend to feel happiest when how we live is in alignment with our deepest values. But the quicksand of modern life can make it difficult for us to devote time to the very things that bring us joy and meaning. Instead, we find ourselves rushing through our lives, caught in an anxious struggle, a whirlwind of work, worrying and wanting.

Reflect on how you spend your time, day to day. You might like to think about how much time you have spent doing the following over the last week, and whether it feels like a healthy balance: paid work, unpaid work (such as cooking, cleaning, caring for family members), sleeping, commuting, shopping, exercising, eating, watching television, browsing social media, relaxing, socialising, doing a hobby, being in nature.

When I have free time, how do I spend it?

Twenty-four-hour access to emails, on-demand movies, next-day delivery and ever-updating social media feeds have accelerated the pace of our lives, leaving us with little in the way of free time. If we do have a few minutes or hours to ourselves, instead of resting or doing something deeply pleasurable, we often either try to cram in more work, or find we are too exhausted to enjoy ourselves.

Reflect on what you do in your free time. Do you spend it in meaningful, joyful ways? Do you find yourself using it passively, doing things such as scrolling through social media? Do you fill it with unnecessary busyness?

What is my relationship with time?

Our perception of time changes depending on our autonomic and emotional states. For example, when we feel anxious or stressed, our internal clocks speed up, life feels like it's passing really quickly, and everything feels incredibly urgent. At other times, like when we're bored, time can feel like it is passing really slowly. And sometimes, perhaps when we're in a state of flow or deep meditation, it can feel as though we exist outside time altogether.

Reflect on your relationship with time. Do you feel like you have enough of it? Are you constantly rushing? How does your relationship with time change when you're bored? Stressed? Excited? Sad? Relaxed?

What do I value more, time or money?

The value we place on our time influences how we live our lives. It can determine big decisions – like whether we choose a high-paying career that demands long hours and a long commute, or a job with fewer hours that is closer to home but with a lower salary – as well as smaller, daily decisions, like whether we cook from scratch or spend slightly more money on pre-cut vegetables and ready-made sauces. Sometimes, when we reflect on what we really value when it comes to time and money, and compare it to what we are prioritising in our lives, we might notice discrepancies. By becoming aware of these, we can begin making changes so we are living more in alignment with what truly matters to us.

Reflect on what you value more: time or money. Is your current lifestyle a reflection of this? What sociocultural and economic factors are preventing you from living in alignment with your financial and time-based values? For example, do you have to work full-time for financial reasons when you really want to spend more time with your children?

What are my time traps?

Most of us have experienced periods of time-poverty – weeks, months or years when we feel as though we have too many things to do and not enough time in which to do them. When we're time-poor, we tend to be more stressed and less productive, and we exercise less and eat fewer nutritious foods – all of which can affect our physical health and mental wellbeing. To reclaim our time and use it deliberately isn't easy. One of the first steps is to identify our 'time traps' – those activities that make us unhappy and steal time away from things that would enhance our wellbeing.

Reflect on your time traps. Common ones include scrolling through your phone, checking emails, surfing the internet, getting interrupted by social media notifications, administrative work, unnecessary meetings, watching television, gaming, overworking, failing to set boundaries, and trying to solve other people's problems.

What sorrows and joys are hiding beneath the busyness of my life?

Being busy protects us from feeling the depths of our grief, but it also prevents us from experiencing the vastness of our joy. Sometimes, subconsciously, we make our lives so hectic so that we do not have to look inside ourselves, to be with our inner chaos, to feel our anger or shame or pain. However, in filling our lives with frantic busyness, we also lose connection with our purpose and our wisdom; with who we really are and what truly matters in our lives.

Reflect on what sorrows and joys are hiding beneath your busyness. What uncomfortable emotions are you trying to outrun? What is your busyness protecting you from? What might you be missing out on by being so busy? Inner stillness? Self-awareness? Deep connection? Spontaneous laughter? Birdsong? Rainbows and sunsets and moon-lit skies?

What is making my life feel so hectic?

In his book, *The Things You Can See Only When You Slow Down*, Buddhist monk Haemin Sunim writes: 'When everything around me is moving so fast, I stop and ask, "Is it the world that's busy, or is it my mind?"' Sometimes, our time pressures are very real – maybe we have to work multiple jobs to pay the bills, or juggle a full-time career with caring for a relative – but there may also be pressures we are putting on ourselves unnecessarily. These could include striving for perfection at work, overcommitting to social occasions to please our friends, and making unrealistically long to-do lists that we expect ourselves to get through each day.

Reflect on what is making your life feel hectic. What real-world time pressures are you experiencing, and what internal pressures are you placing on yourself? How could you lower your expectations? Where could you ask for help? What boundaries could you set so life feels a little less hectic?

How does time anxiety feel?

Time anxiety is an ongoing feeling of uneasiness around the passage of time: a fear that we don't have enough time and that we're not maximising the time we do have. Sometimes, time anxiety feels as though we have to rush through each day, and at other times it's more of an existential worry, where we feel anxious about how many years we have left and how we can make the most of them.

Reflect on your experience of time anxiety and how it shows up for you. Do you worry about hitting certain milestones – getting married, having a baby, owning your own home? Do you feel the need to rush from one place to the next? Do you get annoyed with yourself if you're late or accidentally sleep in or don't get everything on your to-do list done?

What would living more slowly look like?

The US Navy Seals train with the philosophy, 'Slow is smooth and smooth is fast.' When we rush, we become disengaged from the present moment; we are more likely to be distracted, and more likely to make mistakes. The goals we want to achieve, the problems we're trying to solve and the world we want to create will not come from living in a mindless flurry of speed and anxiety, but from slowing down, listening deeply and living consciously.

Reflect on what living more slowly would look like for you. How would it look at home? At work? In your relationships? In your daily routines? In what you eat and how you move?

What is one awakened action I can take to be more meaningful with how I spend my time?

Living in a productivity-obsessed culture can mean that we find ourselves spending time on things that don't really matter to us. We might find ourselves working late at the office instead of getting home in time to have dinner with our families even though spending time with our kids is more important to us. We might find ourselves answering emails and scrolling through social media on our lunch breaks rather than going for a walk even though we want to be more physically active.

Reflect on one practical thing you can do to be more meaningful with your time. Where do you need to reinvest it? This could be in your physical health, by going on longer walks; in your finances, by taking half an hour each weekend to look at your spending; or in your relationship, by arranging a weekly date night.

Awakening creativity

When we don't harness our creative energy, when we neglect it, it tends to turn in on itself. Life begins to feel mechanical, monotonous and empty. Like unblocking a river, as we remove the beliefs and fears that stop us living creative lives, we experience a renewed flow of freedom, inspiration and vitality. As we reawaken our creativity, we dissolve self-doubt. As we let go of the belief that creativity is something rare, something that belongs to the gifted few, we discover the fire of creativity that burns within ourselves.

What does creative living mean to me?

Creativity comes in thousands of different forms. In her book *Big Magic*, Elizabeth Gilbert writes that creative living is 'living a life that is driven more strongly by curiosity than by fear'. Living a creative life doesn't mean we have to become professional poets or painters. Rather, it is about making our creative needs – for self-expression, play and meaning-making – a priority.

Reflect on what creative living means to you. It could include anything, from growing your own vegetables, photographing birds and upcycling furniture, to playing with pancake toppings, putting unique outfits together and adorning your body with tattoos.

What did I enjoy creating as a child?

Many of us believe that we're just not creative. But when we reflect on what we were like as children – how we had tea parties with our teddy bears, turned the washing basket into a pirate ship and made a robot costume out of a cardboard box – we discover that we are all born with the capacity for creativity. At some point, though, we stop nurturing it. Sometimes this is because we were conditioned to believe that conformity is more important than creativity; that imagination and free thinking get in the way of academic achievement and career success.

Reflect on what you enjoyed creating as a child. What were your creative hobbies? When did you stop creating and why?

What is holding me back from living a more creative life?

To create is to be vulnerable, which is why we usually have unlimited reasons not to do it. We're afraid of rejection, of being criticised, of wasting our time. We're scared that we're too old, that it's too late, that we'll upset our families. We think we don't have the time or the training or the financial freedom. We worry we're not disciplined enough, not talented enough, not good enough.

Reflect on what is holding you back from living a more creative life. What limiting beliefs have you absorbed that are blocking you from creating? How can you transform these beliefs into ones that empower you?

What do I do to distract myself from my creative callings?

Creativity can be messy, wild, chaotic and imperfect – everything modern society has taught us not to be. And so, we repress our creative impulses, pushing them into our shadows, distracting ourselves whenever they call for our attention. We often sense this buried creative impulse as a subtle pressure, an inner resistance, because a part of us knows that unblocking our creative energies will challenge our beliefs, our identities, our views of ourselves and the world. As we create our art, our art re-creates us.

Reflect on what you do to suppress your creative impulses. What do you distract yourself with?

What creative dreams have I buried?

Looking back, we often see how we have sacrificed our creativity for good grades or the next promotion; how we have abandoned our creative callings for status and approval; how we have squandered our creative energy on other people's dreams and expectations.

Reflect on the creative dreams you've buried. Like seeds sown deep inside, how can you begin to nurture them so something beautiful can grow?

When do I feel most inspired and creative?

Being creative means loving life enough that we want to contribute to it. Scientific studies have found that love changes the way we mentally represent things, reducing analytical thinking and triggering more creative ways of seeing. We might feel this love for life, this desire to enrich and celebrate it, when we're dancing or meditating or swimming in the ocean; when we're drawing or daydreaming or donating our time to charity; when we're reading poetry or listening to music or relaxing in the arms of someone we love.

Reflect on when you feel your most creative. Where are you? What are you doing? Who are you with? How does this creative energy feel in your body? How does it want to be expressed?

What creative callings would I love to explore, but feel that doing so would be selfish?

Creativity is an act of generosity. It is caring about the world enough to want to contribute to it. However, we have been conditioned to believe that allowing ourselves time for play, for imagination, for creativity, is unproductive and immature; that prioritising creativity over productivity is selfish. We find ourselves feeling too guilty, too selfish to give ourselves the time to pursue our creative callings – to read or write or doodle or bake or learn macramé or try roller-skating or go salsa dancing.

Reflect on five to ten things you'd love to do, but haven't allowed yourself to do because you are afraid it would be selfish. How could you begin including these things in your life?

Who am I waiting for permission from to live a creative life?

For many of us, as children, creativity was treated as a privilege, a reward. Only after we'd done our homework or finished the chores were we allowed to play, to read, to create. As adults, we can still find ourselves looking for permission from someone outside ourselves. We look to our parents, our partners, our friends, even strangers on social media, to tell us that it's okay to prioritise our art. By giving ourselves permission to create, we allow ourselves to care enough to contribute, to try something that might not work, to communicate something that matters to us without needing anyone else's approval.

Reflect on who you are waiting for to give you the green light to create. How can you give yourself permission?

Who inspires me creatively?

When we're awakening our creativity, we often need to connect with people who inspire us, who have been where we are now and have gone on to embody the creative life we long for. By showing us what is possible, these people awaken us to our own potential. Sometimes, these awakeners fill us with awe and inspiration, and at other times, they fill us with jealousy and envy. These feelings of admiration and envy can be powerful tools, revealing what matters to us and showing what is possible when it comes to our creative dreams.

Reflect on who inspires you creatively. Who do you admire? Who are you jealous of? Who awakens you to what is possible? This can be someone you know in your personal life or an author, artist or actor you admire.

What is one awakened action I can take to cultivate creative energy each day?

Creativity is a practice. It is not about measurable results. It doesn't depend on approval or applause. It doesn't matter whether it is magnificent or marketable, or whether it will change other people or the world. What matters is that we are willing to make a mess, to experiment, to honour ourselves enough to make time for whatever it is that ignites our souls.

Reflect on one practical way you can nurture your creativity every day. Maybe you can experiment with new flavour combinations in your meals, or take a photograph of something beautiful on your daily walk, or put together an outfit you feel fabulous in each morning.

Part five: Gentle reminders

- Health is not a quest for perfection. We are not striving to have the perfect diet, the perfect body, the perfect morning routine. Rather, health is a journey towards wholeness: a holistic, integrative, ever-changing state of physical, spiritual and psychosocial wellbeing.
- As we connect more deeply with our bodies, we discover they are a doorway to a rich and beautiful inner universe. As we stop judging, criticising and trying to dominate our bodies, we free up vast amounts of energy to fulfil our deeper spiritual yearnings. As we become more fully embodied, we discover we are in connection with everything, and we open up to the sacredness of ourselves, each other and this glorious, grief-filled world.
- As we heal our relationships with food, we can learn that our bodies can be trusted, that *we* can be trusted. We begin to eat more freely and feel more fully. We discover that a cookie is just a cookie, and not a reflection of our worth.

- Awakening abundance doesn't mean spending money we don't have on things we don't need. Rather, it is untangling our self-worth from our financial success, acknowledging socioeconomic inequalities and releasing any shame we've been carrying around money.

- When money is no longer the source of our worth or focus of our lives, we free up a huge amount of space for other things that truly matter.

- Awakening slowness is about decelerating the pace of our lives. It is about savouring our days instead of rushing through them, no longer worshipping busyness and reclaiming our time from a culture that values constant productivity. It is living deeply instead of quickly, intentionally instead of distractedly, consciously instead of urgently.

- We don't need to make our creativity into our careers – we don't need to make money from our art – but if our lives are feeling empty or monotonous, giving ourselves the time, space and grace to create can be incredibly healing.

- Creativity teaches us that failure isn't fatal. That we can be messy and imperfect and wild and still be lovable.

PART SIX

Letting Things Bloom

Everything in nature takes time to blossom. There is no shortcut. No rush. No hurry. Awakening involves cycles of hard work and deep rest, alternating waves of conscious action and graceful surrender, seasons of rooting down into the dark, damp earth, followed by springtimes of blossoming. As we heal and awaken, we will go through many cycles, many seasons. We will spiral inwards and downwards into the shadowy places within us, and upwards and outwards, carrying gifts for the world. We will grieve for our own personal pain, and we will shed tears for the suffering of the world. There will be moments when we share our love with a sacred few, and times when our hearts will expand to embrace the whole world.

This section explores how our awakening becomes a divine dance of solitude and service, of inner healing and outer contribution, of journeying deeply within ourselves and expanding outwards, devoting ourselves to something larger, to something vaster, to the creation of a more beautiful world.

Awakening playfulness

As adults, we don't have much room in our lives for play. And yet without it, life becomes dreary. Play is a primal need, so when we don't have opportunities to be playful, our mood darkens and we lose our sense of aliveness. Awakening playfulness is about honouring play as essential to our resilience, relationships, creativity, wellbeing and fulfilment. Instead of treating it as unnecessary or indulgent, as a frivolous or childish way to spend our time, we can make play a priority in our lives.

What is the most joyful, playful memory I have from my childhood?

We are biologically wired to play. Nobody has to teach us how to play. We, like kittens, puppies and other mammals, come into the world with an evolutionary knowledge of and need for play. But as we get older and have to sit in classrooms and do homework, and then sit in offices and answer emails, our opportunities for play diminish. By the time we reach adulthood, many of us have forgotten how to play.

Reflect on your childhood and bring to mind a time when you felt playful, joyful and alive. How old were you? Where were you? Who were you with? What were you doing? When was the last time you felt this way?

How was play treated when I was growing up?

Some of us will remember childhoods filled with play – long summer days of playing hide-and-seek, building forts and creating imaginary worlds. Others among us might struggle to find memories of play, because our childhoods felt unsafe or over-scheduled, every moment filled with school work, athletic pursuits, chores or caregiving.

Reflect on how play was treated in your childhood. How did you play? Did you have to finish your homework before you were allowed to have fun? Did pressures to achieve academically or athletically stop you from playing? Were your parents or caregivers playful? How has this shaped your attitude towards play as an adult?

What beliefs have I absorbed around play?

Many of us struggle to play because it is the antithesis of what we've been taught to value in an achievement-orientated, productivity-obsessed world. At its essence, play is rooted in spontaneity, creativity, curiosity, silliness, expressiveness and joy. What makes play play is that it is unproductive and without a finish line. It is something we do simply for the pleasure and joy we get from it.

Reflect on the beliefs you have around play. Do you see play as childish and silly? Do you treat it as a luxury, only allowed once everything else is done? Do you think play is a waste of time compared to more serious spiritual or healing practices? Where do your beliefs around play come from?

How much do I prioritise play in my life?

As adults, most of us experience play deprivation, not only in terms of neglecting play as an activity, but also through neglecting playfulness as a state of being. Instead, we tend to spend most of our days in varying states of anxiety, urgency and exhaustion, where everything feels incredibly serious and important. But when we don't make time for play or fail to regularly build experiences of playfulness into our lives, we miss out on the resilience that it builds – and this resilience can help us to navigate the stressors in our lives with greater equanimity.

Reflect on how much you prioritise play in your life. You might like to rearrange the following list in order of priority, adding in any personal ones too: play, work, sleep, exercise, diet, rest, family, friends, money, community, spiritual practice, personal development, hobbies, social media, nature. Is your list of priorities in alignment with your core values?

How is play deprivation affecting my health and wellbeing?

Play is not generally treated as something essential to our wellbeing, but research shows that too little play can lead to depression, aggression and difficulties in regulating our emotions and relating to others. In his TED talk, play researcher Dr Stuart Brown says, 'The opposite of play is not work, it's depression.'

Reflect on how play deprivation might be affecting your health and wellbeing. How is it affecting your mood? Your motivation? Your aliveness?

How does being playful feel in my body?

Play is a state of being. It is visceral and embodied. It has its own neural circuitry; its own patterns of autonomic activation that we can only access when we feel safe. Sometimes, play can feel energising and exciting, such as when we go bowling with friends. At other times, it might feel more calming and nurturing, like playing with gentle movements on a yoga mat or playing with beads to make a bracelet.

Reflect on how being playful feels in your body. How does it feel different to anxiety? To stress? To sadness? You might like to use the 'How to feel your feelings' practices on page 294.

What suppresses my playfulness?

As humans, we are designed by nature to play. Our brains are built for – and through – play. This is called 'play-associated plasticity'. But when we live in a culture that values work over fun, logic over imagination, and seriousness over silliness, it can be challenging to be playful in our everyday lives.

Reflect on what might be suppressing your playfulness. What stops you from engaging in play-based activities? This might include socioeconomic factors, such as time-poverty and conditioned beliefs, such as play being a waste of time. What prevents you from experiencing a state of playfulness? For example, because we can only access a state of playfulness when our basic survival needs are met, if we are undereating, overexercising and under-sleeping, our bodymind will sense that we are under threat and our playfulness will be repressed in an attempt to preserve energy.

What physical activities and hobbies feel like play?

The goal of play is to increase our joy, but many of us have a habit of turning potentially playful activities into grim duties. We might turn our passions into our careers, only to find that these passions then become just a way to pay the bills, and are now empty of the pleasure they once brought us. We might be so focused on achieving our athletic or aesthetic goals that the exercise we once loved no longer feels fun. The unrealistic expectations we place on ourselves – to bake the perfect sourdough, to write a prize-winning novel, to create a painting that rivals Van Gogh – strip the joy out of hobbies that could breathe playfulness and joy into our days.

Reflect on the hobbies that feel like play to you. What do you find fun? Where do you fall in love with the process rather than striving towards some end goal? Are there things you currently do – cooking, crafting, exercising – that could feel more like play if you prioritised joy over outcome?

Who makes me feel playful?

Being around people who are playful can rekindle a spark of playfulness within us. In the same way that your nervous system can resonate with another's sadness, allowing you to experience and express compassion, when you are in the presence of someone playful, your nervous system shifts towards a state of playfulness.

Reflect on who makes you feel playful. Who can you be silly with? Who makes you laugh? Who inspires your creativity and curiosity? And who does the opposite – who do you feel serious, stressed and self-conscious around?

What is one awakened action I can take to make play more of a priority in my life?

Fostering playfulness in a society that values performance and productivity can feel wasteful, indulgent and unnecessary. But play is essential to our wellbeing. It enables us to connect more deeply, to live more creatively and to embrace the uncertain and unexpected with a sense of wonder and curiosity. As we make time for play, we find it rippling outwards, inspiring our work, enlivening our relationships and invigorating our lives.

Reflect on one way in which you can make play a part of your daily life. You might like to give yourself playtime each day where you can enjoy things like daydreaming, juggling, jigsaw puzzles, colouring books, playing with modelling clay, dancing in the kitchen, playing cards with your partner or jumping on a mini trampoline.

Awakening to nature

There is a mismatch between the human nervous system and the modern world we inhabit. We are wired for sunsets and ocean waves, star-littered skies and wild blackberries, not the artificial lights, processed foods and computer screens that seem to dominate our lives. This rupture in our relationship with nature doesn't only cause harm to the planet, but also to ourselves. As we awaken to nature, to her rhythms and seasons, her beauty and aliveness, we are reminded of our own rhythms, our own beauty. As we swim in the oceans and walk through the forests and watch the sun rise, we discover a sense of belonging, a connection with the natural world, and a deep desire to care for ourselves, each other and this aching, shimmering planet.

Where is my favourite place in nature?

We cannot possibly face climate change, pollution or the destruction of the earth without also remembering the beauty of the world and all there is to love. But it is hard to love what you don't know – the mountains you have never climbed, the flowers you cannot name, the freshly picked apples you have never tasted. When we love something, we naturally want to take care of it. By remembering our favourite places in nature, by visiting them and falling back in love with them, we not only find our own healing, but also discover a desire to heal and protect the natural world around us.

Reflect on your favourite place in nature. Where is it? When was the last time you visited it? What is it you like about being there? If you're feeling playful and creative, you might like to paint, draw or write a poem about this place.

How do I feel when I am in nature?

Being in nature can feel like a kind of homecoming, because we are not separate from the earth – we belong to it. Being in nature, surrounded by fields, forests and flowers, provides our survival brain with a sense of safety, respite from the over-stimulation and cognitive demands of modern, urban environments. Unlike concrete-covered cities, our nervous systems recognise the natural world as our home. Even if you do live in a city or town, there are still ways to deepen your connection to nature, such as exploring local parks, creating a kitchen herb garden, getting some houseplants and shopping at farmers' markets.

Reflect on how you feel when you are in nature. How do you feel when you see a sunset? A rainbow? A five-hundred-year-old tree? How does being in the countryside or on a beach feel different to being in a city? How does watching the sunrise feel different to watching TV?

How connected do I feel with the natural world?

The more connected we feel with the beauty and wonder of nature, the less likely we are to destroy it. However, many of us have lost touch with the natural world. We have been ripped out of our natural rhythms, alienating us from the rituals of our ancestors and forcing us to override our natural cycles of working and wintering, death and rebirth, growth and decay. Without this connection, many of us live in a nature-deficit, starved of the fresh air and green trees our bodies long for.

Reflect on your connection to the natural world. How much time do you spend walking through woodlands, admiring wildflowers and getting down in the dirt to grow your own vegetables? How much do you know about your local flowers and fauna? How does caring for the planet influence your lifestyle choices (e.g. recycling, travelling responsibly and eating sustainably)?

How has my relationship with the natural world changed since I was a child?

As children, we can more easily sense the mystery and magic of the natural world. Everything, from plants and insects to rocks and raindrops, feels sacred and alive. But as we grow up, we tend to lose this way of seeing. Instead, we become conditioned to believe nature is something we own, something to exploit for our own gain. We are taught how to use a computer, how to get a job, how to make money, but we don't learn how to grow our own vegetables or regenerate the soil or care for our local wildlife. Ecospirituality (a reverence for the interrelationship between all living beings on earth) and ecopsychology (the beneficial effects the natural world has on health and healing) rarely make it into the curriculum.

Reflect on how your relationship with the natural world has changed since you were a child. Did you climb trees or make daisy chains or whistle with a blade of grass? Did you ever look for woodland fairies or carry a magic pebble or have a tree hollow you would hide in?

What is disconnecting me from the natural world?

We have basic needs for sunlight, fresh food, community and connection with nature and all the wild things she holds. The systematic separation of our lives from the natural world can be felt as a collective trauma, a deep distress caused by these basic needs not being met. Much of our lives have become mechanical. We work in office buildings. We spend most of our time in front of some kind of screen, alienated from the shimmering web of life.

Reflect on what is disconnecting you from the natural world. Does the society you live in treat economic growth as more important than ecological growth? Do you shop in supermarkets with no idea where the food you eat is grown? Do you spend your free time scrolling through your phone?

How does what is happening to the natural world mirror what is happening in my inner world?

As we reawaken our connections to the natural world, we often realise that what we, as a species, are doing to the planet, is reflected in what we, as individuals, are doing to ourselves. Our disconnection from the natural world mirrors our disconnection from ourselves. As we awaken, we begin to see how our relationship with our bodies, often rooted in control and domination rather than awe and reverence, is reflected in our exploitation of the earth. We realise how our self-destructive habits are mimicked in the systematic destruction of ecosystems. We discover that, in the same way the natural world is treated as something abusable rather than something sacred, we also struggle to find the sacredness in ourselves.

Reflect on how our collective disconnection from and domination of the natural world reflects your relationship with yourself.

What can nature teach me?

As we spend time in the natural world, as we look at flowers and storm clouds and ocean waves, we often see ourselves reflected back. The natural world carries metaphors for human experiences that we might not be able to convey directly with words. We can look at the seasons to understand our own cycles of depression and joy, flourishing and decay. The ever-changing temperament of the ocean captures the fluctuations of our own emotional waves. Simply knowing that a seed has to be planted in the dark, damp earth in order to grow can offer us comfort when we feel that we are in a dark place in our own lives.

Reflect on what metaphors the natural world holds for your life. What can the constantly changing weather teach you? What can you learn from the way the dead leaves drop each autumn? How can the sun rising each morning, no matter how dark the night, inspire you?

How in tune am I with my own seasons and rhythms?

The natural world has many seasons, many cycles. The sun rises and it sets. Autumn becomes winter, and winter becomes spring. The moon passes through phases of waxing and waning, fullness and newness. And yet, stuck at our desks, it's easy to lose touch with the rhythms of nature. Artificial lights confuse our circadian rhythms. Stress interferes with our menstrual cycles. Diet culture disrupts our natural eating patterns. And our obsession with productivity and positive thinking prevents us from honouring our cycles of hard work and deep rest, great joy and profound grief.

Reflect on how connected you are to your own rhythms and cycles. When are you usually hungry? What time of day can you concentrate best? How does your mood change depending on the phases of the moon or where you are in your menstrual cycle?

How might my life look if I were to reconnect with the rhythms of the natural world and of my inner world?

As we work with the energy of the earth rather than against it, as we honour the seasons and cycles of the natural world as well as our own, we discover that we don't have to push so hard, to strive so much, to always be progressing. With nature as our guide, we begin to trust our inner winters, because we know spring will come. We begin to honour the waxing and waning of our energy rather than overriding our fatigue. We begin to let ourselves feel, to let ourselves eat, to let ourselves rest.

Reflect on how your life might look different if you were to honour your rhythms. How would you schedule your day to reflect your energy levels? How would you change your sleep pattern in order to honour your circadian rhythms? What changes would you need to make to your diet in order to eat more seasonally?

What is one awakened action I can take to make nature more of a priority in my life?

Much of our lives are designed to keep us away from the natural world. And yet, to feel our connections with nature, to sense that we belong to a shared earth that transcends racial, religious and national boundaries, we need to experience it. We need to touch the soil and feel the raindrops and celebrate the sunsets. We need to make the natural world a priority in our technology-centred lives, so that we can heal and protect the earth, each other and ourselves.

Reflect on one practical thing you can do to make nature more of a priority in your life. You might like to explore some of the following ideas: creating a Saturday morning hiking ritual, eating seasonal vegetables, growing herbs, watching wildlife documentaries, reading eco poetry, or walking barefoot on grass while watching the sunset to remind you of the beauty in the world.

Awakening your inner child

Reconnecting with your inner child allows you to embrace the playful, curious, wonder-filled parts of yourself that we so often abandon as we grow up. Inner child work helps us to see ourselves and the world more clearly, instead of through the lens of our childhood conditioning. It offers us a way to heal the wounds of our pasts, to discover a more childlike, excited, awe-inspired way of being in the world, and to give ourselves what we needed but did not receive growing up. Inner child work is not about blaming our parents. Rather, it is about becoming gentle, loving parents to ourselves. Sometimes inner child work can leave us feeling quite vulnerable, so make sure to ground, centre and anchor yourself using the practices on pages 27–29. If you have experienced childhood abuse, please work through this section with a therapist or someone you trust.

What is my current relationship with my inner child?

Many of us abandoned our inner child long ago, leaving behind our playfulness, our curiosity and our creativity. When we are disconnected from our inner child and the wounds that it carries, it calls for our attention by hijacking our adult selves. This can make it feel as though the dangers of the past are still with us in the present, and we might find ourselves reacting to stressful situations as if we were still that powerless child, rather than responding consciously and compassionately as the adults we have grown into.

Reflect on your relationship with your inner child. How do you make time for it? How does it call for your attention? How do you honour its needs for rest, creativity and play?

When did I lose touch with my inner child?

As John Bradshaw writes in his bestselling book *Homecoming*, when we lose touch with our inner child, 'life becomes a problem to be solved instead of an adventure to be lived'. Rather than living with a sense of wonder, curiosity and joy, we find ourselves conforming to what we've been led to believe a grown-up should be: serious, productive, hard-working and achievement-orientated. Our inner child becomes lost under the pressure of society's expectations – and, with it, so does our passion, our playfulness and our aliveness.

Reflect on when you lost touch with your inner child. When did you start hiding the curious, childlike parts of yourself?

What made me feel alive as a child?

At some point during our childhoods, we painted our last picture, we built our last fort, we had our last sleepover. At some point, we stopped playing and cartwheeling and climbing trees. We extinguished the energy of our inner child and became the kind of grown-up the world expected us to be – but by stifling our inner child, we also stifled our aliveness.

Reflect on what made you feel alive as a child. What did you love doing? What adventures filled you with joy? How can you re-create these sources of aliveness in your life now?

What role did I play in my family when I was growing up?

Often, long after we have grown up and left home, we'll find ourselves still playing the same role in our families that we played as a child. If, as a child, we learned to matter by always doing as we were told, we may still be playing the role of people-pleaser as an adult. We may be terrified of setting boundaries and neglectful of our own needs, wants and dreams.

Reflect on the role you played in your family growing up. How did you learn to matter? How did you keep the family together? Are you still playing this role, or have you outgrown it? Notice if any of these roles resonate with you: hero, rebel, good girl/boy, perfectionist, overachiever, underachiever, baby, victim, caregiver, scapegoat, peacemaker, clown, martyr.

As a child, did I feel safe being myself?

Most of the time, our parents did the best they could. And yet, there still will have been moments when we felt unsafe, when we were criticised or punished for expressing our needs, when we were not given the love we deserved to receive. When it does not feel safe to have our own opinions, to show strong emotions, to play and have fun, and to speak up for what we believe in, we learn to suppress those parts of who we are in order to be loved. Until we welcome back these outcast parts of our being, we tend to feel that part of us is missing. By creating a safe space for our inner child, by nurturing these abandoned parts of ourselves back to life, we rediscover our worthiness, our aliveness, our wholeness.

Reflect on how safe it felt for you to be your whole self as a child. Did you feel loved for your achievements or for simply being you? Were you allowed to express your emotions, beliefs and opinions? Were there parts of yourself you felt you had to hide?

How were emotions expressed when I was growing up?

From an early age, many of us learn to numb our emotions so that we can keep up with the machine pace of life. When we grow up in families where shaming and repressing emotions is the norm (often because of generational conditioning), we learn that it's not okay to feel how we feel. As children, repressing strong emotions can be a powerful coping strategy if we are at a time in our lives when we don't have the capacity to feel them. But unfelt emotions don't just go away. As adults, these repressed emotions keep our nervous system stuck in a state of fight-or-flight, robbing us of our vitality and aliveness.

Reflect on how emotions were expressed in your family when you were growing up. How was anger expressed? How was sadness expressed? How was joy expressed? Were you ever shamed for expressing your emotions? How might you be able to start feeling the unfelt feelings of your past in the safety of the present?

What unmet needs did I have as a child, and how can I meet these needs for myself now?

As children, we have dependency needs. Needs that we cannot meet on our own. These include our needs for food, protection, security, warmth, shelter, love and affection. If these needs aren't met, or if we are shamed for having these needs, we can grow up believing that we either don't have a right to have needs, or that, as adults, we don't have the capacity to meet them for ourselves. Having unmet needs in childhood doesn't mean that our parents didn't do their best. Even the most loving parents will make mistakes and find themselves in situations that get in the way of them being fully present.

Reflect on any dependency needs that weren't met in your childhood. You might like to refer to the list of safety, psychological and belonging needs on page 22 as a guide. For each need that wasn't met in your childhood, how might you meet these needs for yourself now?

What do I need to give myself permission to do?

We live in a permission-seeking society. As children, we have to ask for permission to do most things – to have a snack, to watch TV, to go to the toilet. As adults, we often continue to seek permission. This permission-seeking often manifests as a need for constant reassurance. We find ourselves second-guessing our own feelings and needs, seeking advice from others instead of trusting ourselves. By noticing when we are tempted to ask others' permission and giving it to ourselves instead, we begin reclaiming our agency, our power – our lives.

Reflect on your permission-seeking behaviour. Who do you usually ask for permission from? What do you usually ask permission or seek reassurance for? And how can you give this to yourself?

What would a letter to my inner child say?

Often, there are things we needed to hear as children that we did not hear. As adults, we still need to hear these things: to listen to words of comfort that soothe us when we are feeling scared or angry or overwhelmed.

Reflect on what you needed to hear as a child and write it down in a letter to your younger self. You might like to start a dialogue with your inner child by writing a letter back to your adult self. Some people find it helpful to write this reply using their non-dominant hand. This can be a way to move beyond the analytical mind and allow greater access to their subconscious and deeper connection with the energy of their inner child.

What is one awakened action I can take to nurture my inner child?

Developing a relationship with your inner child is like developing any other relationship. It requires time, communication and love.

Reflect on one thing you can do to cultivate a deeper relationship with your inner child. You might like to use the following ideas as inspiration: checking in with your inner child each morning to see how they feel and what they need; buying a bouncy ball and giving yourself five minutes a day of playtime; flying a kite; snuggling under a blanket each evening; having a weekly art night; reading a fantasy book or fun novel before bed; or sitting on the doorstep after work and letting yourself daydream.

Awakening to wholeness

If we are perfect, we cannot be whole, because we must leave out all our imperfections. And if we are whole, we cannot be perfect, because wholeness means good *and* evil, ugly *and* beautiful, powerful *and* vulnerable, loving *and* selfish, generous *and* greedy, terrible *and* glorious. Awakening to wholeness means exploring our shadows – the places within us that hold the secrets we have hidden, the impulses and emotions we have suppressed, the parts of ourselves we have been conditioned to believe are unacceptable – and welcoming back these neglected pieces of our souls so that they no longer have power over us. It takes courage, compassion and a trust in our inherent worthiness to explore our shadows, so make sure you use the techniques on pages 27–29 to ground you.

What qualities do I admire in others?

Our shadows are made up of not only what we dare not see, but also who we have the potential to be. Many of us don't only fear our flaws and failures, but also our beauty and our brilliance. Our shadows form naturally as we grow up, as a way of protecting ourselves whenever parts of us are met with disapproval, jealousy or rejection. Often, we then project these denied parts of ourselves, including our gifts, talents and untapped potential, on to others, because these rejected qualities are in conflict with who we believe ourselves to be. As we pay attention to what we admire in others and realise that these qualities live within us, too, we discover our hidden strengths and experience ourselves as more powerful, more creative and more talented than we imagined we could be.

Reflect on who you admire (this could be in real life or in the media). What qualities do they have that inspire you? Write these down in a list titled 'shadow qualities' (we will be adding to this list over the following few questions). How can you begin embodying these qualities?

Who am I jealous of?

Our shadows often make themselves known through jealousy. As uncomfortable as it is to experience, we can use our envy as a door into our shadows, a message that there are parts of ourselves that need welcoming in order for us to achieve what we are capable of achieving, and become who we are capable of being.

Reflect on who you are jealous of. What specifically is your jealousy focused on? Their confidence and creativity? Their success and financial security? Their generosity and gentleness? Add these to your 'shadow qualities' list. Have you ever expressed these qualities? How can you begin embodying them?

What three words would I use to describe myself and what are their opposites?

Awakening is a process of integration, not elimination. It means giving our whole selves permission to exist: letting ourselves be selfless, strong, joyful, and hard-working, *and* also selfish, weak, angry and lazy. We are most powerful when we integrate our opposites, when we embrace the parts of ourselves that we have previously denied. Once we know and accept our shadow sides, we don't need to waste psychological energy holding ourselves together so tightly anymore. We can take off our masks and relax our defences, because we have nothing to hide.

Reflect on three adjectives you would use to describe yourself and add the opposites of these words to your 'shadow qualities' list, acknowledging you have the capacity to be both (because we *all* have the capacity to be both). For example, if you would describe yourself as kind, professional and shy, you might add thoughtless, playful and assertive to your list of 'shadow qualities'.

What behaviours and qualities upset or frustrate me most in others?

Whenever we deny a part of ourselves, we often see that part more vividly in others, and find ourselves reacting to it with greater emotional intensity. Psychoanalyst Carl Jung, famous for coining the term 'shadow' writes: 'Everything that irritates us about others can lead us to an understanding of ourselves.' As we pay attention to the qualities that frustrate us most in others, we begin to discover the outcast parts of our souls that need welcoming with compassion and kindness.

Reflect on someone you find difficult or frustrating. What irritates you about them? What might this be revealing about a denied part of yourself? For example, if you find your partner lazy, it might be revealing a disowned part of you that longs to relax. Add these qualities to your shadow list. (Please be aware there are some situations where we are *not* projecting our shadows, including experiences of abuse, racism and discrimination.)

What am I most afraid someone will find out about me?

Awakening to our wholeness requires radical self-acceptance. As we shine the candlelight of our awareness into the shadowed places within us and discover the banished, withered parts hiding there, we need deep compassion and loving acceptance at every step. The parts of yourself that live in your shadow do so because they threaten your ego identity, because they are inconsistent with the persona you are trying to portray. This means that healing and awakening comes with its own kind of pain, as we shed our false skins and discover the truth of who we are in all our messiness and monstrosity and magnificence.

With compassion and curiosity, reflect on what you are most afraid someone will find out about you. What secrets are you carrying? What parts of yourself do you find shameful or repulsive? Add these to your 'shadow qualities' list.

When and why did these qualities get pushed into my shadow?

As we grow up, go to school and experience the world, we learn that there are certain qualities that are welcomed, applauded and rewarded, and others that are shamed, criticised and condemned. And so, in order to keep ourselves safe, we hide the parts of ourselves that we have been conditioned to believe are unwanted and unworthy.

Reflect on your list of shadow qualities. When did each quality get pushed into your shadow? How was this part of yourself criticised or shamed? Can you remember a time when you fully embraced this part of yourself? What impact have sociocultural forces had on the qualities you embrace and those you hide?

What are the signs that my shadow has been activated?

Whatever orphaned and abandoned parts reside in our shadows tend to make themselves known through memories, visions, dreams, pain, illness and emotional reactions. This is your shadow being activated. Until we dive into our inner darkness to discover the parts of ourselves that have not known love, these outcast pieces of our souls will continue to call for our attention through reactivity, anxiety, depression and addiction, longing for us to embrace them with tenderness and warmth.

Reflect on how it feels when your shadow has been activated. How does this activation manifest in your physical sensations, thoughts, emotions and behaviours? This might include being passive-aggressive, reacting in a way that is out of proportion to the situation, feeling irritated, angry or annoyed, being judgemental, feeling jealous or envious, or experiencing a fast heart rate, a tight jaw or shortness of breath.

How can I embrace each of my shadow qualities?

As we explore our shadows and reclaim our orphaned parts, we can begin nurturing them into consciousness, enabling these pieces of ourselves to be of service in our lives. Instead of denying our selfishness, we can embrace it to help us assert strong boundaries. Rather than repressing our anger, we can use it as fuel for activism and social change. Instead of banishing the parts of ourselves that are weak and pathetic, we can integrate them, deepening our compassion for others' fragilities and vulnerabilities.

Reflect on how each of the qualities on your shadow list can serve you. How can they empower you? How can they deepen your relationships? How can they help you cultivate deeper compassion for yourself and the world?

How would it feel to be my whole self?

It is exhausting to constantly suppress the parts of ourselves we are afraid of; to live with the loss of the rejected pieces of our souls, constantly grieving for the parts of ourselves that are missing. As we explore our shadows and embrace all that we find there – no matter how ugly or flawed – we begin to feel integrated instead of fragmented. We no longer feel broken or empty. Maybe for the first time in our lives, we feel whole.

Reflect on how it would feel to be your whole self. How would it feel to stop pretending? To stop hiding? To stop chasing perfection? How would it feel to no longer be afraid of your own shadow? To honour your imperfections? To treat all your qualities, even those you don't like, as sacred?

What is one awakened action I can take to help me integrate and embody my shadow qualities?

Integration means embracing the parts of ourselves that we have rejected in the past, taking responsibility for them and harnessing them so they can serve us and the world. It means honouring the multitudes we contain, allowing seemingly opposing qualities to coexist within us. Integration doesn't mean that we will never be triggered. Rather, it means that we are no longer controlled by the parts of ourselves we have denied, and that we get to choose how to respond when we are triggered. We begin to see that we can love someone *and* be angry with them; that we can feel powerless *and* choose change; that we can experience failure *and* be worthy.

Reflect on one practical thing you can do to begin integrating some of your shadow qualities. Perhaps you can simply pause when you notice a shadow part being activated and ask yourself, 'What part of me is being triggered by this?'. Then, if, for example, the shadow quality is 'laziness', maybe you can make a conscious choice each day to rest.

Awakening to privilege, prejudice and power

Awakening is often uncomfortable, especially when it means being honest with ourselves about our privilege and prejudice, about the power we hold and the power others have over us, about our role as oppressors and our experiences of being oppressed. But, for as long as we remain blind to discrimination and injustice, we cannot challenge it. By becoming aware of the power we have been given – or starved of – because of socioeconomic inequities, we can begin to question the status quo, to dismantle prejudicial systems, to stop blaming ourselves for our distress and instead turn our attention towards creating a society that holds us and heals us and serves us all.

How do I feel about exploring my privileges and prejudices?

When we are part of an oppressed group, we are usually acutely aware of prejudice. However, if we are in a privileged place, we are often blind to it, because, on the surface, we are the ones benefiting. Much of our privilege is complacency. For example, if someone grows up in a small village, surrounded by people of similar race, class and sexuality, they might be ignorant of their own privilege, as well as the implicit biases they hold, and the distress experienced by marginalised groups. Awakening to this privilege can be – and, in some way, needs to be – heartbreaking work, filled with guilt, rage and shame. Equally, if we have spent our lives individualising our mental distress by blaming it on personal deficiencies, then awakening to the sociocultural forces that have contributed to our distress can be heavy, grief-filled work.

Reflect on how you feel about exploring your privileges and prejudices. What emotions arise? How do discomfort, judgement and resistance manifest for you? What do you need to do to take care of yourself during this process?

What social groups am I a part of?

Seeing our differences, and recognising who benefits from these differences, is essential when it comes to changing oppressive systems – and so is remembering our common humanity. Most of us are members of at least one marginalised group, and some of us are members of multiple-minority groups, reducing our socioeconomic status, limiting our access to resources and increasing our risk of stress-related illness. If we are part of one or many privileged groups, it doesn't mean we have it easy or that we have never experienced adversity or distress. Rather, it is about recognising how our privilege has protected us, provided us with access to resources and positively influenced our lives.

Reflect on the social groups you are part of. How have they privileged you? How have they led to prejudice against you? You might like to think about the following: race, gender, age, sexuality, social class, neurodiversity and disability, as well as religion, mental and physical health, access to education, and anything else that comes to mind.

What prejudices do I hold against others?

Our prejudices are pre-judgements – opinions, attitudes and stereotypes about others based on them belonging to a particular social group. We might feel comfortable talking about some prejudices, but feel shame around others – and there might be some we are totally blind to. As we become more aware of the prejudices we hold, the judgements we make about those who are different to us, and the preconceptions that blind us to reality, we can begin to dismantle them.

Non-judgementally, reflect on the prejudices you hold against others. You can use any of these questions as a starting point: what judgements do you make about people of a different race? Of a different religion? Of a different sexual orientation? People with a diagnosed mental illness? People who are experiencing addiction? People who were born into money? And those who have none?

Where did I absorb these prejudices from?

We are told stories about the world before we experience it. We hear about it from our parents and teachers, we read about it in books, we see it on television and social media. We internalise the prejudices and preconceptions of others until they feel like our own. By becoming conscious of the prejudices we have absorbed and the implicit evolutionary biases we are born with, we can find ways of taming them, of unlearning them, and of seeing things as they are rather than how they appear through multiple layers of conditioning.

Reflect on where you absorbed each of your prejudices from. How did your parents speak about people of different races, sexualities and socioeconomic classes? How much was your schooling biased in its educational curriculum on slavery, religion and war? In what ways were you exposed to literature and art created by people from different cultures and ethnicities? How have religion, academia, films and social media influenced the prejudices you hold?

Where do I need to do the work to dismantle my own prejudices?

Awakening asks us to question the status quo instead of adapting to it. To educate ourselves in a way that does not require those against whom we hold prejudices to do yet more labour on our behalf. To reject the preconceptions that keep power structures in place, even if it means sacrificing the comforts we have gained from those power structures. To see the suffering of those who have no voice, who are thought of as less beautiful, who are always at the bottom of the social hierarchy. To realise the ways in which we have been complicit in the oppression of others. To accept our part in the remaking of the world. This is fierce work.

Reflect on where you need to do the work in dismantling your own prejudices. Where do you need to educate yourself? What unpleasant truths do you need to face? What comforts are you willing to sacrifice?

How do prevailing sociocultural norms affect the way I see myself and others?

We long to feel 'normal'. To belong. If we are members of a marginalised group, we can experience prejudice, oppression and discrimination. Rather than allowing for diversity and uniqueness, social norms dictate what is acceptable, how we should behave, what we should believe and whose voices we should listen to. Sometimes, we conform to these norms without even knowing it – we might suppress our emotions for fear of being seen as mentally ill if we fully express our pain, or we might dye our grey hair blonde for fear of being discriminated against as we age.

Reflect on how sociocultural norms affect the way you see yourself and others. What parts of yourself do you hide because they go against social norms? How do social norms influence who you consider an 'expert'?

How does internalised prejudice affect the way I see myself?

When we are stigmatised and marginalised by society, we may begin to see ourselves through the same lens. We might internalise the hatred, inferiority and violence others have enacted on people in our social group, and treat ourselves with that same level of self-loathing. When distress comes from the outside in, from internalised oppression, prejudice and stigma, it is often masked by mainstream narratives that try to frame it as being due to a personal deficiency or maladaptive coping strategies. By exploring the ways in which we have internalised social stigmas, we can release some of the shame and blame we've been carrying.

Reflect on the ways in which you criticise, judge and shame yourself. How does this relationship with yourself mirror the way your social group is marginalised and oppressed in society?

How is power operating in my life?

Most of us are privileged in at least one way. This privilege doesn't mean that we don't face struggle or hardship, but it does come with a certain amount of power. Equally, many of us will experience oppression at some point in our lives. This oppression means that other people have power over us. The amount of power and privilege we have and oppression we experience will differ vastly for each of us, depending on our social group and sociocultural norms. In *The Power Threat Meaning Framework*, clinical psychologists Dr Lucy Johnstone and Professor Mary Boyle identified several types of power. Embodied power gives some people advantages because of characteristics like skin colour, physical ability and appearance. Legal power gives some people the power to arrest, to imprison and to make and enforce laws. Having greater economic power offers us better access to healthcare, housing, education, possessions and services. Those with ideological power have greater control over dominant ideas and beliefs in society as well as the power to silence, 'cancel' and undermine. Interpersonal power is the power to protect, abandon, care for and give or withhold love from another.

Reflect on how power operates in your life. Where do you have power? Where do other people, groups or institutions have power over you? Think about embodied, legal, economic, ideological and interpersonal power.

What kind of threat do these forms of power pose, both to myself and others?

The inequalities in power in our society mean that many of our core needs are not being met. Whenever these needs for safety, belonging, justice, agency, hope, meaning and purpose are not met, we experience it as a threat to our safety and survival, which shifts our nervous systems into a state of defence. Living under the chronic stress of oppression changes our physiology, with negative consequences for our physical, mental and emotional wellbeing. Re-establishing the link between lack of power, threat, physical illness and emotional distress can help us hold ourselves and others with less blame and more compassion.

Reflect on the threat that power inequalities pose to yourself and others. Consider things like physical danger, emotional overwhelm, social exclusion, economic threat, material deprivation, loss of access to resources, threat to personal agency or sense of self, and loss of cultural rituals and understandings.

What is one awakened action I can take to empower myself and support those who need empowering?

Empowerment doesn't have to be earth-shattering. It can mean speaking out against the prejudiced views of a family member. It can mean highlighting the power inequalities in our workplaces. It can mean sharing skills with those who otherwise might not be able to access them. And alongside this, we must keep doing the hard, inner work of reflecting on our own complicity, of refusing to stay apathetic, of letting our hearts break open to the ways in which we have been oppressive and are being oppressed.

Reflect on one practical thing you can do to empower yourself and others. What access to power resources do you already have? These could include loving relationships, educational opportunities, self-regulation tools, physical health, community and connections to nature. How can you share these? How could you increase access to power resources for yourself and others? Consider options including campaigning and activism, joining support groups, exploring alternative therapies, and creating and sharing new narratives.

Awakening grace and gratitude

The pressures and expectations of modern life leave little space for gratitude and grace. Constant demands and deadlines distract us from noticing the sacredness in our lives. It is often only when we awaken from our trance of busyness that we are able to drop below the surface drama of our lives and reconnect with our divinity. As grace and gratefulness flow through our lives, we stop striving so hard and working so much, because we know, deep in our bones, we will never be able to fill the holes in our souls with external things.

Reflecting on grace and God can feel uncomfortable when so much of our grace-filled experiences cannot be captured in words; when the word 'God' comes with so many connotations; when most of what cannot be measured by science has been rationalised out of existence. However, it is when we are in connection with each of these things – God and grace and gratitude – that we feel most safe, most hopeful, most alive. They allow us to be all that we are: fully human and fully divine.

What am I grateful for?

Gratitude is one of the most powerful feelings we can have. It helps us function optimally on physiological, psychological, relational and even cultural levels. It is only from this place of gratitude that we can extend grace to others. However, our incessant doing, striving and achieving can blind us to everything we have to be grateful for – to the beauty and radiance that shimmers beneath the surface of our lives.

Reflect on what you are grateful for. Who are you thankful for? What simple joys do you appreciate? How often do you miss these unremarkable yet ravishing moments because you are too busy to notice them?

What would unconditional gratitude feel like?

It is hard to be grateful when we are exhausted or in pain; when life feels unbearable and unfair. But it is in these moments of suffering that gratitude can hold us and heal us. Unconditional gratitude reminds us that our lives are larger than this moment. As we cultivate this universal gratitude, not as something we feel only when life is going well, but as a way of being in the world, we discover a vaster, richer perspective. Gratitude allows us to zoom out, to glimpse a hidden wholeness, to see that this dark place is just a fragment of a larger picture we are yet to see.

Reflect on how it would feel if unconditional gratitude was your default state. How would your thoughts, emotions and behaviours change? How would you treat yourself differently? How would your relationships shift? How would unconditional gratitude help you to hold your suffering, and the suffering of the world, within a larger wholeness?

When have I experienced grace in my life?

Healing is always part effort and part grace, part human will and part divine embrace. Like love or truth or God, grace cannot easily be defined, measured or quantified. Instead, it can only be experienced directly in moments when we know we are loved, forgiven, transformed. Grace is never earned or achieved – rather, it is given. Unmerited. Unconditional. From an unobligated giver who is sometimes human and sometimes divine. These experiences of grace are beyond words, beyond science, beyond what our rational minds can understand. Research shows that they are transformative, reducing shame, anxiety and depression, and improving mental health, hopefulness and spiritual wellbeing.

Reflect on when you have experienced grace in your life. When have you felt love and forgiveness, even though you didn't feel you deserved it? When have you received divine guidance? What mystical experiences have you had that have transformed you in some way?

How does grace feel?

Sometimes grace arrives in gentle waves, and sometimes it comes in fierce insights that leave us forever changed. Grace may arrive as an intuition, vision or synchronicity, or through a dream, an inner voice or in the form of another human being. We may feel a sense of being guided, held or loved. Grace may give us the strength to surrender, to release our clenched fists and open our hands to receive, to stop pushing and let ourselves be pulled towards meaning and wholeness.

Reflect on how grace feels for you. Maybe there is a deep feeling of being taken care of that allows you to be of service because you know you are being looked after. Perhaps grace gives you freedom from the need to prove your worthiness. Or maybe grace arrives after periods of despair, or as the cessation of addiction, or in moments when you stop waging war with yourself and surrender to something greater.

How can I hold myself and my life with grace?

In a society where striving and busyness are worshipped as status symbols, we have to be intentional about practising grace and gratitude, in leaving enough space in our lives to receive. Like a butterfly emerging from a chrysalis, or a mango ripening on a tree, we must allow some things to unfold in their own time, because healing does not come through force. Healing happens by treating the space between where we are now and where we want to be as sacred ground; by allowing grace to fill the gap.

Reflect on how you can hold yourself and your life with grace. How can you create more space to receive? What can you stop striving for? Where do you need to offer yourself unconditional love, acceptance and mercy?

Who or what do I worship?

Many of us are hungry for something we cannot name. We long for something deeper and more meaningful than the mundanity of daily life. We live with an inner restlessness, an inner emptiness, a hole in our soul. And yet, because modern life doesn't leave much space for the sacred rituals and spiritual communities that help connect us with this divinity (which we might call 'energy' or 'God' or 'universal love'), we find ourselves worshipping false 'gods', trying to satisfy our hunger for divine connection with superficial substitutes that leave us feeling empty.

Reflect on who or what you worship. This might include food, alcohol, caffeine, sex, money, celebrities, gambling, gaming, shopping, social media influencers, designer clothes, academic achievement, or thigh gaps and flat stomachs. There is nothing necessarily wrong with any of these things in themselves. Rather, it is when we are overly devoted to them that they can distort our priorities and cause suffering.

What kind of relationship do I have with God?

The word 'God' can make many of us feel incredibly uncomfortable, especially if our religious experiences have been oppressive, coercive or disempowering. But God does not have to be associated with a particular religion or belief system. We might experience God as love, as connection, as the breath, as the breeze, as the divine spark inside every human heart. In many ways, the journey of awakening is one of unlearning our way back to God. Not some preconceived, patriarchal notion of God, but our personal god, a god that holds us and heals us and loves us unconditionally.

Reflect on your relationship with God. What have family, cultural and religious forces conditioned you to believe? How is this different to what you feel is true? How has your relationship with God changed over time? How do you nurture and deepen this relationship?

When do I feel most connected to God?

Often, we find God not in a church or a temple, but here, in the mud and mundanity of everyday life. As we release our conditioning around the idea of God and open our hearts to a personal connection with the divine, we often find that God is everywhere – in every blade of grass and every grain of sand; in the ocean waves and the old oak trees; in our breath and our bodies and our hearts. We discover the physical is spiritual and the spiritual is physical; that everything, everywhere, everyone is sacred.

Reflect on when you feel most connected to God. Where are you? Who are you with? What are you doing?

How would my life be different if gratitude, grace and God came first?

Neither God nor grace nor gratitude can be fully quantified or defined, but gratefulness and sacredness are deeply healing. They help us to celebrate the beauty and bear the terrors of the world; to trust in the mystery of life; to stop racing to the top of the mountain and let ourselves pause for long enough to see the view is glorious from exactly where we are.

Reflect on how your life would be different if gratitude, grace and God came first. How would they help you deal with loss, failure and uncertainty? What could you stop striving to achieve? What would making space for grace look like?

What is one awakened action I can take to deepen my relationship with gratitude, grace and God?

The modern world promotes striving, productivity and materialism as signs of success – the very opposites of gratitude, grace and God. This means we have to be intentional about cultivating gratitude, creating space for grace and inviting God into our lives. As we do so, we often find ourselves in a healing spiral. The more grateful we become, the more grace seems to enter our lives. And the more grace grounds us and reminds us of the

sacredness of life, the more grateful we feel. With time, we realise our search for meaning, for love, for God, for our true selves,
are all part of the same search, the same journey of healing,
freedom and awakening.

Reflect on one thing you can do to connect more deeply with
gratitude, grace and God. Maybe you can treat everyone you meet
as God in human form. Perhaps you can explore prayer or meditation, asking for divine assistance or forgiveness. Or maybe you
can stop overworking so that there is space for grace.

Awakening integration

In daily life, we tend to work hard and be productive, but allow little time for relaxation and integration. The same tends to be true over the long term: we finish the course or achieve the goal, only to jump straight into the next project without allowing our minds and bodies the rest they need to integrate what we have learned.

Throughout this book, we have explored many different themes, and our awareness will have expanded through the insights and realisations we've had. It's important to allow ourselves the time and space to integrate these insights, so that, rather than remaining intellectual understandings, we begin to embody them in our daily lives. This process of spiritual and psychological integration happens quite naturally as long as we do not block it, but sometimes we might feel called to support this process through relaxation, visualisations and awakened action.

In reflecting on these questions, it's important to remember that integration is not something we can force or rush. Rather, it is something that unfolds moment by moment, breath by breath.

How do I feel looking back at the intentions I made at the beginning of this book?

At the start of this book, we explored our intentions – what called us to begin reading this book, and where we wanted to be by the end of it. And then we put those goals to one side and opened ourselves to the experience of awakening in the present moment, welcoming anything and everything that arose and embracing the paradox that moving towards our goals happens as we accept, rather than deny, how things are right now.

Reflect on the intentions you made at the beginning of *Daily Awakening* (page 30). How have your healing and awakening aligned with your intentions? How have they differed? Would the you from one year ago be proud of who you are today?

What are the core insights I've had since I started *Daily Awakening*?

Integration helps us to metabolise our insights, discoveries and realisations into wisdom – core lessons and gentle reminders that can bring us back to what is truly important when the stresses and storms of life knock us off path. Often, these insights are far simpler and more subtle than we imagine them to be – and yet, they are no less transformative.

Reflect on the key insights you have had since beginning *Daily Awakening*. How can you integrate them into a few gentle reminders for moments when you forget who you are and what matters to you? Are there any insights you are struggling to understand or accept? How does intellectually understanding something feel different to realising and embodying it?

What has changed in the way I relate to myself and act in the world?

Integration allows us to accept all parts of ourselves, each other and the world around us. To see the connections between our biological, cognitive, emotional and spiritual processes. To honour the impact of our early relationships, the society in which we live and the state of the natural world. As the way we see ourselves and the world changes, as we begin looking through a lens of love instead of fear, the actions that flow from this new perspective will be transformed as well.

Reflect on how the way you see yourself and the world has changed since you started *Daily Awakening*. What has changed in the way you see your body? Your career? Your finances? Your goals? Your worth? How has your relationship with uncertainty changed? How about with time? With rest? With God? How do you feel differently about nature and modern society? What has changed in the way you relate to unpleasant emotions? To the present moment? To awakening itself?

What inner resources have I awakened?

All too often, we approach awakening hoping for supernatural results – to be happy all the time, to never feel grief or stress or pain, to rise above the messiness of being human. But, as we begin awakening, what we usually find is the opposite. Rather than transcending our humanness, awakening leads us back to what makes us most human: our bodies, our breath, and our basic needs for food and water, nature and connection, meaning and love. Instead of escaping into realms of love and light, awakening mobilises our inner capacities for growth and healing so that we can work with the full catastrophe of being human in a way that does not increase our suffering.

Reflect on what inner resources and psychological skills you have cultivated and mobilised. This may include becoming more psychologically flexible: shifting from avoidance to acceptance; from preoccupation with the past or future to present-moment awareness; from cognitive fusion (treating thoughts as truths) to cognitive defusion (seeing thoughts as passing clouds); from the self as solid to the self as fluid; from living by other people's values to living by our own; from inaction and impulsivity to awakened action. Or it might include mobilising psychological strengths: creativity, curiosity, bravery, honesty, perseverance, kindness, love, compassion, forgiveness, self-regulation, appreciation of beauty, gratitude, hope, humour, spirituality.

How can I integrate my insights into my daily life?

We cannot force our integration, but we can support it by resting, by taking care of ourselves, by not going against what we know in our hearts to be true. Integration is a gentle process that happens as we embody our insights in our everyday lives – in how we treat ourselves and others, in how we respond to situations, in what we dedicate our time to. We know when an insight remains unintegrated by the way we feel. We might sense an inner restlessness, a conflict within us. We might be aware that we're using food or alcohol to cope with difficult emotions, but until we act on that awareness by finding ways of working with our pain and stress without using food or drink, it will remain unintegrated.

Reflect on anything you can do to support your integration. This might include finding an embodied movement to symbolise the insight you would like to integrate (for example, clenching and releasing your fist to represent letting go, or placing your hand on your heart to symbolise living a more heart-centred life), or practising a visualisation where you imagine the different parts of yourself coming together as one. Or perhaps the best thing you can do to support integration would be to take a break from inner work for a little while, and simply live your life.

Part six: Gentle reminders

- We need to balance hard work with soft work. With deep work. With loving work.
- It is easy to get bogged down by the stresses and seriousness of life. But, as we awaken playfulness, we discover that, while play might not take away the inevitable pain of life, it allows us to experience happiness, freedom and belonging alongside it.
- As we awaken to nature, we begin to see how the natural world and our inner worlds are intertwined. We suffer with the earth, and we heal with it too. Spending time in nature can often be a doorway to a deeper connection with ourselves and the world around us. As we walk in the woods and watch the sunsets and eat wild blackberries, we sense we are part of something vaster and more beautiful than we've been conditioned to believe. We feel, maybe for the first time, a sense of belonging. We find a home, both in the natural world and within ourselves.
- We treat ourselves the way we were treated in childhood. We criticise ourselves in the same way we've been criticised. We shame ourselves in the same way we've been shamed. As we reconnect with our inner child, we discover we have a choice: to repeat the patterns from

our past, or to become a compassionate, loving parent to ourselves.

- Reconnecting with our inner child allows us to see our innate worthiness; to reawaken our playfulness, wonder and joy; and to heal the wounds of our past so we feel safe enough to fall in love with being alive.

- Awakening to wholeness doesn't mean becoming perfect, it means allowing our darkness to coexist with our light. Welcoming our flaws, fears and fragilities is rarely easy, and is often painful. But doing so not only frees us from the never-ending quest for perfection, it also allows us to embrace the shadow qualities we have rejected, and to harness them in service of healing and harmony, both within ourselves and in the world.

- If we are to challenge prejudice, we must first acknowledge its existence – both within society and within ourselves. As we do this work, as we let our hearts break open and feel the fiery rage flow through our veins, we can harness these fierce energies for awakened action and social change.

- As intense as working on our prejudice and privileges may be, nobody will thank us for doing it. We do not do it for praise. We do it because we must. Because the world we have built doesn't work for everyone. And we will continue to suffer until we have a world that feels like home for us all.

- When we feel battered by the demands of everyday life, we tend to lose our sense of gratefulness, our trust in grace, our connection with God. And yet, each of these things – God and grace and gratitude – can hold us and heal us in the darkest times of our lives. And it is often in those moments, when we hold ourselves and our lives with gratitude, when we create space for God and grace in our hearts, that we feel most safe, most hopeful, most alive.

- Awakening is a process of integration. Of fully accepting all aspects of ourselves and our experience. Of embracing our shadow and our light. Our masculinity and our femininity. Our humanity and our divinity. In doing so, we are able to stay connected to beauty in the midst of pain; to let love be a candle in the darkness of our grief; to take awakened action, even when we are afraid.

- Our awakening and integration come from clearly seeing and deeply accepting the sacred messiness of being human – the glorious catastrophe of being alive.

CONCLUSION

The Garden of Awakening

There are many words for awakening. Healing. Freedom. Becoming. Intimacy. Acceptance. Connection. Aliveness. Love. And there are many ways in which we can experience awakening, many ways in which we can express it. We can experience awakening as an untangling, an embracing, an opening, a deepening, a rebirth. We can express it by being fully present in our lives; by welcoming everything that comes to us, no matter how beautiful or painful; by offering our whole selves and the gifts we carry within us to the world.

As we begin to awaken, we become aware of how much of ourselves we have been trying to fix, how many of our emotions we have been trying to solve, and how much of our lives we have been trying to control. We begin to see how we have mistaken our humanness for brokenness, and that nothing actually needs 'fixing', because we have always been whole. We become gardeners instead of mechanics. Rather than running around all the time, doing and struggling and striving, we slow down and start tending to the soil of our souls, welcoming whatever grows. With nothing to fix and nowhere to go, the garden itself becomes our home.

We discover that awakening isn't an abstract philosophy, academic theory or spiritual dogma, but a way of being – of seeing clearly and feeling deeply and living fully. Awakening asks us to dig deeply, to weed out our ignorance, prejudice and fear, to sow seeds of healing, freedom and belonging, and to water them with our love and laughter and tears.

Our capacity for awakening is infinite. Anything conditioned can be unconditioned. Our limiting beliefs can be uprooted. The monsters within us can be tamed. And awakening is always closer than we think – not on a mountaintop or in a faraway temple, but right here, in this moment, amidst all our suffering and confusion. Because what we have been looking for all along has never been missing, but simply hidden, waiting to be discovered.

There is no way of failing at awakening. And yet, to awaken, and to remain awake, is not easy. Living in a world where there is so much pain, hatred and violence makes it difficult to keep our hearts open, to stay connected with the healing force within us, to speak out for what we stand for. However, as we tend to the soil and sow the seeds and remove the weeds in our inner worlds, our actions in the outer world change, and peace, love and compassion begin to bloom.

Awakening allows us to transcend our conditioning. To respond consciously instead of reacting automatically. To make space for painful experiences. To stay grounded when intense emotions arise. As we awaken, we discover new capacities, strengths and resources. We learn how to be present, how to honour our needs, how to live from our deepest values instead of letting our thoughts and feelings yank us around. We learn how to be with uncertainty, how to savour intense joy, how to welcome the parts of ourselves we have tried so hard to hide. We discover the power of rest, of slowness, of grace. We realise we can take awakened action even when we feel anxious or afraid. With awakening, there comes deep healing. We discover a profound sense of freedom, of belonging, of wholeness. We stop fighting and fixing and forcing, and instead open ourselves to the whole sacred messiness of life. Instead of hovering on the edge of the dancefloor, longing to join in but terrified of being seen, we step fully into our lives and join the dance.

I hope this book has been a healing space for you; that it has helped you remember what you already know in your heart to be true. And I hope that you will continue. I hope that you will continue to ask questions, to take risks, to hold yourself and others with compassion. I hope that you will continue to open your heart, to trust your soul, to take off your masks and embrace all that you are. Fully human, fully awake, fully alive.

Acknowledgements

I feel deep gratitude as I reflect on all the people who have contributed to bringing this book to life.

This project grew out of my own journey of healing and awakening, and so there are hundreds, if not thousands, of people who have played a role in its creation. To those who have taught me and guided me, thank you. To those who planted seeds of hope and healing within me, thank you. To those who showed me that life can be more beautiful than we have been conditioned to believe, thank you.

To Justin, for holding me close but never holding me back, thank you. To my mum and my sister, who loved me on my darkest days, who forgave me for the hurt I caused when I was in pain, and who continue to support me, challenge me and remind me of my courage when I am afraid, there are no words to express how grateful I am for your existence. And to my dad, I wish you were still alive to see the healing and freedom I have found.

This book has been deeply inspired by the people I have taught and worked with over the years. I feel honoured to be able to hold space for their healing, and to witness them awaken in their own glorious ways. Thank you for your courage, for your trust, and for showing me just how brave and resilient humans can be.

Woven together in this book are the threads of many ideas, theories, practices, research findings and personal conversations and collaborations. While there are far too many to mention, I feel incredibly grateful for the people who I have received teaching from personally and also those who have inspired me through the books they have written, the research they have published and the words they have shared.

I am deeply grateful to my wonderful editor, Bernadette Marron, and my agents Catherine Cho, Hayley Steed and Emma Bal for believing in this book. Without them, *Daily Awakening* would remain nothing but a dream.

And finally to you, my reader. Thank you for joining me on this messy, magnificent journey of awakening.

How to feel your feelings

Most of us have never been taught how to safely and skilfully feel our feelings. Instead, we have been conditioned to suppress unpleasant emotions, to 'think positively', to downplay our pain. And so, without conscious practice, we find ourselves being yanked around by our emotions, ping-ponging between emotional avoidance (subconsciously distracting and numbing ourselves with food, alcohol, TV, social media and excessive busyness) and emotional hijack (when our feelings explode unexpectedly, distorting the way we see ourselves and the world, and triggering us to act in ways that move us away from the lives we want to live and the people we want to become).

By learning how to feel our feelings, we discover that we do not have to fight them or fix them or fear them. As we create space for our emotions, as we turn towards them and hold them softly and gently, we discover our feelings can guide us, inspire us and remind us of what truly matters, so we can create a rich and meaningful life.

Below are three techniques to help you feel your feelings. Explore which ones work best for you. As you become more familiar with them, you may want to combine them or create your own. Be mindful that as you explore these practices, you might experience different forms of emotional release, such as crying, laughing, yawning, sighing and trembling. This is very normal, very human. However, if an emotional state becomes too intense, use the tools on page 29 to anchor yourself in safety and shift your attention from your inner to the outer world.

Each technique begins with the following four steps:

1. Begin by awakening safety using one of the
   techniques on pages 27–29.
2. Notice the general tone of your emotional experience.
   Is it pleasant or unpleasant? Is it a high-arousal
   emotion or a low-arousal emotion? Is it mild
   or intense?
3. See if you can name the specific emotion (use the list
   on page 297 if you need to).
4. Allow the emotion to be there without trying to
   change, fix or avoid it.

Emotional holding

Notice where in your body the emotion feels most intense and
place a hand here, holding the emotion gently for a few minutes,
or for as long as you need. You might like to imagine a warm,
healing light radiating from your hand, helping the area to relax,
open up and make room for the emotion.

Breathing into feelings

Notice where in your body the emotion feels most intense, and
gently breathe into this area for a few moments, seeing if you can
expand around the emotion.

Embodied experiencing

Gently begin to experience the emotion directly by sensing the
physical feelings in your body. Where is the emotion located?
How much space does it take up? What shape is it? What temper-
ature is it? How does it move? Is it light or heavy? Soft or hard?
Solid or fluid? What else can you feel – tingling, tension, tight-
ness, tenderness? (These questions are simply a guide to help you

sense what is going on in your body. Aim to feel the sensations themselves rather than conceptualising or analysing them.) Ride the waves of the emotion for a few minutes, or longer if you need, noticing how they ebb and flow, arise and pass away.

Our emotions always signal a need, so after feeling your feelings you might like to ask yourself: 'What do I need? What awakened action can I take? What is the most compassionate thing I can do for myself right now?'

Feelings list

As we learn more words for our emotions, we can begin to experience the subtleties of our feelings and to respond to them more consciously and skilfully when they arise. You might like to expand the feelings list below by adding any other emotions that resonate with you, as well as making up your own feeling words and phrases (e.g. spread-too-thin and at-one-with-the-universe).

Joy
Amazed
Blissful
Cheerful
Content
Delighted
Ecstatic
Enchanted
Energised
Excited
Grateful
Happy
In awe
Inspired
Playful
Satisfied
Thrilled

Fear
Afraid

Anxious
Apprehensive
Frightened
Hesitant
Nervous
Panicked
Paralysed
Scared
Terrified
Threatened
Unsafe
Worried

Sadness
Depressed
Devastated
Disappointed
Disheartened
Empty
Grief-stricken

Heartbroken
Hopeless
Lonely
Numb
Shut down
Unhappy
Upset

Love
Accepting
Affectionate
Calm
Caring
Centred
Compassionate
Desirous
Full
Open
Passionate
Peaceful

Present
Relaxed
Safe
Thankful
Trusting
Worthy

Shame
Ashamed
Disgusted
Embarrassed
Guilty
Humiliated
Inadequate
Insecure
Regretful
Self-conscious
Unworthy

Anger
Agitated
Annoyed
Contemptuous
Disapproving

Enraged
Envious
Frustrated
Furious
Grouchy
Hostile
Impatient
Irritated
Jealous

Courage
Adventurous
Brave
Capable
Confident
Daring
Determined
Free
Powerful
Proud
Strong

Stressed
Burned out

Depleted
Drained
Exhausted
Overwhelmed

Surprise
Astonished
Astounded
Baffled
Confused
Shocked
Startled
Stunned

Alive
At one
Awake
Fierce
Free
Full
Vibrant
Vulnerable
Whole

Sensations list

Getting to know our emotions in an embodied way by paying attention to our physical sensations helps us to recognise an emotion when it arises, and to respond to it consciously rather than suppressing it or getting lost in it.

Achy	Fiery	Prickly
Airy	Flowing	Pulsing
Alive	Fluid	Queasy
Asleep	Fluttery	Radiating
Awake	Frozen	Relaxed
Bloated	Full	Releasing
Blocked	Hard	Rigid
Bruised	Heavy	Sensitive
Burning	Hollow	Shaky
Buzzy	Hot	Shivery
Clammy	Imploding	Smooth
Clenched	Itchy	Soft
Cold	Jumpy	Sore
Constricted	Knotted	Spacious
Contracted	Light	Stiff
Dense	Loose	Still
Dizzy	Melting	Stuck
Drained	Nauseous	Suffocated
Dull	Numb	Sweaty
Electric	Open	Tender
Empty	Painful	Tense
Expanded	Pounding	Throbbing

Tight	Trembly	Vibrating
Tingling	Twitchy	Warm
Trapped	Untethered	Wobbly

Bibliography

Introduction

Cope, S. (2000). *Yoga and the Quest for the True Self*. New York, NY: Bantam Books.

Klawonn, A., Kernan, D., & Lynskey, J. (2019). 'A 5-week seminar on the biopsychosocial-spiritual model of self-care improves anxiety, self-compassion, mindfulness, depression, and stress in graduate healthcare students'. *International Journal of Yoga Therapy, 29*(1), 81–89.

Koole, S. L., Greenberg, J., & Pyszczynski, T. (2006). 'Introducing science to the psychology of the soul: Experimental existential psychology'. *Current Directions in Psychological Science, 15*(5), 212–216.

Kornfield, J. (2002). *A Path With Heart: The Classic Guide Through the Perils and Promises of Spiritual Life*. London: Ebury Publishing.

Lepore, S. J., Greenberg, M. A., Bruno, M., & Smyth, J. M. (2002). 'Expressive writing and health: Self-regulation of emotion-related experience, physiology, and behavior'. In S. J. Lepore & J. M. Smyth (Eds.), *The Writing Cure: How expressive writing promotes health and emotional well-being* (pp. 99–117). American Psychological Association.

Li, A. M. (2017). 'Ecological determinants of health: food and environment on human health'. *Environmental Science and Pollution Research*, 24(10), 9002–9015.

Morton, J., Snowdon, S., Gopold, M., & Guymer, E. (2012). 'Acceptance and commitment therapy group treatment for symptoms of borderline personality disorder: A public sector pilot study'. *Cognitive and Behavioral Practice*, 19(4), 527–544.

Pennebaker, J. W. (1997). 'Writing about emotional experiences as a therapeutic process'. *Psychological Science*, 8(3), 162–166.

Pennebaker, J. W., & Seagal, J. D. (1999). 'Forming a story: The health benefits of narrative'. *Journal of Clinical Psychology*, 55(10), 1243–1254.

Pittman, T. S., & Zeigler, K. R. (2007). 'Basic human needs'. In A. W. Kruglanski & E. T. Higgins (Eds.), *Social Psychology: Handbook of Basic Principles* (pp. 473–489). The Guilford Press.

Popova, M. (2016, October 22). 'Live the Questions: Rilke on Embracing Uncertainty and Doubt as a Stabilizing Force'. Brain Pickings. https://www.brainpickings.org/2012/06/01/rilke-on-questions/

Porges, S. W. (2017). *The Pocket Guide to the Polyvagal Theory: The Transformative Power of Feeling Safe.* New York, NY: W. W. Norton & Company.

Richo, D. (2005). *The Five Things We Cannot Change and the Happiness We Find By Embracing Them.* Boston, MA: Shambhala.

'Stressed nation: 74% of UK "overwhelmed or unable to cope"'. (2020, January 16). Mental Health Foundation. https://www.mentalhealth.org.uk/news/stressed-nation-74-uk-overwhelmed-or-unable-cope-some-point-past-year

Sulmasy, D. P. (2002). 'A biopsychosocial-spiritual model for the care of patients at the end of life'. *The Gerontologist*, 42(suppl_3), 24–33.

Walton, G. M., & Wilson, T. D. (2018). 'Wise interventions:

Psychological remedies for social and personal problems'. *Psychological Review*, 125(5), 617.

Weller, F. (2015). *The Wild Edge of Sorrow: Rituals of Renewal and the Sacred Work of Grief*. Berkeley, California: North Atlantic Books.

Yalom, I. D. (2003). *The Gift of Therapy*. London: Piatkus Books.

Part one

Awakening compassion

Barker, J. (2020). *Exploring self-compassion: an action research study with women who have been sexually abused as children* (Doctoral dissertation, Middlesex University/Metanoia Institute).

Neff, K. D. (2012). 'The science of self-compassion'. *Compassion and Wisdom in Psychotherapy*, 1, 79–92.

Neff, K., & Germer, C. (2017). 'Self-compassion and psychological wellbeing'. *The Oxford Handbook of Compassion Science*, 371.

Porges, S. W. (2017). 'Vagal pathways: Portals to compassion'. *The Oxford Handbook of Compassion Science*, 189.

Verduyn, P., Gugushvili, N., Massar, K., Täht, K., & Kross, E. (2020). 'Social comparison on social networking sites'. *Current Opinion in Psychology*, 36, 32–37.

Awakening awareness

Grossman, P., Niemann, L., Schmidt, S., & Walach, H. (2004). 'Mindfulness-based stress reduction and health benefits: A meta-analysis'. *Journal of Psychosomatic Research*, 57(1), 35–43.

Kabat-Zinn, J. (2021). *Full Catastrophe Living: How to Cope with Stress, Pain and Illness Using Mindfulness Meditation* (Revised edition). London: Piatkus

Nolen-Hoeksema, S., Wisco, B. E., & Lyubomirsky, S. (2008).

'Rethinking rumination'. *Perspectives on Psychological Science*, 3(5), 400–424.

Price, C. J., & Thompson, E. A. (2007). 'Measuring dimensions of body connection: body awareness and bodily dissociation'. *The Journal of Alternative and Complementary Medicine*, 13(9), 945–953.

Purser, R. (2015). 'The myth of the present moment'. *Mindfulness*, 6(3), 680–686.

Richards, J. M., & Gross, J. J. (1999). 'Composure at any cost? The cognitive consequences of emotion suppression'. *Personality and Social Psychology Bulletin*, 25(8), 1033–1044.

Vago, D. R., & Zeidan, F. (2016). 'The brain on silent: mind wandering, mindful awareness, and states of mental tranquil'. *Annals of the New York Academy of Sciences*, 1373(1), 96–113.

Awakening ego strength

Knight, Z. G. (2017). 'A proposed model of psychodynamic psychotherapy linked to Erik Erikson's eight stages of psychosocial development'. *Clinical Psychology & Psychotherapy*, 24(5), 1047–1058.

Muraven, M., Buczny, J., & Law, K. F. (2019). 'Ego depletion'. *The Oxford Handbook of Human Motivation*, 113.

Vaillant, G. E. (2011). 'Involuntary coping mechanisms: a psychodynamic perspective'. *Dialogues in Clinical Neuroscience*, 13(3), 366.

Ziadni, M. S., Jasinski, M. J., Labouvie-Vief, G., & Lumley, M. A. (2017). 'Alexithymia, defenses, and ego strength: Cross-sectional and longitudinal relationships with psychological well-being and depression'. *Journal of Happiness Studies*, 18(6), 1799–1813.

Awakening authenticity

Cope, S. (2000). *Yoga and the Quest for the True Self*. New York, NY: Bantam Books.

Kernis, M. H., & Goldman, B. M. (2006). 'A multicomponent conceptualization of authenticity: Theory and research'. *Advances in Experimental Social Psychology, 38*, 283–357.

Maharaj, N., Frydman, M., & Dikshit, S. S. (2015). *I Am That: Talks with Sri Nisargadatta Maharaj* (5th American edition (revised) ed.). Durham, NC: The Acorn Press.

Rivera, G. N., Christy, A. G., Kim, J., Vess, M., Hicks, J. A., & Schlegel, R. J. (2019). 'Understanding the relationship between perceived authenticity and well-being'. *Review of General Psychology, 23*(1), 113–126.

Sparby T., Edelhäuser F., & Weger U. W. (2019). 'The True Self. Critique, Nature, and Method'. *Frontiers in Psychology, 10*, 2250.

Strohminger, N., Knobe, J., & Newman, G. (2017). 'The true self: A psychological concept distinct from the self'. *Perspectives on Psychological Science, 12*(4), 551–560.

Awakening self-worth

Haugen, T., Säfvenbom, R., & Ommundsen, Y. (2011). 'Physical activity and global self-worth: The role of physical self-esteem indices and gender'. *Mental Health and Physical Activity, 4*(2), 49–56.

Ismail, N. A. H., & Tekke, M. (2015). 'Rediscovering Rogers's self theory and personality'. *Journal of Educational, Health and Community Psychology, 4*(3), 28–36.

Lamont, M. (2019). 'From "having" to "being": self-worth and the current crisis of American society'. *The British Journal of Sociology, 70*(3), 660–707.

Leite, C., & Kuiper, N. A. (2008). 'Positive and negative self-worth beliefs and evaluative standards'. *Europe's Journal of Psychology, 4*(2).

Miller Smedema, S., Catalano, D., & Ebener, D. J. (2010). 'The relationship of coping, self-worth, and subjective well-being: A structural equation model'. *Rehabilitation Counseling Bulletin*, 53(3), 131–142.

Stefanone, M. A., Lackaff, D., & Rosen, D. (2011). 'Contingencies of self-worth and social-networking-site behavior'. *Cyberpsychology, behavior, and social networking*, 14(1–2), 41–49.

Williamson, M. (2015). *A Return to Love: Reflections on the Principles of a Course in Miracles*. London: Thorsons.

Awakening self-trust

Govier, T. (1993). 'Self-trust, autonomy, and self-esteem'. *Hypatia*, 8(1), 99–120.

Nys, T. (2015, December). 'Autonomy, trust, and respect'. *The Journal of Medicine and Philosophy: A Forum for Bioethics and Philosophy of Medicine*, 41(1), 10–24.

Pasveer, K. A. (1997). *Self-trust: definition and creation of the self-trust questionnaire*. (Unpublished doctoral thesis). University of Calgary.

Part two

Awakening curiosity, courage and confidence

Cuddy, A. J., Wilmuth, C. A., & Carney, D. R. (2012). 'The benefit of power posing before a high-stakes social evaluation'. *Harvard Business School Working Paper*, No. 13–027.

Kashdan, T. B., Stiksma, M. C., Disabato, D. J., McKnight, P. E., Bekier, J., Kaji, J., & Lazarus, R. (2018). 'The five-dimensional curiosity scale: Capturing the bandwidth of curiosity and identifying four unique subgroups of curious people'. *Journal of Research in Personality*, 73, 130–149.

Lydon-Staley, D. M., Zurn, P., & Bassett, D. S. (2020). 'Within-person variability in curiosity during daily life and associations with well-being'. *Journal of Personality*, 88(4), 625–641.

Nin, A., & Stuhlmann, G. (1971). *The Diary of Anaïs Nin, Vol. 3: 1939–1944*. Boston, MA: Houghton Mifflin Harcourt.

Putman, D. (1997). 'Psychological courage'. *Philosophy, Psychiatry, & Psychology*, 4(1), 1–11.

Rate, C. R., Clarke, J. A., Lindsay, D. R., & Sternberg, R. J. (2007). 'Implicit theories of courage'. *The Journal of Positive Psychology*, 2(2), 80–98.

Awakening emotional awareness

Campbell-Sills, L., Barlow, D. H., Brown, T. A., & Hofmann, S. G. (2006). 'Effects of suppression and acceptance on emotional responses of individuals with anxiety and mood disorders'. *Behaviour Research and Therapy*, 44(9), 1251–1263.

Kircanski, K., Lieberman, M. D., & Craske, M. G. (2012). 'Feelings into words: contributions of language to exposure therapy'. *Psychological Science*, 23(10), 1086–1091.

Kramer, A. D., Guillory, J. E., & Hancock, J. T. (2014). 'Experimental evidence of massive-scale emotional contagion through social networks'. *Proceedings of the National Academy of Sciences*, 111(24), 8788–8790.

Torre, J. B., & Lieberman, M. D. (2018). 'Putting feelings into words: Affect labeling as implicit emotion regulation'. *Emotion Review*, 10(2), 116–124.

Wilson-Mendenhall, C. D., Barrett, L. F., & Barsalou, L. W. (2013). 'Neural evidence that human emotions share core affective properties'. *Psychological Science*, 24(6), 947–956.

Awakening relaxation

Kim, H., & Newman, M. G. (2019). 'The paradox of relaxation training: Relaxation induced anxiety and mediation effects of negative contrast sensitivity in generalized anxiety disorder and major depressive disorder'. *Journal of Affective Disorders, 259*, 271–278.

Lewis, G. F., Hourani, L., Tueller, S., Kizakevich, P., Bryant, S., Weimer, B., & Strange, L. (2015). 'Relaxation training assisted by heart rate variability biofeedback: Implication for a military predeployment stress inoculation protocol'. *Psychophysiology, 52*(9), 1167–1174.

Luberto, C. M., McLeish, A. C., & Kallen, R. W. (2020). 'Development and initial validation of the relaxation sensitivity index'. *International Journal of Cognitive Therapy, 14*(2) 320–340.

Manzoni, G. M., Pagnini, F., Castelnuovo, G., & Molinari, E. (2008). 'Relaxation training for anxiety: a ten-years systematic review with meta-analysis'. *BMC Psychiatry, 8*(1), 1–12.

Porges, S. W. (2017). *The Pocket Guide to the Polyvagal Theory: The Transformative Power of Feeling Safe*. New York, NY: W. W. Norton & Company.

Sevinc, G., Hölzel, B. K., Hashmi, J., Greenberg, J., McCallister, A., Treadway, M., Lazar, S. W., *et al.* (2018). 'Common and dissociable neural activity after mindfulness-based stress reduction and relaxation response programs'. *Psychosomatic Medicine, 80*(5), 439.

Awakening joy

Bowen, H. J., Kark, S. M., & Kensinger, E. A. (2018). 'NEVER forget: negative emotional valence enhances recapitulation'. *Psychonomic Bulletin & Review, 25*(3), 870–891.

Fava, G. A., McEwen, B. S., Guidi, J., Gostoli, S., Offidani, E., &

Sonino, N. (2019). 'Clinical characterization of allostatic overload'. *Psychoneuroendocrinology*, *108*, 94–101.

Johnson, M. K. (2020). Joy: 'A review of the literature and suggestions for future directions'. *The Journal of Positive Psychology*, *15*(1), 5–24.

Kraus, S., & Sears, S. (2009). 'Measuring the immeasurables: Development and initial validation of the Self-Other Four Immeasurables (SOFI) scale based on Buddhist teachings on loving kindness, compassion, joy, and equanimity'. *Social Indicators Research*, *92*(1), 169–181.

Watkins, P. C., Emmons, R. A., Greaves, M. R., & Bell, J. (2018). 'Joy is a distinct positive emotion: Assessment of joy and relationship to gratitude and well-being'. *The Journal of Positive Psychology*, *13*(5), 522–539.

Awakening success

Bostock, J. (2014). *The Meaning of Success*. Cambridge University Press.

Dyke, L. S., & Murphy, S. A. (2006). 'How we define success: A qualitative study of what matters most to women and men'. *Sex Roles*, *55*(5–6), 357–371.

Enke, K. A., & Ropers-Huilman, R. (2010). 'Defining and achieving success: Perspectives from students at Catholic women's colleges'. *Higher Education in Review*, *7*, 1–22.

Ivers, J. H., & Downes, P. (2012). 'A phenomenological reinterpretation of Horner's fear of success in terms of social class'. *European Journal of Psychology of Education*, *27*(3), 369–388.

Awakening meaning and purpose

Buechner, F. (2017, July 18). 'Vocation'. The Frederick Buechner Center. https://www.frederickbuechner.com/quote-of-the-day/2017/7/18/vocation

Drageset, J., Haugan, G., & Tranvåg, O. (2017). 'Crucial aspects promoting meaning and purpose in life: perceptions of nursing home residents'. *BMC Geriatrics*, *17*(1), 1–9.

Holmes, K., Gore, J., Smith, M., & Lloyd, A. (2018). 'An integrated analysis of school students' aspirations for STEM careers: Which student and school factors are most predictive?'. *International Journal of Science and Mathematics Education*, *16*(4), 655–675.

Kim, E. S., Delaney, S. W., & Kubzansky, L. D. (2019). 'Sense of purpose in life and cardiovascular disease: underlying mechanisms and future directions'. *Current Cardiology Reports*, *21*(11), 1–11.

Prinzing, M. M., De Freitas, J., & Fredrickson, B. L. (2021). 'The ordinary concept of a meaningful life: The role of subjective and objective factors in third-person attributions of meaning'. *The Journal of Positive Psychology*.

Steger, M. F., Frazier, P., Oishi, S., & Kaler, M. (2006). 'The meaning in life questionnaire: Assessing the presence of and search for meaning in life'. *Journal of Counseling Psychology*, *53*(1), 80.

Van Zyl, L. E., Hulshof, I., & Dickens, L. R. (2019). '#NoFilter: an online photographic meaningful-moments intervention'. In *Evidence-Based Positive Psychological Interventions in Multi-Cultural Contexts* (pp. 57–82). Cham: Springer.

Part three

Awakening from limiting beliefs

Hauser, O. P., Gino, F., & Norton, M. I. (2018). 'Budging beliefs, nudging behaviour'. *Mind & Society*, *17*(1), 15–26.

Kaplan, J. T., Gimbel, S. I., & Harris, S. (2016). 'Neural correlates of maintaining one's political beliefs in the face of counterevidence'. *Scientific Reports*, *6*(1), 1–11.

Klein, T., Kendall, B., & Tougas, T. (2019). 'Changing brains, changing lives: Researching the lived experience of individuals practicing self-directed neuroplasticity'. Retrieved from Sophia, the St. Catherine University repository website.

Leite, C., & Kuiper, N. A. (2008). 'Positive and negative self-worth beliefs and evaluative standards'. *Europe's Journal of Psychology, 4*(2).

Rollwage, M., Dolan, R. J., & Fleming, S. M. (2018). 'Metacognitive failure as a feature of those holding radical beliefs'. *Current Biology, 28*(24), 4014–4021.

Awakening from perfectionism

Azam, M. A. (2015). 'The psychophysiology of maladaptive perfectionism and mindfulness meditation: An investigation using heart rate variability'. Thesis. York University, Ontario.

Curran, T., & Hill, A. P. (2019). 'Perfectionism is increasing over time: A meta-analysis of birth cohort differences from 1989 to 2016'. *Psychological Bulletin, 145*(4), 410.

Hewitt, P. L., & Flett, G. L. (1991). 'Perfectionism in the self and social contexts: conceptualization, assessment, and association with psychopathology'. *Journal of Personality and Social Psychology, 60*(3), 456.

Hill, A. P., & Curran, T. (2016). 'Multidimensional perfectionism and burnout: A meta-analysis'. *Personality and Social Psychology Review, 20*(3), 269–288.

Limburg, K., Watson, H. J., Hagger, M. S., & Egan, S. J. (2017). 'The relationship between perfectionism and psychopathology: A meta-analysis'. *Journal of Clinical Psychology, 73*(10), 1301–1326.

Winnicott, D. W. (2021). *The Child, the Family, and the Outside World*. London: Penguin Classics.

Awakening from people-pleasing

Domínguez D. J. F., Taing, S. A., & Molenberghs, P. (2016). 'Why do some find it hard to disagree? An fMRI study'. *Frontiers in Human Neuroscience*, 9, 718.

Eberhard, V., Matthes, S., & Ulrich, J. G. (2015). 'The need for social approval and the choice of gender-typed occupations'. In C. Imdorf, K. Hegna & L. Reisel (Eds.), *Gender Segregation in Vocational Education*. Emerald Group Publishing Limited.

Estés, C. P. (1998). *Women Who Run With the Wolves: Contacting the Power of the Wild Woman*. London: Rider.

Exline, J. J., Zell, A. L., Bratslavsky, E., Hamilton, M., & Swenson, A. (2012). 'People-pleasing through eating: Sociotropy predicts greater eating in response to perceived social pressure'. *Journal of Social and Clinical Psychology*, 31(2), 169–193.

Karpman, S. (1968). 'Fairy tales and script drama analysis'. *Transactional Analysis Bulletin*, 7(26), 39–43.

Awakening from burnout

Abedini, N. C., Stack, S. W., Goodman, J. L., & Steinberg, K. P. (2018). '"It's not just time off": a framework for understanding factors promoting recovery from burnout among internal medicine residents'. *Journal of Graduate Medical Education*, 10(1), 26.

Hubert, S., & Aujoulat, I. (2018). 'Parental burnout: When exhausted mothers open up'. *Frontiers in Psychology*, 9, 1021.

Liu, C., & Ma, J. (2020). 'Social media addiction and burnout: The mediating roles of envy and social media use anxiety'. *Current Psychology*, 39(6), 1883–1891.

Madigan, D. J., & Curran, T. (2020). 'Does burnout affect academic achievement? A meta-analysis of over 100,000 students'. *Educational Psychology Review*, 1–19.

Maslach, C., & Leiter, M. P. (2016). 'Understanding the burnout experience: recent research and its implications for psychiatry'. *World Psychiatry*, 15(2), 103–111.

Toker, S., & Melamed, S. (2017). 'Stress, recovery, sleep, and burnout'. In C. L. Cooper & J. C. Quick (Eds.), *The Handbook of Stress and Health: A Guide to Research and Practice* (pp. 168–185). Hoboken: Wiley Blackwell.

Awakening from shame

Brown, B. (2006). 'Shame resilience theory: A grounded theory study on women and shame'. *Families in Society*, 87(1), 43–52.

Brown, B. (2013). *Daring Greatly: How the Courage to Be Vulnerable Transforms the Way We Live, Love, Parent, and Lead*. London: Portfolio Penguin.

Brown, B., & McPhail, B. (2005). *Speaking Shame: A 10-week Psychoeducational Shame Resilience Curriculum*. University of Houston, Texas.

Hartling, L. M., Rosen, W., Walker, M., & Jordan, J. V. (2004). 'Shame and humiliation: From isolation to relational transformation'. In J. V. Jordan, M. Walker & L. M. Hartling (Eds.), *The Complexity of Connection*, (pp. 103–128) New York, NY: Guildford Press.

Horney, K. (2013). *Our Inner Conflicts: A Constructive Theory of Neurosis* (Vol. 17). Abingdon: Routledge.

Kross, E., Berman, M. G., Mischel, W., Smith, E. E., & Wager, T. D. (2011). 'Social rejection shares somatosensory representations with physical pain'. *Proceedings of the National Academy of Sciences*, 108(15), 6270–6275.

Velotti, P., Garofalo, C., Bottazzi, F., & Caretti, V. (2017). 'Faces of shame: Implications for self-esteem, emotion regulation, aggression, and well-being'. *The Journal of Psychology*, 151(2), 171–184.

Awakening self-forgiveness

Cornish, M. A., Woodyatt, L., Morris, G., Conroy, A., & Townsdin, J. (2018). 'Self-forgiveness, self-exoneration, and self-condemnation: Individual differences associated with three patterns of responding to interpersonal offenses'. *Personality and Individual Differences, 129*, 43–53.

Hall, J. H., & Fincham, F. D. (2005). 'Self-forgiveness: The stepchild of forgiveness research'. *Journal of Social and Clinical Psychology, 24*(5), 621–637.

Pope, A. (1711). *An Essay on Criticism*. Poetry Foundation. (https://www.poetryfoundation.org/poems/44897/an-essay-on-criticism-part-2)

Toussaint, L. L., Webb, J. R., & Hirsch, J. K. (2017). 'Self-forgiveness and health: A stress-and-coping model'. In L. Woodyatt, E. Worthington, M. Wenzel & B. Griffin (Eds.), *Handbook of the Psychology of Self-forgiveness* (pp. 87–99). Cham: Springer.

Webb, J. R., Bumgarner, D. J., Conway-Williams, E., Dangel, T., & Hall, B. B. (2017). 'A consensus definition of self-forgiveness: Implications for assessment and treatment'. *Spirituality in Clinical Practice, 4*(3), 216.

Part four

Awakening bodymind healing

Dana, D. (2020). *Polyvagal Exercises for Safety and Connection: 50 Client-Centered Practices*. New York: W. W. Norton & Company.

Guilliams, T. G., & Edwards, L. (2010). 'Chronic stress and the HPA axis'. *The Standard, 9*(2), 1–12.

Jha, A. P., Stanley, E. A., Kiyonaga, A., Wong, L., & Gelfand, L. (2010). 'Examining the protective effects of mindfulness training on working memory capacity and affective experience'. *Emotion, 10*(1), 54.

McEwen, B. S. (2000). 'Allostasis and allostatic load: implications for neuropsychopharmacology'. *Neuropsychopharmacology, 22*(2), 108–124.

Siegel D. J. (1999) *The Developing Mind*. New York: Guilford

Stanley, E., & van der Kolk, B. (2019). *Widen the Window: Training Your Brain and Body to Thrive During Stress and Recover from Trauma*. London: Yellow Kite.

Van der Kolk, B. A., Roth, S., Pelcovitz, D., Sunday, S., & Spinazzola, J. (2005). 'Disorders of extreme stress: The empirical foundation of a complex adaptation to trauma'. *Journal of Traumatic Stress: Official Publication of the International Society for Traumatic Stress Studies, 18*(5), 389–399.

Awakening from anxiety

Adolphs, R. (2013). 'The biology of fear'. *Current Biology, 23*(2), R79–R93.

Brown, R. P., & Gerbarg, P. L. (2005). 'Sudarshan Kriya yogic breathing in the treatment of stress, anxiety, and depression: part I—neurophysiologic model'. *Journal of Alternative & Complementary Medicine, 11*(1), 189–201.

Chalmers, J. A., Quintana, D. S., Abbott, M. J., & Kemp, A. H. (2014). 'Anxiety disorders are associated with reduced heart rate variability: a meta-analysis'. *Frontiers in psychiatry, 5*, 80.

Karasewich, T. A., & Kuhlmeier, V. A. (2020). 'Trait social anxiety as a conditional adaptation: A developmental and evolutionary framework'. *Developmental Review, 55*, 100886.

Schwartz, R. C. (2015). 'Facing Our Dark Side'. Psychotherapy Networker. https://www.psychotherapynetworker.org/magazine/article/2/facing-our-dark-side

Awakening to love

Bransen, J. (2006). 'Selfless self-love'. *Ethical Theory and Moral Practice*, *9*(1), 3–25.

Duschek, S., Nassauer, L., Montoro, C. I., Bair, A., & Montoya, P. (2019). 'Dispositional empathy is associated with experimental pain reduction during provision of social support by romantic partners'. *Scandinavian Journal of Pain*, *20*(1), 205–209.

Esch, T., & Stefano, G. B. (2005). 'The neurobiology of love'. *Neuroendocrinology Letters*, *26*(3), 175–192.

Fromm, E. (1995). *The Art of Loving*. London: Thorsons.

Master, S. L., Eisenberger, N. I., Taylor, S. E., Naliboff, B. D., Shirinyan, D., & Lieberman, M. D. (2009). 'A picture's worth: Partner photographs reduce experimentally induced pain'. *Psychological Science*, *20*(11), 1316–1318.

Porges, S. W. (1998). 'Love: An emergent property of the mammalian autonomic nervous system'. *Psychoneuroendocrinology*, *23*(8), 837–861.

Richo, D. (2002). *How to Be an Adult in Relationships: The 5 Keys to Mindful Loving*. Boston, MA: Shambhala.

Shaver, P. R., Morgan, H. J., & Wu, S. (1996). 'Is love a "basic" emotion?'. *Personal Relationships*, *3*(1), 81–96.

Awakening to grief

Cunsolo, A., & Ellis, N. R. (2018). 'Ecological grief as a mental health response to climate change-related loss'. *Nature Climate Change*, *8*(4), 275–281.

Fuchs, T. (2018). 'Presence in absence. The ambiguous phenomenology of grief'. *Phenomenology and the Cognitive Sciences*, *17*(1), 43–63.

Stroebe, M., Schut, H., & Boerner, K. (2017). 'Cautioning health-care professionals: Bereaved persons are misguided through the stages of grief'. *OMEGA-Journal of Death and Dying*, *74*(4), 455–473.

Weller, F. (2015). *The Wild Edge of Sorrow: Rituals of Renewal and the Sacred Work of Grief*. Berkeley, California: North Atlantic Books.

Awakening to belonging

Allen, K. A., Kern, M. L., Rozek, C. S., McInerney, D. M., & Slavich, G. M. (2021). 'Belonging: a review of conceptual issues, an integrative framework, and directions for future research'. *Australian Journal of Psychology*, 1–16.

Griffin, J. (2010). *The Lonely Society*. Mental Health Foundation. https://www.mentalhealth.org.uk/sites/default/files/the_lonely_society_report.pdf

Hagerty, B. M., Lynch-Sauer, J., Patusky, K. L., Bouwsema, M., & Collier, P. (1992). 'Sense of belonging: A vital mental health concept'. *Archives of Psychiatric Nursing*, *6*(3), 172–177.

Malone, G. P., Pillow, D. R., & Osman, A. (2012). 'The general belongingness scale (GBS): Assessing achieved belongingness'. *Personality and individual differences*, *52*(3), 311–316.

Montaigne, M., Frame, D. M. (1958). *The Complete Essays of Montaigne*. Stanford, California: Stanford University Press.

Awakening to uncertainty

Carleton, R. N., Norton, M. P. J., & Asmundson, G. J. (2007). 'Fearing the unknown: A short version of the Intolerance of Uncertainty Scale'. *Journal of Anxiety Disorders*, *21*(1), 105–117.

De Berker, A. O., Rutledge, R. B., Mathys, C., Marshall, L., Cross, G. F., Dolan, R. J., & Bestmann, S. (2016). 'Computations of uncertainty mediate acute stress responses in humans'. *Nature Communications*, *7*(1), 1–11.

Peters, A., McEwen, B. S., & Friston, K. (2017). 'Uncertainty and stress: Why it causes diseases and how it is mastered by the brain'. *Progress in Neurobiology*, *156*, 164–188.

Part five

Awakening health

Card, A. J. (2017). 'Moving beyond the WHO definition of health: A new perspective for an aging world and the emerging era of value-based care'. *World Medical & Health Policy*, *9*(1), 127–137.

Dhar, N., Chaturvedi, S. K. & Nandan, D. (2011). 'Spiritual health scale 2011: Defining and measuring 4th dimension of health'. *Indian Journal of Community Medicine: Official Publication of Indian Association of Preventive & Social Medicine*, *36*(4), 275.

Holt-Lunstad, J., Smith, T. B., Baker, M., Harris, T. & Stephenson, D. (2015). 'Loneliness and social isolation as risk factors for mortality: a meta-analytic review'. *Perspectives on Psychological Science*, *10*(2), 227–237.

Kawachi, I., Subramanian, S. V., & Almeida-Filho, N. (2002). 'A glossary for health inequalities'. *Journal of Epidemiology & Community Health*, *56*(9), 647–652.

McCartney, G., Popham, F., McMaster, R., & Cumbers, A. (2019). 'Defining health and health inequalities'. *Public Health*, *172*, 22–30.

Teresa, M. (1995). *A Simple Path*. New York: Ballantine Books.

Witt, C. M., Chiaramonte, D., Berman, S., Chesney, M. A., Kaplan, G. A., Stange, K. C., Berman, B. M, *et al.* (2017). 'Defining health in a comprehensive context: a new definition of integrative health'. *American Journal of Preventive Medicine*, *53*(1), 134–137.

Awakening body kindness

Harrison, N. A., Gray, M. A., Gianaros, P. J., & Critchley, H. D. (2010). 'The embodiment of emotional feelings in the brain'. *Journal of Neuroscience, 30*(38), 12878–12884.

Hufendiek, R. (2015). *Embodied emotions: A naturalist approach to a normative phenomenon.* New York: Routledge.

Pace-Schott, E. F., Amole, M. C., Aue, T., Balconi, M., Bylsma, L. M., Critchley, H., VanElzakker, M. B., *et al.* (2019). 'Physiological feelings'. *Neuroscience & Biobehavioral Reviews, 103*, 267–304.

Ramseyer Winter, V., Gillen, M. M., Cahill, L., Jones, A., & Ward, M. (2019). 'Body appreciation, anxiety, and depression among a racially diverse sample of women'. *Journal of Health Psychology, 24*(11), 1517–1525.

Roberts, T. A., Calogero, R. M., & Gervais, S. J. (2018). 'Objectification theory: Continuing contributions to feminist psychology'. In C. B. Travis, J. W. White, A. Rutherford, W. S. Williams, S. L. Cook, & K. F. Wyche (Eds.), *APA Handbook of the Psychology of Women: History, Theory, and Battlegrounds* (pp. 249–271). American Psychological Association.

Woodman, M., & Mellick, J. (1998). *Coming Home to Myself: Reflections for Nurturing a Woman's Body and Soul.* Berkeley, CA: Conari Press.

Awakening nourishment

Hazzard, V. M., Telke, S. E., Simone, M., Anderson, L. M., Larson, N. I., & Neumark-Sztainer, D. (2020). 'Intuitive eating longitudinally predicts better psychological health and lower use of disordered eating behaviors: findings from EAT 2010–2018'. *Eating and Weight Disorders – Studies on Anorexia, Bulimia and Obesity*, 1–8.

Johnston, A. (2000). *Eating in the Light of the Moon: How Women Can Transform Their Relationship with Food Through Myths, Metaphors, and Storytelling* (1st ed.). Carlsbad, CA: Gurze Books.

Juarascio, A. S., Parker, M. N., Manasse, S. M., Barney, J. L., Wyckoff, E. P., & Dochat, C. (2020). 'An exploratory component analysis of emotion regulation strategies for improving emotion regulation and emotional eating'. *Appetite*, 150, 104634.

Kozak, A. T., Davis, J., Brown, R., & Grabowski, M. (2017). 'Are overeating and food addiction related to distress tolerance? An examination of residents with obesity from a US metropolitan area'. *Obesity Research & Clinical Practice*, 11(3), 287–298.

Simmons, W. K., & DeVille, D. C. (2017). 'Interoceptive contributions to healthy eating and obesity'. *Current Opinion in Psychology*, 17, 106–112.

Warren, J. M., Smith, N., & Ashwell, M. (2017). 'A structured literature review on the role of mindfulness, mindful eating and intuitive eating in changing eating behaviours: effectiveness and associated potential mechanisms'. *Nutrition Research Reviews*, 30(2), 272–283.

Awakening abundance

Gasiorowska, A., Zaleskiewicz, T., & Kesebir, P. (2018). 'Money as an existential anxiety buffer: Exposure to money prevents mortality reminders from leading to increased death thoughts'. *Journal of Experimental Social Psychology*, 79, 394–409.

Park, L. E., Ward, D. E., & Naragon-Gainey, K. (2017). 'It's all about the money (for some): Consequences of financially contingent self-worth'. *Personality and Social Psychology Bulletin*, 43(5), 601–622.

Sadek, N. (2020). 'The phenomenology and dynamics of wealth

shame: Between moral responsibility and moral masochism'. *Journal of the American Psychoanalytic Association*, *68*(4), 615–648.

Wang, Z., Jetten, J., & Steffens, N. K. (2020). 'The more you have, the more you want? Higher social class predicts a greater desire for wealth and status'. *European Journal of Social Psychology*, *50*(2), 360–375.

Awakening slowness

Bellezza, S., Paharia, N., & Keinan, A. (2017). 'Conspicuous consumption of time: When busyness and lack of leisure time become a status symbol'. *Journal of Consumer Research*, *44*(1), 118–138.

Fayolle, S., Gil, S., & Droit-Volet, S. (2015). 'Fear and time: Fear speeds up the internal clock'. *Behavioural processes*, *120*, 135–140.

Gender Pay Gap Reporting (2020). CIPD. https://www.cipd.co.uk/Images/cipd-gender-pay-gap-report-2020_tcm18-86626.pdf

Huijsmans, I., Ma, I., Micheli, L., Civai, C., Stallen, M., & Sanfey, A. G. (2019). 'A scarcity mindset alters neural processing underlying consumer decision making'. *Proceedings of the National Academy of Sciences*, *116*(24), 11699–11704.

Mogilner, C. (2019). 'It's time for happiness'. *Current Opinion in Psychology*, *26*, 80–84.

Mogilner, C., Whillans, A., & Norton, M. I. (2018). 'Time, money, and subjective well-being'. In E. Diener, S. Oishi & L. Tay (Eds.), *Handbook of Well-being*. Salt Lake City: DEF.

Sunim, H., Lee, Y., & Kim, C. (2017). *The Things You Can See Only When You Slow Down: How to Be Calm in a Busy World*. London: Penguin Life.

Awakening creativity

Corry, D. A., Lewis, C. A., & Mallett, J. (2014). 'Harnessing the mental health benefits of the creativity–spirituality construct: Introducing the theory of transformative coping'. *Journal of Spirituality in Mental Health*, 16(2), 89–110.

Forgeard, M. J., & Kaufman, J. C. (2016). 'Who cares about imagination, creativity, and innovation, and why? A review'. *Psychology of Aesthetics, Creativity, and the Arts*, 10(3), 250.

Förster, J., Epstude, K., & Özelsel, A. (2009). 'Why love has wings and sex has not: How reminders of love and sex influence creative and analytic thinking'. *Personality and Social Psychology Bulletin*, 35(11), 1479–1491.

Gilbert, E. (2015). *Big Magic*. London: Bloomsbury Publishing.

Groyecka, A., Gajda, A., Jankowska, D. M., Sorokowski, P., & Karwowski, M. (2020). 'On the benefits of thinking creatively: Why does creativity training strengthen intercultural sensitivity among children?'. *Thinking Skills and Creativity*, 37, 100693.

Kapoor, H., & Kaufman, J. C. (2020). 'Meaning-making through creativity during COVID-19'. *Frontiers in Psychology*, 11.

Kaufman, J. C. (2018). 'Finding meaning with creativity in the past, present, and future'. *Perspectives on Psychological Science*, 13(6), 734–749.

Part six

Awakening playfulness

Brown, S. (2009, March 12). 'Play is more than just fun'. TED Talks. https://www.ted.com/talks/stuart_brown_play_is_more_than_just_fun

Brown, S. L. (2009). *Play: How it shapes the brain, opens the imagination, and invigorates the soul*. London: Penguin.

Hadiprodjo, N. (2018). *Clinical applications of the polyvagal theory and attachment theory to play therapy for children with developmental trauma* (Doctoral dissertation, University of Roehampton).

Koeners, M. P., & Francis, J. (2020). 'The physiology of play: potential relevance for higher education'. *International Journal of Play*, 9(1), 143–159.

Lauer, L. M. (2011). 'Play deprivation: Is it happening in your school?'. Institute of Education Sciences. https://eric.ed.gov/?id=ED524739

Proyer, R. T., Brauer, K., & Wolf, A. (2019). 'Assessing other-directed, lighthearted, intellectual, and whimsical playfulness in adults'. *European Journal of Psychological Assessment*, 36(4), 624–634.

Siviy, S. M. (2016). 'A brain motivated to play: insights into the neurobiology of playfulness'. *Behaviour*, 153(6–7), 819–844.

Yarnal, C., & Qian, X. (2011). 'Older-adult playfulness: An innovative construct and measurement for healthy aging research'. *American Journal of Play*, 4(1), 52–79.

Awakening to nature

Berger, R., & McLeod, J. (2006). 'Incorporating nature into therapy: A framework for practice'. *Journal of Systemic Therapies*, 25(2), 80–94.

Glendinning, C. (1995). 'Technology, trauma, and the wild'. *Ecopsychology: Restoring the earth, healing the mind*, 41–54.

Milton, M. J., & Corbett, L. (2011). 'Ecopsychology: A perspective on trauma'. *European Journal of Ecopsychology*, 2, 28–47.

Stigsdotter, U. K., Palsdottir, A. M., Burls, A., Chermaz, A., Ferrini, F., & Grahn, P. (2011). 'Nature-based therapeutic interventions'. In K. Nilsson, M. Sangster, C. Gallis, T. Hartig, S. de Vries, K. Seeland & J. Schipperjin (Eds.), *Forests, Trees and Human health* (pp. 309–342). Dordrecht: Springer.

Suganthi, L. (2019). 'Ecospirituality: A scale to measure an individual's reverential respect for the environment'. *Ecopsychology*, 11(2), 110–122.

Awakening your inner child

Bradshaw, J. (2015). *Homecoming: Reclaiming and Championing Your Inner Child*. (3rd ed.) London: Piatkus.

Fortune, C. (2003). 'The analytic nursery: Ferenczi's "wise baby" meets Jung's "divine child". *Journal of Analytical Psychology*, 48(4), 457–466.

Schwartz, R. C. (2013). 'Moving from acceptance toward transformation with internal family systems therapy (IFS)'. *Journal of Clinical Psychology*, 69(8), 805–816.

Wesley, D. (2019). 'The divine child'. *Psychological Perspectives*, 62(4), 446–454.

Awakening wholeness

Daniels, M. (2005). *Shadow, Self, Spirit: Essays in Transpersonal Psychology*. Exeter: Imprint Academic.

Ford, D. (2001). *The Dark Side of the Light Chasers*. London: Hodder & Stoughton.

Jung, C. G. (2012). *Psychology of the Unconscious*. Chelmsford, MA: Courier Corporation.

Jung, C. G., & Jaffe, A. (1965). *Memories, Dreams, Reflections*. New York: Vintage Books.

Awakening to privilege, prejudice and power

Barker, M. J. (2015). 'Depression and/or oppression? Bisexuality and mental health'. *Journal of Bisexuality*, 15(3), 369–384.

Cummins, D. (2005). 'Dominance, status, and social hierarchies'. *The Handbook of Evolutionary Psychology*, 676–697.

Heath, C. D. (2006). 'A womanist approach to understanding and assessing the relationship between spirituality and mental health'. *Mental Health, Religion & Culture*, 9(02), 155–170.

Johnstone, L., & Boyle, M., with Cromby, J., Dillon, J., Harper,

D., Kinderman, P., Longden, E., Pilgrim, D., & Read, J. (2018). *The Power Threat Meaning Framework: Towards the identification of patterns in emotional distress, unusual experiences and troubled or troubling behavior, as an alternative to functional psychiatric diagnosis.* Leicester: British Psychological Society.

Puhl, R. M., & Heuer, C. A. (2009). 'The stigma of obesity: a review and update'. *Obesity, 17*(5), 941.

Smith, L., Chambers, D. A., & Bratini, L. (2009). 'When oppression is the pathogen: The participatory development of socially just mental health practice'. *American Journal of Orthopsychiatry, 79*(2), 159.

Zitek, E. M., & Hebl, M. R. (2007). 'The role of social norm clarity in the influenced expression of prejudice over time'. *Journal of Experimental Social Psychology, 43*(6), 867–876.

Awakening grace and gratitude

Bronte, J. C., & Wade, J. (2012). 'The experience of grace: Divine assistance in making a change'. *Journal of Transpersonal Psychology, 44*(2).

Bufford, R. K., Sisemore, T. A., & Blackburn, A. M. (2017). 'Dimensions of grace: Factor analysis of three grace scales'. *Psychology of Religion and Spirituality, 9*(1), 56.

Emmons, R. A., & Mishra, A. (2011). 'Why gratitude enhances well-being: What we know, what we need to know'. In K. Sheldon, T. Kashdan & M. Steger (Eds.), *Designing Positive Psychology: Taking Stock and Moving Forward* (pp. 248–262). Oxford: Oxford University Press.

Emmons, R. A., Hill, P. C., Barrett, J. L., & Kapic, K. M. (2017). 'Psychological and theological reflections on grace and its relevance for science and practice'. *Psychology of Religion and Spirituality, 9*(3), 276.

Nickolas, M., Hayes, A., Hughes, P., Hammer, D., Clarke, A.,

Pargament, K., & Doehring, C. (2009). 'Perceiving sacredness in life: Correlates and predictors'. *Archive for the Psychology of Religion*, 31(1), 55–73.

Steindl-Rast, D. (2004). 'Gratitude as thankfulness and as gratefulness'. In R. Emmons & M. McCullough, (Eds.), *The Psychology of Gratitude* (p.282). Oxford: Oxford University Press.

Awakening integration

Gorman, I., Nielson, E. M., Molinar, A., Cassidy, K., & Sabbagh, J. (2021). 'Psychedelic harm reduction and integration: A transtheoretical model for clinical practice'. *Frontiers in Psychology*, 12, 710.

McCracken, L. M., & Morley, S. (2014). 'The psychological flexibility model: a basis for integration and progress in psychological approaches to chronic pain management'. *The Journal of Pain*, 15(3), 221–234.

Tamminen, J., Payne, J. D., Stickgold, R., Wamsley, E. J., & Gaskell, M. G. (2010). 'Sleep spindle activity is associated with the integration of new memories and existing knowledge'. *Journal of Neuroscience*, 30(43), 14356–14360.

Watts, R., & Luoma, J. B. (2020). 'The use of the psychological flexibility model to support psychedelic assisted therapy'. *Journal of Contextual Behavioral Science*, 15, 92–102.